D1116720

THE IVP NEW TESTAMENT COMMENTARY SERIES

Philippians

Gordon D. Fee

Grant R. Osborne
series editor

D. Stuart Briscoe
Haddon Robinson
consulting editors

INTERVARSITY PRESS
DOWNERS GROVE, ILLINOIS, USA
LEICESTER, ENGLAND

InterVarsity Press, USA
P.O. Box 1400, Downers Grove, IL 60515-1426, USA
World Wide Web: www.ivpress.com
Email: email@ivpress.com

Inter-Varsity Press, England
Norton Street, Nottingham NG7 3HR, England
Website: www.ivpbooks.com
Email: ivp@ivpbooks.com

InterVarsity Press®, U.S.A., is the book-publishing division of InterVarsity Christian Fellowship/USA®, a student movement active on campus at hundreds of universities, colleges and schools of nursing in the United States of America, and a member movement of the International Fellowship of Evangelical Students. For information about local and regional activities, write Public Relations Dept., InterVarsity Christian Fellowship/USA, 6400 Schroeder Rd., P.O. Box 7895, Madison, WI 53707-7895, or visit the IVCF website at <www.intervarsity.org>.

Inter-Varsity Press, England, is closely linked with the Universities and Colleges Christian Fellowship (formerly the Inter-Varsity Fellowship), a student movement linking Christian Unions in universities and colleges throughout the United Kingdom and the Republic of Ireland, and a member movement of the International Fellowship of Evangelical Students. For information about local and national activities write to UCCF, 38 De Montfort Street, Leicester LE1 7GP, visit them on the web at www.uccf.org.uk, or email them at email@uccf.org.uk.

USA ISBN-10: 0-8308-1811-1
USA ISBN-13: 978-0-8308-1811-2
UK ISBN-10: 0-85111-684-1
UK ISBN-13: 978-0-85111-684-6

Printed in the United States of America

Library of Congress Cataloging-in-Publication Data

Fee, Gordon D.
Philippians/Gordon D. Fee.
p. cm.—(The IVP New Testament commentary series)
Includes bibliographical references (p.).
ISBN 0-8308-1811-1 (cloth: alk. paper)
1. Bible. N.T. Philippians Commentaries. I. Title.
II. Series.
BS2705.3.F44 1999
277'.607—dc21

99-21884
CIP

British Library Cataloguing in Publication Data

A catalogue record for this book is available from the British Library.

P *22 21 20 19 18 17 16 15 14 13 12 11 10 9 8 7 6*
Y *21 20 19 18 17 16 15 14 13 12 11 10 09 08 07 06*

General Preface

In an age of proliferating commentary series, one might easily ask why add yet another to the seeming glut. The simplest answer is that no other series has yet achieved what we had in mind—a series to and from the church, that seeks to move from the text to its contemporary relevance and application.

No other series offers the unique combination of solid, biblical exposition and helpful explanatory notes in the same user-friendly format. No other series has tapped the unique blend of scholars and pastors who share both a passion for faithful exegesis and a deep concern for the church. Based on the New International Version of the Bible, one of the most widely used modern translations, the IVP New Testament Commentary Series builds on the NIV's reputation for clarity and accuracy. Individual commentators indicate clearly whenever they depart from the standard translation as required by their understanding of the original Greek text.

The series contributors represent a wide range of theological traditions, united by a common commitment to the authority of Scripture for Christian faith and practice. Their efforts here are directed toward applying the unchanging message of the New Testament to the ever-changing world in which we live.

Readers will find in each volume not only traditional discussions of authorship and backgrounds, but useful summaries of principal themes and approaches to contemporary application. To bridge the gap between commentaries that stress the flow of an author's argument but skip over exegetical nettles and those that simply jump from one difficulty to another, we have developed our unique format that expounds the text in uninterrupted form on the upper portion of each page while dealing with other issues underneath in verse-keyed notes. To avoid clutter we have also adopted a social studies note system that keys references to the bibliography.

We offer the series in hope that pastors, students, Bible teachers and small group leaders of all sorts will find it a valuable aid—one that stretches the mind and moves the heart to ever-growing faithfulness and obedience to our Lord Jesus Christ.

Author's Preface

More years ago now than I should be willing to admit, Jim Hoover, my former student who had become an editor with InterVarsity Press, invited me to edit a new series of commentaries that IVP was interested in publishing. I was writing my 1 Corinthians commentary (New International Commentary series) at the time, so wisdom dictated that I decline. But when pressed at least to contribute a volume, I agreed, "as long as it is one of Paul's shorter letters!" So we agreed that I should undertake the Philippians volume in this series.

A few years later I was approached by Eerdmans Publishing Company to succeed F. F. Bruce as editor of the New International Commentary series. This time I agreed; but when the Philippians commentary in that series came open and the publishers approached me to write it, I faced a considerable dilemma. The editors of IVP graciously agreed to my request to write the NIC commentary first, and for this I owe them an enormous debt. Now the shoe is on the other foot; for it became clear in the process of writing this smaller version (what I came fondly to dub "Little Phil") that it would be impossible for me not to repeat myself over and again. So now I am indebted to Eerdmans for their generosity in allowing me to use so many words that have been published elsewhere.

The reader, however, should not assume by these acknowledgments of indebtedness that this is simply a smaller version of the larger one. In many ways, of course, it is that, since I changed my mind only a couple of times in the course of this writing. But I have had the reader of this series in view at every turn, which has meant that the exposition has "lightened up" a bit and the many footnotes of "Big Phil" have been all but eliminated. What remain are those few that are necessary to help the reader know where to go for alternative views on many texts.

I wish also to thank the board of governors at Regent College for their generous sabbatical policy, which allowed me the time to write these pages during the early months of 1998. For a time Maudine and I enjoyed an almost idyllic life in our cottage on Galiano Island overlooking Trincomali Channel, watching two eagles fly past our windows every day and a seal that wouldn't yield his place in the channel despite our intrusion. But the idyll was rudely interrupted in late January. A biopsy revealed that Maudine had breast cancer. Suddenly rejoicing always, being anxious for nothing, offering everything to God with thanksgiving, having his peace which goes beyond the limits of human thoughts (Phil 4:4-7) took on an existential note, moving these words—words originally written to a suffering community of believers—off the page into our own lives.

As of this writing there has been "successful" surgery; but we also know that our lives are in God's hands, and that we, like all who read this commentary, are utterly dependent on God's mercy for all things. And so "to our God and Father be glory for ever and ever. Amen" (Phil 4:20).

Introduction

Ask any number of people to name their favorite Pauline letter, and the majority will say Philippians. For good reason. Whereas we meet an erudite Paul in Romans, a bombastic Paul in Galatians, a sometimes caustic Paul in 2 Corinthians and a sometimes baffling Paul in 1 Corinthians, here we find a very personal and warm human being who pours out a heart of affection for his friends in Philippi. In short, many of us like Philippians because we like the Paul we meet here.

Not only so, but the letter is full of wonderfully memorable passages. Who among believers in Christ does not know and love such grand Pauline moments as "For me, to live is Christ, to die is gain," or "for whom I have suffered the loss of all things for the surpassing worth of knowing Christ Jesus my Lord," or "I can do all things through him who strengthens me," or "My God will supply all your needs according to his riches in glory in Christ Jesus" (here cited from memory, with the King James flavor still showing)—or any number of clauses or phrases from the Christ story in 2:6-11 and the Paul narrative in 3:4-14?

On the other hand, ask the same people to trace the flow of thought of this letter—how does the letter "work," as it were—and one draws a blank, often even among scholars who insist that the letter is too "personal" to analyze in that way. For most of us, Philippians simply reads better in parts than as a whole. So we have the interesting ambiguity that this best loved of Paul's letters is also one of the least understood *as a letter*. We know its many pieces, and we have a good "feel" for what it's about, but we are less sure how the pieces fit together.

Not surprisingly, scholarship has had the same difficulty in keeping the letter together. But in scholars' case the problem is usually overanalysis or a kind of professional instinct (arrogance?) that Paul would not write much differently from us in our better moments. And since we would not intentionally write a letter as difficult to follow as this one, we assume Paul probably did not either. So many have divided the letter into three—all by Paul and all to Philippi, but written at different times with different purposes.

This commentary takes the opposite view: that the letter as it has come down to us makes good sense as a letter, written by Paul, probably from Rome in the early 60s, to his longtime friends and compatriots in the gospel who lived in Philippi, a Roman military colony on the interior plain of eastern Macedonia. The aim of this introduction is therefore to introduce both the letter as I see it and this commentary on the letter. Although the various critical questions that belong to such an introduction will be touched on, one will need to go elsewhere for fuller treatment of most of these issues.

□ Philippians as a Letter

The other day I received an e-mail message from the leader of our house group, sent from home on his wife's account. Since he did not "sign" it, and it bore her name in the return address, I read it through and responded as though she had written it. When Maudine came home the next day and read it, she said, "This is from David, not Heather."

After my first brief embarrassment, I realized how instructive that moment was in terms of how we read. Once it was pointed out to me that David had written the message, all the "of course" bells went off; but in the meantime other signals had suggested to me that Heather was the writer, so I read it quite differently in the first instance.

So it is with reading almost any document, including a letter like Philippians. My purpose here is to ring a few bells that will help one "see" Philippians as a letter within its own first-century context, so that we might not only read it more intelligently but also "hear" it for ourselves in a more informed way.

Philippians and Ancient Letter Writing As early as grammar school, and even more at the secondary level, I was introduced to the art of letter writing. This instruction included matters of "form," of which there were two: the personal (or "friendly") letter and the business letter, the latter being divided into further kinds, depending on the nature of one's business. Usually questions of form had to do with "salutation" and "closing," although instruction was also given as to what was appropriate for the opening sentences of each genre.

I wonder whether my teachers knew that such instruction preceded them not just by the some two hundred years of instruction in American schools, but by some two millennia in the Greco-Roman world. In fact two (pseudonymous) letter-writing manuals have come down to us under the names of Demetrius and Libanius (for English translations see Malherbe 1988)—although they were probably not written for schoolchildren but for the training of professional scribes. The one by Pseudo-Demetrius lists and illustrates twenty-one different types of letters. First on his list is (in his language) "the friendly type," which was the most common and, according to Cicero, was the reason for the "invention of letter-writing" (*Ad Familiares* 2.4.1). Sixth on the list is the "letter of moral exhortation," usually written in the context of "friendship" of a more patron-client nature.

In sharp contrast to most of Paul's other letters, Philippians reflects the essential characteristics of these two types of letters (friendship and moral exhortation); to be sure, as with almost everything else, in Paul's hands these are also transformed into something distinctively Christian.

Philippians as a Letter of Friendship The letter of friendship was the most "artless" of ancient letters; nonetheless, certain characteristics are discernible, and most of these fit very well with one dimension of Paul's letter to the Philippians. Here, for example, is Pseudo-Demetrius's sample letter:

> Even though I have been *separated from you for a long time,* I suffer this in body only. For I can never forget you or the impeccable way

we were raised together from childhood up. Knowing that I myself am genuinely concerned about *your affairs,* and that I have worked unstintingly for what is most advantageous to you, I have assumed that you, too, have the same opinion of me, and will refuse me nothing. You will *do well,* therefore, to give close attention to the members of my household lest they *need* anything, to assist them in whatever they might *need,* and to write about whatever you should choose.

Besides leaning heavily toward the reciprocation of friendship (see next section), three features (italicized above) of this theoretical example are noteworthy for Philippians: (1) the note at the beginning that friendly letters are related to separation of friends (cf. Phil 1:27; 2:12), (2) such letters are concerned with the "affairs" of both the sender and recipient (cf. Phil 1:12, 27; 2:19, 24), and (3) the recipient "does well" in looking after the "needs" of the sender (cf. Phil 4:14).

Recently Loveday Alexander (1989), in an empirical analysis of a series of family letters from among the papyri, has shown that a certain *formal* pattern emerges in these letters which is also in evidence in Philippians. She isolates seven items, including the salutation and concluding greetings (I have put the corresponding parts of Philippians in brackets):

1. The address and greeting [1:1-2]
2. Prayer for the recipients [1:3-11]
3. Reassurance about the sender (= "my affairs") [1:12-26]
4. Request for reassurance about the recipients (= "your affairs") [1:27—2:18; 3:1—4:3]
5. Information about movements of intermediaries [2:19-30]
6. Exchange of greetings with third parties [4:21-22]
7. Closing wish for health [4:23]

To be sure, Cicero considers "friendly letters" like these as not worthy of correspondence between true friends, since most of them deal with mundane matters, while letters between friends should engage in conversation about weightier matters—and this, of course, is also true of Philippians. What we have in Philippians, then, is a letter whose *form* has all the characteristics, including the "logic," of a friendly letter of the family type, but whose *content* engages in much weightier conversation.

Friendship itself, of the kind Cicero was talking about, was a matter that the Greeks and Romans took with a seriousness most moderns can scarcely appreciate. Since there are several indications within our letter that Paul understood his relationship with the Philippians to be a modified expression of this kind of friendship, a brief overview of this phenomenon is also necessary for us to understand Paul's letter to them.

Friendship in the Greco-Roman World As in most ancient societies, friendship played a primary role in basic societal relationships in the Greco-Roman world, including politics and business. So important was this matter that it became a regular topic of philosophical discussions. Aristotle devoted a considerable section of his *Nicomachean Ethics* to a discussion of friendship, while Cicero and Plutarch have entire treatises on the subject, and Seneca addresses the issue in several of his "moral letters." According to Aristotle (and others who followed his lead), there were three kinds of "friendship" between "equals": (1) true friendship between virtuous people, whose relationship is based on goodwill and loyalty (including trust), (2) friendship based on pleasure, that is, on the enjoyment of the same thing, so that people enjoy the society of those who are "agreeable to us," and (3) friendship based on need, a purely utilitarian arrangement, which Aristotle disdains, as do most of his successors. Somewhat condescendingly, Aristotle also admitted the word *friendship* for relationships between "unequals" (patronal)—parent and child, older person and younger, husband and wife(!), and ruler and persons ruled.

The philosophical discussions of friendship deal primarily with the first kind, where a certain core of ideals emerge that were thought to be applicable to all genuine friendships, which were entered intentionally in an almost contractual way. These included virtue, especially fidelity or loyalty; affection, in the form of mutual goodwill; and especially the basic matter—social reciprocity in the form of "giving and receiving benefits" (usually goods and services, although reciprocity sometimes took the form of gratitude only). The matter of "benefits" called for some of the lengthiest discussions, because friendship could not be understood apart from "benefits," but these could also be abused so as to undermine mutuality and trust. Because it entailed reciprocity, friendship also included a sense of "obligation" and expressions of "gratitude" (further goodwill).

Moreover, and in ways very difficult for moderns to appreciate, friendship of this more contractual kind was also agonistic (competitive). Plutarch puts it plainly: "Enmities follow close upon friendships, and are interwoven with them, inasmuch as it is impossible for a friend not to share his friend's wrongs or disrepute or disfavor" *Amicitiae Multitudinae* 96A-B). Friends automatically had enemies in common, so that "constant attention to friends meant constant watchfulness of enemies" (Stowers 1991:113).

One may easily see that many of these "ideals" are reflected in Paul's relationship to the Philippian believers. His letter is predicated on his and their mutual goodwill; this is the bottom line, which is so secure that Paul has no hesitation in addressing, even exhorting, them as he does. Theirs has been a participation or partnership in the gospel from the very beginning, a partnership that involved the Philippians themselves in evangelism and in furthering the gospel through their benefactions to Paul. That partnership now also includes mutual suffering for the gospel (1:29-30; 2:17). Friendship is further demonstrated by the oft-noted expressions of deep affection (e.g., "I long for all of you with the affection of Christ Jesus" [1:8]; cf. 1:7; 4:1). But friendship is especially demonstrated in their mutuality and reciprocity, exhibited in a variety of ways: Paul's earnestness to see them again for their own progress in the faith, since they have just recently benefited him in a material way; his praying for them (1:4) and their praying for him (1:19); but especially their recent gift, Paul's acknowledgment of which (4:10-20) is full of language indicating reciprocity in friendship. And friendship surely lies behind his concern that within their own community they be "like-minded" (see 2:2-5; 4:2-3); for his and their friendship will be on rocky ground if theirs with one another is not sustained. Significantly, much of the "special" vocabulary of Philippians occurs precisely at these points where friendship is in evidence (see Fee 1995:18-21).

These expressions of friendship are further heightened by the fact that Paul studiously avoids any indication of a patron-client (or patron-protégé) relationship, which emerges so frequently in his other letters (either in discussions of apostleship or in the imagery of father with children). Thus he begins by identifying himself and Timothy as slaves of Christ Jesus (1:1), who himself became a slave for all by dying on a cross (2:7-8). And though the major parts of the letter are exhortative, there is no appeal to Paul's authority as the basis of his exhortation; rather he appeals to their mutuality in Christ (2:1) and to his own example, as he himself follows Christ's example (3:4-14; so also 1:12-26 and 4:10-13, 17-19).

The Question of Opponents Given these clear evidences of friendship in Philippians, in both form and content, it seems likely that the agonistic nature of Greco-Roman friendship also holds the key to one of the more perplexing issues in this letter: the matter of opponents. There is nearly universal agreement that the Philippians are being harassed by opponents of some kind (some would say "kind*s*"); there is likewise nearly universal *dis*agreement as to the "who," "how many" and "where" of these opponents. "Those who oppose you" in 1:28 almost certainly refers to pagan opponents in Philippi (they are destined for destruction, after all) who are directly responsible for the Christians' current suffering (1:29-30). At issue are two passages in chapter 3 (vv. 2-3 and 18-19) where first Paul castigates as "dogs" and "men who do evil" those who compel Gentiles to be circumcised and are thus involved in mutilation. The second are people over whom Paul weeps, apparently because by setting their minds on earthly things (v. 19) they have become enemies of the cross (v. 18)—in sharp contrast to Christ (2:8) and Paul (3:10).

Who these people are, whether they are one or two groups, whether they are Christians or Jews, and how they are related to the "opponents" in 1:28 have been matters of considerable debate. But several pieces of data seem to moderate the significance of these questions for understanding Philippians. First, Paul expresses no anxiety that his Philippian friends might capitulate to false teaching; in this regard Philippians stands in bold relief over against Galatians and 2 Corinthians 10—13. Second, in both cases (3:1, 18) Paul indicates that he has told the Philippian believers about such people on some previous occasion(s). And third and most important, in neither case can one assume that the people referred to are currently present in Philippi, since nothing in the text itself indicates as much.

More likely, therefore, Paul's mention of them has to do with friends having enemies in common. In exhorting the Philippians to stand firm in the one Spirit for the gospel in the face of opposition and suffering (1:27—2:18), and thus not to lose sight of their sure eschatological future (3:10-21), he appeals to their long-term friendship (see especially 2:1) and places that in a context over against "enemies." Paul has warned them about such people many times before (3:1, 18), people who turn out to be his and their "enemies" mostly because they are first of all "enemies" of Christ himself (3:18). Thus it is probably a mistake to read chapter 3 as though opponents were actually present in Philippi, and then to mirror read what Paul says so as to reconstruct some kind of false teaching that Paul is combating. The nonpolemical language of Philippians (excepting 3:2-4) will not easily bear such weight.

For our understanding Philippians as a letter, however, friendship is only part of the story; the rest is to be found in another well-known kind of letter.

Philippians as a Letter of Moral Exhortation Another area in which first-century sociology differed considerably from ours is ethics and morality. Deeply influenced by the Law, the Prophets, the Gospels and the Epistles, we find it difficult to dissociate religion from ethics. But in the Greco-Roman world, ethical instruction did not belong to religion but to philosophy. Moreover, moral instruction often took place in the context of friendship—of the second kind, where a superior instructed an inferior, often by means of letters. Two fundamental elements characterize these letters: (1) the writer is the recipient's friend or moral superior, and (2) they aim at persuasion or dissuasion. Because the persuasion or dissuasion is toward or away from certain models of behavior, the author frequently appeals to examples, including his own. Pseudo-Libanius's brief example of such a letter reads: "Always be an emulator, dear friend, of virtuous men. For it is better to be well spoken of when imitating good men than to be reproached by all people while following evil men."

The Use of Exemplary Paradigms Philippians is easily recognizable in this description. Indeed, the larger part of the letter is taken up with two substantial hortatory sections (1:27—2:18 and 3:1—4:3), in which the appeal is made on the basis of mutuality and friendship (2:1;

cf. "all of *us* . . . should" in 3:15) and the aim is to persuade toward one kind of behavior and to dissuade from another. At the heart of these two sections are the best-known materials in the letter, the Christ story in 2:6-11 and Paul's story in 3:4-14. In both sections he explicitly says that the narratives have been given to serve as models for the Philippians' own way of thinking and of behavior appropriate to such a mindset (2:5; 3:15, 17; cf. 4:9). What is being modeled in each case is a mindset in keeping with the gospel. Christ serves as paradigm for the injunction of 2:3, "Do nothing out of selfish ambition or vain conceit, but in humility consider others better than yourselves." In Paul's case the Philippians are urged to follow his example, which has knowing Christ as its singular focus (3:10), especially by living "cruciform" (see note on 1:11) while at the same time straining to obtain the prize, a final and complete knowing of Christ at the end.

Given these explicitly paradigmatic narratives, we are alerted to read other personal references in the same way. Thus, even though Paul's opening reflection on his "affairs" in 1:12-26 fits with a letter of friendship, there is good reason to believe that it is also intended to be paradigmatic. So also with the two important interlude narratives as to what's next between him and them, namely the coming of Timothy shortly (2:19-24) and of Epaphroditus now (2:25-30, with this letter). Both men are well known to the Philippians yet are commended to them precisely because both exemplify the gospel. Timothy is set in contrast to nonfriends (= enemies) who look out for their own interests (vis-à-vis the exhortation of 2:3-4); moreover, he is well known to the Philippians as one who will take "a genuine interest in your welfare" (v. 20), which is the same as looking out for the interests of Christ (v. 21; cf. 2:4). And Epaphroditus is one who in service to Paul risked his own life for the work of Christ (v. 30). The Philippians are to "honor people like him."

Rhetoric and Orality But the issue of persuasion in this letter has been read differently by some. One of the current rages in New Testament studies is to read all of Paul's letters as though he had been a student of ancient rhetoric under the likes of an Aristotle or Quintilian (see Murphy-O'Connor 1995:65-86 for a useful overview; for a significant critique see Weima 1997). But the various attempts to superimpose Quintilian's grid over our letter (e.g., Watson 1988; Bloomquist 1993;

Witherington 1994) have only demonstrated the tenuousness of this procedure.

This is not to deny the presence of rhetorical features within the letter. While rhetorical analyses may yet prove helpful in showing how the hortatory (persuasion) parts of the letter work, far more important are several other rhetorical devices that seem intended to catch the attention of, and thus to carry conviction with, the *hearer* of the letter. Many of these (assonance, chiasmus, repetition, wordplays) will be pointed out in the course of this commentary.

These rhetorical features are especially to be understood in relationship to another (seldom noted) reality: that the Greco-Roman world was primarily an oral (and thus aural) culture (only about 15 percent of the population could read and write). This would have been especially true for the majority to whom this letter was addressed. All of Paul's letters, and Philippians in particular, were first of all oral—*dictated* to be *read aloud* in the community. Much of Paul's rhetoric comes into play precisely for this purpose. His assonance and wordplays, for example, are designed to be memorable. Oral cultures had a very high level of retention. In literary cultures we are bombarded by so many words in print that very few, if any, are kept in memory in a precise way.

Most significant for our present purposes, these features, rhetoric and orality, best explain an aspect of the letter that has often perplexed scholars: why Paul left his thanksgiving for the gift to the very end. For most of us that borders on rudeness, if not impropriety, and for scholars it has been the source of considerable speculation. But rhetoric and orality best account for it (see the introduction to 4:10-20). These are intentionally the last words left ringing in the Philippians' ears as the letter concludes—words of gratitude, theology and doxology that simply soar. And this in turn explains the extreme brevity (for Paul) of the final greetings (vv. 21-22).

Philippians as a Christian Hortatory Letter of Friendship In light of the foregoing, Philippians is rightly called "a hortatory letter of friendship" (Stowers 1991:107; White 1990:206). The marks of the letter of friendship are everywhere. Philippians is clearly intended to make up for their mutual absence, functioning as Paul's way of being present while absent (see comment on 1:27; 2:12). Thus he informs them about his affairs, speaks into their affairs and offers information about the movements of intermediaries. Evidence of mutual affection abounds. The reciprocity of friendship is especially evident at the beginning and the end, and thus is probably to be seen in the other parts as well. Moreover, in the two sections in which Paul speaks into their affairs the letter functions as moral exhortation, which is tied very specifically to exemplary paradigms.

But "hortatory letter of friendship" is only part of the story and, in some ways, the least significant part. For in Paul's hands everything turns into gospel, including both the formal and the material aspects of such a letter. Most significant, friendship in particular is radically transformed from a two-way to a three-way bond between him, the Philippians and Christ. And obviously it is Christ who is the center and focus of everything. Paul's and their friendship is predicated on their mutual participation/partnership *in the gospel.* This involves them in most of the conventions of Greco-Roman friendship, including especially social reciprocity, but it does so in light of Christ and the gospel. This three-way bond, which is the glue that holds the letter together from beginning to end, may best be illustrated as follows:

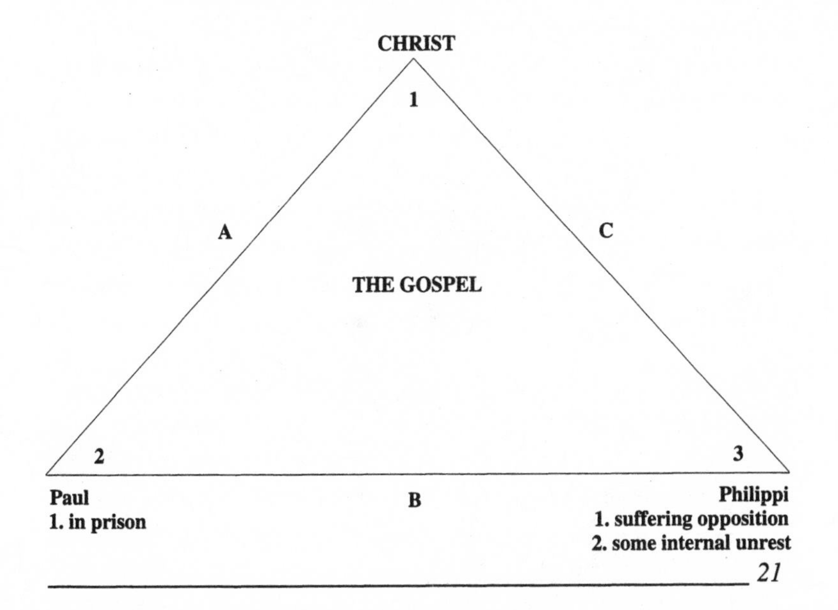

Paul's overarching concern is with the *gospel,* a word that occurs more often in this letter than in any of his others. His specific concern for the Philippians is with their ongoing relationship with Christ (figure 1, line C); all of the hortatory sections and many of the others have the strengthening of this relationship as their primary aim. Because of his and their long-time relationship in the gospel (line B), evidenced most recently by their gift to him (both of material substance and of the coming of Epaphroditus), Paul writes a letter of friendship that assumes the secure nature of that relationship. The reason for the exhortations is point 3, their present historical situation, which occasions the letter (see below). The paradigm for these appeals is threefold (Christ himself, point 1; Paul's imprisonment, point 2; and Paul's relationship with Christ, line A). Everything in the letter can be explained in light of one of these items.

Thus even though the description "hortatory letter of friendship" gives insight into a large number of this letter's special features, above all Philippians is an especially Pauline, and therefore intensely Christian, expression of such a letter. In his hands form yields to Christ and the gospel, first and always. Thus the first-century conventions that give us all kinds of insights into details are themselves of little moment to Paul. He is altogether concerned for his friends in Philippi and their ongoing relationship with Christ.

Use of the Old Testament A final feature of this letter, related to its being both hortatory and Christian, is Paul's use of the Old Testament. Elsewhere whenever Paul is carrying on an argument with his churches, and especially so when some form of Judaizing persuasion is afoot (as in 2 Corinthians, Galatians and Romans), he invariably argues from the Old Testament to support his understanding of the gospel. Sometimes it is enough simply to say, "it is written"; at other times he explicates the meaning of what stands written in light of the event of Christ and the Spirit.

All such forms of argumentation are noticeably missing from Philippians, especially from chapter 3, where in warning against his Judaizing enemies Paul tells his own story as an example of one who had been there but gave it up for Christ. In this letter Paul's use of the Old Testament is of an altogether different kind, one that occurs throughout his letters but is used exclusively here. Literary critics call this strategy "intertextuality," meaning the *conscious* embedding of fragments from an earlier text into a later one. Intertextuality assumes (1) that the readers/hearers will know the former text intimately—its language and very often its setting—and (2) that they will hear those echoes used in a new, or newly applied, way in the present setting. Thus while one might expect the Philippians to hear Paul's (conscious or unconscious) use of Old Testament language in many places (1:11; 3:1; 4:5), intertextuality seems to occur at several key points in the letter (1:19; 2:10-11, 14-16, 17 [4:18]). This kind of usage, especially the appeal in 2:14-16, where Paul presupposes the Philippians' place in the story of Israel, is not the stuff of polemics but of mutuality. He never argues on the basis that "it is written," because he assumes that he and they are on common ground with regard to their *understanding* of the gospel. His concern is with some practical implications of that common understanding.

Such a use of the Old Testament presupposes that as in all the Pauline churches, these early Gentile believers were thoroughly acquainted with their Bibles, and that they would recognize this application of the Old Testament texts to Paul's and their situation. They would do so in part because of the basically oral nature of the culture, in which the constant hearing of the same stories would reinforce them deeply in their memories. To put it bluntly, we may rightly assume that these early Gentile believers knew the Old Testament—their only Bible!—infinitely better than most Christians do today.

The Question of Integrity This leads us finally back to the matter noted at the outset: that many scholars resolve the "difficulty" of reading Philippians by breaking it up into two or (usually) three smaller letters. Advocates of such dismantling are especially disturbed by three matters: (1) the *to loipon* (NIV "finally") with which Paul begins 3:1, only (2) to interrupt himself with a vigorous attack against some Judaizers before returning to "finally" in 4:8, plus (3) an alleged final interruption with a "thankless thanks" at the end—not to mention the rudeness of waiting so long to do so. But those who find such issues insurmountable also seem blinded to the inherent weaknesses of their own point of view, which in fact creates more difficulties than it solves (see Fee 1995:21-23;

cf. O'Brien 1991:12-13).

The ultimate reason for rejecting the pastiche hypothesis is that the various parts of our current letter hold together well as one piece. For example, Paul's thanksgivings regularly anticipate many, if not most, of the items in the body of a given letter. In this case both the language and content of 1:3-11 anticipate topics from all three of the alleged letters. Thus the language of partnership in the gospel in verses 4-5 anticipates 4:10-20; the language of increasingly loving one another anticipates the exhortation of 1:27—2:18; the mention of the Philippians' sharing in his "bonds" for the defense of the gospel leads directly to 1:12-18; the language of longing for them in 1:7 anticipates the vocative of 4:1; the "fruit of righteousness" of verse 11 and the eschatological urgency of verses 6 and 10 point directly to 3:4-14. Did the "redactor" rewrite the obviously Pauline thanksgiving in order to make this work?

In the same vein, the two major hortatory sections of the letter, despite addressing different specific issues, are held together by (1) several linguistic phenomena (especially the use of "have the same mindset") as well as by (2) the two paradigmatic narratives—Christ's and Paul's—whose main thrust is to urge a cruciform way of looking at and living out present existence in the midst of opposition and suffering. Was the alleged redactor himself responsible for this insight, and if he *was* this clever, why then did he bungle the stitching job so badly? And is this bungler also responsible for the most ingenious rhetorical stroke of all: putting the "first letter" (allegedly 4:10-20) last, so that its powerful concluding theological rhetoric (4:18-20) is basically the last words in the letter?

The answer to these rhetorical questions, of course, is the obvious one: The person who both "bungled" the seams and arranged things so ingeniously is the apostle himself.

□ The Historical Situation of Philippians

Given that Philippians is a (very Christian) "hortatory letter of friendship," the question remains, why *this* letter to *this* people at *this* time? Thus we turn to the historical situation to which the apostle was writing—an exercise beset with pitfalls, since it requires a degree of "mirror reading" (trying to discover the Philippian situation on the basis of what Paul says to them). Each of the following sections, therefore, begins with what seems more certain before offering some best guesses as to how and why.

The City and Its People Philippi was located at the far eastern end of a large fertile plain (Datos) in central Macedonia, nestled against the initial ascent of a formidable acropolis. The major east-west turnpike, the Egnatian Way, ran through it, angling south from Philippi for its ten-mile (sixteen-kilometer) run across a low range of coastal mountains to the Aegean seaport Neapolis (modern Kavalla). An original colony had been taken over and renamed after himself by Philip of Macedon (father of Alexander the Great) in 356 B.C.E. Its reasons for existence are related to its strategic location: it sat as sentinel to a large agricultural plain; it was well protected by its acropolis; and, most important to Philip, it was near Mount Pangaion on the northern side of the plain, which at that period was rich in mineral deposits, including gold. In 168 Philippi (and all Macedonia) came under the control of the Romans, who abolished the ancient Macedonian dynasty and eventually created a Roman province, divided into four parts. According to Luke, Philippi was "the leading city of that district of Macedonia" (Acts 16:12).

Our interest in the city stems from 42 B.C.E, when two major battles were fought nearby in the plain—between Cassius and Brutus (the assassins of Julius Caesar) and the victors, Octavian (later the emperor Augustus) and Mark Antony. Following these victories Octavian honored Philippi by "refounding" it as a Roman military colony, thus endowing its populace with Roman citizenship. Always astute politically, Octavian populated the town and its surrounding agricultural area with discharged veterans from the war. This both alleviated a population problem in Rome and ensured allegiance to the empire (through its emperor) at this strategic spot along the major highway that connected Rome with Asia Minor and other points east. In an even more astute move, Octavian did the same after he defeated Antony at the battle of Actium in 30 B.C.E.—this time with veterans from Antony's army, thus building up loyalty among those who had once fought with him and more recently against him.

Although these events happened some ninety-plus years before the writing of our letter, they have a considerable influence on several key matters in Philippians. By the time Paul came to the city in 49 C.E. (Acts 16:11-15), Philippi was the urban political center of the eastern end of the plain. Its population was both Roman and Greek, and although Latin was the official language, Greek was the predominant language of commerce and everyday life—all the more so in a city located in Greece. Of the four people from the early Christian community whose names we know, three bear Greek names (Lydia, Euodia, Syntyche) and the other Roman (Clement). We know very little otherwise about the socioeconomic makeup of the congregation. Lydia, a merchant from Thyatira, bears the name of her home province. That she had a household large enough to include Paul and his companions suggests she owned a villa; it is likely that at least some of the women who were gathered with her at the river for worship, perhaps including Euodia and Syntyche, were members of her household. The jailer, on the other hand, who also had a household, probably belonged to the artisan class; and the young girl from whom Paul cast the divining spirit belonged to the slave class, which often made up a large part of early Christian congregations (as members of Christian households or, as in her case, on their own). What this suggests is that the socioeconomic range was somewhat similar to what one finds in churches in urban centers today.

The Situation of the Church The specific historical context of the church to which Paul wrote reflects a combination of three factors: its own history, its location in Philippi and its long-term relationship with Paul in terms of Greco-Roman friendship.

Their History The story of the founding of this church, recorded in Acts 16:11-40, is well known. According to Luke's report, its nucleus was formed by a group of God-fearing women, who, because of the lack of a Jewish synagogue in the city, had been meeting by the river on the sabbath for prayer. Given the well-known prominent place of women in Macedonian life in general, it is not surprising that the core group of first converts consisted of women, nor that the location of Macedonia's first house church was the home of a woman merchant. That Paul and his entourage also accepted patronage from Lydia, including becoming temporary members of her household, also is significant for some of the matters in our letter (see comment on 4:14-17).

We cannot be sure from any of our sources how long Paul and his companions (Silas, Timothy and Luke) stayed in Philippi. But whatever the length of their stay, it was long enough to establish a close friendship between the apostle and this community of believers, undoubtedly aided by Luke's staying on in Philippi after Paul, Silas and Timothy had departed for Thessalonica (see comment on 4:3). Evidence for the kind of contractual friendship outlined above is to be found in particular in Paul's statement in 4:15 ("not one church shared with me in the matter of giving and receiving, except you only"); social reciprocity was the primary stuff of Greco-Roman friendship.

What we know of Paul's relationship with this community after his somewhat hasty departure is sketchy. On the basis of statements in 1 and 2 Corinthians, he apparently paid at least two visits to Philippi not recorded in Acts. According to 2 Corinthians 1:16—2:5, everything erupted when he appeared suddenly—and unexpectedly—in Corinth, and not in keeping with earlier plans (1 Cor 16:5). So Paul went on to Macedonia and then decided to write to Corinth instead of returning. Later (2 Cor 2:13; 7:5) he came again into Macedonia, where he met Titus, and dispatched him and two other brothers (Luke? see 2 Cor 8:18, "the brother who is praised by all the churches for his service to the gospel") along with our 2 Corinthians, which he wrote from there. According to Acts, because of a plot against him he paid yet another visit to the city (20:3) on his way to Jerusalem with the collection.

Paul's deep affection for this congregation, evident throughout his letter, is also evidenced in his extravagant testimony about them in 2 Corinthians 8:1-5:

> And now, brothers and sisters, we want you to know about the grace that God has given the Macedonian churches. Out of the most severe trial, their overflowing joy and their extreme poverty welled up in rich generosity. For I testify that they gave as much as they were able, and even beyond their ability. Entirely on their own, they urgently pleaded with us for the privilege of sharing in this service to the saints. And they did not do as we expected, but they gave themselves first to the Lord and then to us in keeping with God's will.

Significant for our purposes is not only the affection on display here—further evidence of friendship—but the equation of "joy," "poverty" and "generosity." These, too, have bearing on our letter.

The occasion of our letter is to be found both in the elements of friendship (the return of Epaphroditus; Paul's reporting on his "affairs"; his acknowledgment of the Philippians' gift) and in its hortatory sections. At least two issues coalesce as the driving force behind the exhortations: suffering because of current opposition in Philippi, and internal unrest of some sort. Both of these are mentioned in the initial imperative (1:27-28): "that you *stand firm* in *one spirit, contending as one man* for the faith of the gospel without being frightened in any way by *those who oppose you*." This is followed by a clause explaining their suffering (vv. 29-30) and by an appeal to have the same mindset (2:1-2). Significantly, Paul uses these same verbs ("stand firm," "have the same mindset") in the appeals that conclude the second hortatory section (4:1-3). Thus these two concerns frame the two hortatory sections in the letter, and do so with identical language. But the precise nature of these two issues, how they interrelate and how much the matter of opposition comes into play, are less certain.

Opposition and Suffering That the Philippian congregation is undergoing suffering as the result of opposition in Philippi is stated explicitly in 1:27-30 and metaphorically in 2:17. Moreover, in 1:29-30 Paul not only gives *theological reasons* for their suffering ("on behalf of Christ") but indicates that his present imprisonment and their current suffering are related ("you are going through *the same* struggle you saw I had, and now hear that I still have"). While suffering is not the dominant motif in Philippians, it constitutes the church's primary historical context *in Philippi* and thus underlies much of the letter. Two items are noteworthy.

First, this context helps to explain Paul's emphasis on his imprisonment and suffering in the thanksgiving (v. 7) and in the narrative about his affairs (vv. 12-26). Part of his reason for thanksgiving is their partnership with him in his chains, for both the defense and confirmation of the gospel, which he terms "God's grace" (v. 7). Both parts of the narrative about "my affairs" which immediately follows (vv. 12-18a, 18b-26) seem intended to illustrate how Paul is responding, first, to his suffering at the hands of the empire and, second, to the selfish ambition/rivalry of other believers who are trying to cause him grief.

Thus the narrative, which functions as a typical (expanded) expression of friendship, also functions as an exemplary paradigm (= this is how you should respond in your own suffering at the hands of "Rome" in Philippi).

Second, opposition and suffering probably lie behind a further—seldom noted—major motif in the letter: Paul's repeated emphasis on the believer's sure future with its eschatological triumph. This motif begins in the thanksgiving and prayer report (vv. 6, 10); it dominates the second part of his report on his affairs (1:21-24); it serves as the glorious climax (vv. 9-11) to the Christ story in 2:6-11; it is the penultimate word in the appeal that follows (v. 16); it holds the dominant place in his own story in 3:4-14, as the climax of both the story itself (vv. 12-14) and the appeal that follows (vv. 20-21; 4:1), which is explicitly paradigmatic at this very point; it serves as the singular affirmation (4:5) to the concluding imperatives (4:4-9); and it is integral to the letter's final words of theology and doxology (4:19-20).

The tie of this motif to opposition and suffering is especially to be seen in Paul's personal story and its application in 3:4—4:1. Here Paul yearns to know Christ, both the power of his resurrection and *sharing in his sufferings* (vv. 10-11), the former being necessary for the latter and the latter explained further as "becoming like him in his death" (cf. 2:6-8). In the appeal that immediately follows, the Philippians are urged to "take such a view" as has Paul (vv. 15, 17), who, while "becoming like [Christ] in his death," vigorously pursues the ultimate eschatological prize of knowing Christ finally and completely (vv. 13-14), which is explicated at the end in terms of receiving a glorified body like Christ's (vv. 20-21).

The *source* and *reason* for this suffering are less clear, but the clue probably lies with the first explicit mention of it in 1:29-30. The Philippians are suffering, Paul says, because they are involved in "the same struggle . . . that I still have." If we take this seriously—and literally—then the reason for the preceding reflections on imprisonment (1:12-26) also takes shape. Paul's suffering is both for the defense of the gospel and at the hands of the empire. The Philippian believers are opposed by a "crooked and depraved generation" (2:15) who are destined for destruction (1:28). These passages can refer only to the pagan populace of Philippi, who happen also to be citizens of Rome in a Roman military colony and descendants of repatriated soldiers fiercely loyal to the emperor. Thus they are the source of the suffering.

That the opposition, and thus the believers' suffering, is a direct result of the Roman character of their city is further indicated by the twin play on their dual citizenship in 1:27 and 3:20. Roman citizens, they also constitute a colony of heaven in this colony of Rome in Macedonia. Since their true "citizenship" is in heaven (3:20), they are to live their heavenly citizenship in Philippi "in a manner worthy of . . . Christ" (1:27).

The pro-empire character of Philippi also explains another phenomenon in the letter: the unusually high number of references to Christ, especially the emphasis on Christ's having obtained sole privilege to the title *Kyrios* ("Lord," 2:9-11) and the unique appellation of Christ as *Sōtēr* ("Savior," 3:20).

With this we come to the most probable *cause* of the suffering. Philippi owed its existence as a Roman colony to the special grace of the first Roman emperor, thus ensuring that the city would always have special devotion for the emperor. By the time of our letter, the primary titles for the emperor were *Kyrios* and *Sōtēr* ("Lord and Savior"). Not only so, but the cult of the emperor, honoring the emperor in a way approaching deification, had found its most fertile soil in the eastern provinces. In a city like Philippi this would have meant that every public event (the assembly, public performances in the theater, etc.) and much else within its boundaries took place in the context of giving honor to the emperor, with the acknowledgment that (in this case) Nero was "lord and savior." Which is precisely the place where believers in Christ could no longer join in as citizens of Rome in Philippi. Their allegiance was to another *Kyrios,* Jesus Christ, before whom every knee would someday bow and every tongue confess, including the citizens of Philippi who were causing their suffering, as well as the emperor himself. The Philippian believers in Christ were thus citizens of a greater dominion, and their allegiance was to another *Sōtēr,* whose coming from heaven they awaited with eager expectation.

If this were not enough to make the citizens of Philippi begin a methodical persecution of these (now) expatriates living among them, the fact that the Christians' Lord and Savior had taken the form of a slave in his becoming human, and in that humanity died on a cross (2:6-8), would have been the final straw. But to this one, Paul says, whom the Philippian pagans scorn, God has given the name above all names, the name of the Lord *(Kyrios)* God himself.

Although one cannot be sure of all the details, there is good reason to believe this picture reflects the historical context of our letter. It is in this light that the Philippians would hear Paul's triumphant note about the whole Praetorian Guard—the emperor's own select troops—coming to know about the gospel through Paul's imprisonment (1:13). So also with the final word of the letter (before the concluding grace-benediction): "All the saints [in Rome] send you greetings, especially those who belong to *Caesar's household*" (4:22)—who themselves join the Philippians in saying "Jesus is Lord." The gospel, with its proclamation of a heavenly Lord who has become the incarnate Savior, had penetrated the household of the (merely earthly) Roman "lord and savior," who stands ultimately behind the same struggle both Paul and the Philippians are currently experiencing. And this just a couple of short years before the struggle would break out with a vengeance in Rome itself, with Nero's pogrom against believers in Christ.

Internal Unrest While opposition and suffering at the hands of the Roman citizens of Philippi is the historical context, the crux of the letter, Paul's ultimate concern in its hortatory sections, has to do with internal posturing. The Philippians are in a life-and-death struggle for the gospel in Philippi, and if their present unrest goes uncorrected it could bid fair to blunt, if not destroy, their witness to Christ in their city. There can be little question that this issue lies behind the major moments in the letter. It is the first item mentioned in the opening imperative (1:27), to which Paul returns in 2:1-4 after the momentary focus on their suffering. It explicitly lies behind both the Christ story in 2:6-11 and its application in 2:12-16. It seems also to lie behind the description of Timothy in 2:20-22 and parts of Paul's story in 3:4-14, as well as the concluding imperative in 4:2-3, where Euodia and Syntyche are singled out by means of the identical imperative as in 2:2.

But the exact nature of the problem, and how far-reaching it is, is much more speculative. On the basis of what Paul says and how he speaks to this matter, three things seem fairly certain. First, what lies behind the unrest is some form of "selfish ambition"—or posturing, as I prefer to call it. When appealing to the community to be "like-minded" so as to complete Paul's joy (2:2), he singles out "selfish ambition" (rivalry) and "vain conceit" (empty glory) as the attitudes that must be rejected (v. 3). In their place he calls for "humility," which evidences itself by each one looking out for "the interests of others" (v. 4). It is scarcely accidental (1) that "selfish ambition"/rivalry is attributed to those in Rome who are trying to make life miserable for Paul in his imprisonment (1:17) or (2) that looking out for the concerns of the Philippians, over against caring only for one's own interests, is the way Paul describes Timothy to the Philippians, who know Timothy well (2:20-21). The Christ narrative thus speaks directly to this matter, since as God he "made himself nothing" (emptied himself—over against doing anything on the basis of selfish ambition) and as man he "humbled himself" (over against doing anything on the basis of vainglory).

But second, these attitudes have not yet led to "divisions" or "quarrels," the language Paul uses in 1 Corinthians 1:10-12, which there he goes on to describe in clear terms of disunity. The closest thing to such language in our letter is "complaining or arguing" (Phil 2:14). This is still some distance from "divisions"; but if unchecked, it is the stuff that leads to division, which is precisely why Paul feels compelled to speak to it, and to send Timothy to look into it (2:19-20) before he himself comes (2:23-24).

Third, this is probably where the warning in chapter 3 against enemies fits in. While there is no evidence for the actual presence of outsiders "stirring up the pot" in Philippi, the unrest in the church is likely reflected in one or some of them being open to listen to foreign matter. Their readiness to do so is most likely related to the issue of suffering. The apparent security of being Jewish (the matrix out of which some of them originated as God-fearers) while also being in Christ may have begun to look better to them now, since Judaism was a legitimate religion in the empire. But people who think so are enemies, Paul reminds the Philippians with the stern warning of 3:2-3. He himself had been there, and there is no future to the past. The future lies strictly with Christ; hence Paul's weeping over others who have become enemies of the cross of Christ by setting their minds strictly on earthly things

(3:18-19).

While we may not have certainty about these "guesses," they reflect an attempt to tie together the various items of the letter as a whole. In any case, the situation in Philippi is serious but not disastrous. And since these people are his friends, having recently renewed the evidence of their friendship by a gift to minister to Paul's needs in prison, and since his imprisonment forbids his current presence with them, he does what friends do in such situations: writes a hortatory letter of friendship to serve as his "presence" in his "absence" (2:12).

The Situation of Paul At the time of his writing Philippians, Paul is clearly in detainment, which he describes four times as being "in chains" (1:7, 13, 14, 17). The questions of where and when have been assumed throughout this introduction (and the commentary that follows) to refer to his Roman imprisonment in the early 60s (between 60 and 62); but since many reject this tradition (in favor of either Caesarea or Ephesus), a few words are needed regarding the matter.

The internal evidence of the letter specifically favors the tradition, especially the mention in 1:13 that "it has become clear throughout the *whole* palace [Praetorian] guard . . . that I am in chains for Christ," and the final greeting in 4:22 from "the saints . . . especially those who belong to Caesar's household." The natural reading of these texts implies that Paul is incarcerated in Rome.

First, the way Paul mentions the *whole* praetorium seems intended to elicit delight and wonder from the Philippians. Although *praetorium* can refer to a "governor's palace" in the provinces (as in Mark 15:16 and Acts 23:35), the word more naturally refers to the Praetorian Guard, the emperor's elite troops stationed in Rome (see on 1:13). Those who favor an Ephesian imprisonment are especially hard put by this reference, since Ephesus was one of the competing capitals of Asia, a *senatorial* province in which there was no (imperial) praetorium of either kind. Likewise, although the word could refer to the governor's palace in Caesarea, there would be little cause for wonder to mention that the "whole praetorium" in Caesarea had come to learn that Paul's imprisonment was for Christ. Paul's sentence implies that this became clear to a large number of people over a period of time and through his direct involvement, whereas in Caesarea the number of people involved would be relatively small. In any case, his coming by night under the care of two centurions, their two hundred men, plus cavalry and spearmen, followed by a very quick hearing, would have been a major event in the praetorium in Caesarea and scarcely what Paul is referring to in 1:13.

Second, regarding the mention of "members of Caesar's household," there can be little question that Nero had members of his household scattered all over the empire looking out for his interests in the provinces. But nowhere outside of Rome was there a known concentration of them of such size that some of its "members" are noteworthy for having become believers in Christ, nor is there any evidence for the use of this terminology outside of Rome. Indeed, in contrast to the mention of the Praetorian Guard, this is *not* a technical term, and Paul uses it on several occasions, always to refer to a house and its occupants. One would seem to need hard evidence and particularly compelling reasons for rejecting the Roman provenance of this letter to argue that Paul in this case has abandoned his normal usage.

But compelling reasons for rejecting the tradition are precisely what is lacking. Only two have a degree of substance, and neither is compelling. First, it is argued that in writing to Rome Paul expected to start a mission in the west (Rom 15:23-24, 28), not to return east, whereas in our letter Paul expects to be released and to return to Philippi (1:26; 2:24). Second, the distance between Rome and Philippi (c. eight hundred miles) is argued to be too great for the five trips to and fro that this letter is alleged to presuppose.

With regard to the first matter, there is every imaginable difference between what Paul hoped to do when speaking as a free man some three or four years before our letter and what he now plans to do at the end of a long and trying imprisonment—especially so with some storm clouds hovering over his churches in the east. Likewise, the distance factor is more imagined than real, since it presupposes more trips between Paul and Philippi than are warranted and assumes the historically unlikely scenario that Epaphroditus was traveling alone (see comment on 2:26). Philippi, after all, sat astride the Egnatian Way, which brought people from Rome to Macedonia, and vice versa, in a relatively short time by ancient standards.

Finally, it should be pointed out that Paul's contemplation of the possible outcomes of his tribunal ("life or death" = release or execution, 1:20-26) would be out of place in Ephesus, again because it is an imperial matter and Asia was a senatorial province (not to mention the lack of hard evidence for *any* kind of imprisonment there).

Most tradition has good reason for its existence; the data clearly favor it in this case, and there is no good reason to reject it. Hence the commentary proceeds from this perspective.

As to the time frame of this imprisonment, the traditional suggestion of between 60 and 62 fits most of the data best. Although some of this evidence is capable of another interpretation, the internal evidence of Philippians would put the writing of this letter toward the latter end of the imprisonment, rather than early on, thus closer to 62 than to 60.

□ Some Theological Reflections

As the foregoing analysis and the following commentary point out, Paul's concern throughout Philippians is ultimately with the *gospel.* But because he and the Philippians are friends and partners in the gospel of such long standing, there is little need for him to spell out its content in this letter. The closest thing to such a statement is 3:3-9, especially verses 3 and 9, where all of the essential gospel matters are spoken to in very brief fashion.

The gospel for Paul is ultimately all about salvation (cf. 1:28), which comes from God and is effected by Christ and made effective by the Spirit. Because the Jewish law is the point of contention in this passage, Paul's regular word in such contexts is "righteousness." The contrasts in this case, however, are not between works of law and faith in Christ but between "confidence in the flesh" (= putting confidence in one's standing with God on the basis of human religious achievement, 3:4) and serving by the Spirit/boasting in Christ Jesus (= putting one's confidence totally in Christ and evidencing that by serving God through the power of the Holy Spirit). In 3:9 this contrast is spelled out in the more familiar terms of "a righteousness of my own that comes from the law" and "righteousness that comes from God and is by faith."

Most of this is expressed in the context of Paul's story that is to serve as a paradigm in contrast to their common enemies, the Judaizers, and in favor of a lifestyle in conformity to that of Christ. And since controversy controls very little of the argument of this letter, Paul easily shifts from these positional ways of talking about salvation to the more standard Old Testament relational way: "knowing" Christ. Thus *Christ* becomes the front-and-center concern throughout the letter; and knowing Christ, now and forever, is the passion that drives everything. To know Christ is to know God; thus Paul's singular passion: "to live is Christ and to die is [to] gain [Christ]."

But knowing Christ is not some kind of intellectual exercise. Rather it is to live in relationship with him in such a way that one comes to know him intimately. And to know him is to be conformed into his likeness. Thus the role of the two marvelous paradigmatic passages: Christ's story in 2:6-11 and Paul's story in 3:4-14. Crucial to Christ's story is the fact that he is equal with God and therefore that in his self-emptying and humbling himself to death on a cross, God's character is on display. The God we serve is not grasping or capricious but is "gentle and humble in heart" (Mt 11:29) and self-sacrificially gives himself on behalf of those he loves. And so with Paul's story, to know Christ means to share in his sufferings and thus to be conformed to the likeness of his death (Phil 3:10).

This is where the theme of imitation also fits in. Just as Paul has left them an example, the Philippian believers are to join together to live cruciform, in the pattern of Christ's cross; and they are to "take note of those who live according to the pattern we gave you" (3:17). Those who walk otherwise, whose minds are set on merely earthly things, are thus also "enemies of the cross of Christ" (3:18-19).

This *theological* concern—God's essential character on display in Christ, who redeems us to share that likeness—also underlies the other well-known themes in this letter: suffering, joy, unity, pressing on toward the prize. The proper response to hardship is, as in the Psalter, to "rejoice in the Lord always," for "the Lord is near" (4:4-5). The Lord is none other than Christ; and to rejoice in him is to put one's trust totally in him. To rejoice in the Lord in this way is the sure antidote also to the "selfish ambition" and inflated self-importance (2:3-4) that has led to complaining and arguing (2:14). To live cruciform means to put the needs and concerns of others before one's own (cf. 2:20-21); and in such living there is little room for petty bickering that divides. This same Lord is near in the other sense: whose coming "from heaven" we eagerly await, when we will be finally conformed to his likeness in every way.

Thus the theology of Philippians is held together by its singular focus on Christ. May those of us who read it over and again be more and more conformed into his likeness, so that we might faithfully hold fast to the word of life and thus shine like stars in the midst of our own "crooked and perverse generation" (2:15-16). The theology that bursts forth in this letter is not one option among others for Christian living; this is the only God there is, and he calls us to bear his likeness in every possible way.

Outline of Philippians

1:1-11	**Introductory Matters**
1:1-2	The Greeting
1:3-8	Prayer as Thanksgiving
1:9-11	Prayer as Petition
1:12-26	**Paul's Affairs: Reflections on Imprisonment**
1:12-18	The Present: Paul's Imprisonment Advances the Gospel
1:18-26	The Future: For Christ's Glory and the Good of the Philippians
1:27—2:18	**The Philippians' Affairs: Exhortation to Steadfastness and Unity**
1:27-30	The Appeal: In the Face of Opposition
2:1-4	The Appeal Renewed: Unity Through Humility
2:5-11	The Example of Christ
2:12-18	Application and Final Appeal
2:19-30	**What's Next Regarding Paul's and Their Affairs**
2:19-24	Timothy and Paul to Come Later
2:25-30	Epaphroditus to Come Now
3:1—4:3	**The Philippians' Affairs—Again**
3:1-4	At Issue: The Circumcision of Gentiles
3:4-14	The Example of Paul
3:15—4:3	Application and Final Appeal
4:4-23	**Concluding Matters**
4:4-9	Concluding Exhortations
4:10-20	Acknowledging Their Gift: Friendship and the Gospel
4:21-23	Closing Greetings

COMMENTARY

□ Introductory Matters (1:1-11)

In grammar school I was taught some rudimentary rules about writing letters: that there are basically two types (personal/friendly and business); that one (business) has an inside address, while friendly letters do not; but that both begin and end the same way (with a greeting, such as "Dear Father," and a closing, "Your son, Gordon").

Letters in the Greco-Roman period had this pattern in reverse, with a threefold salutation at the beginning: "Gordon, to his father: Greetings." Very often the next item in the letter was a wish (sometimes a prayer) for the health or well-being of the recipient. Paul's letters, which follow this standard form, usually include a thanksgiving report and sometimes, as here, a prayer report (telling his recipients specifically how he prays for them). In contrast to most first-century letters, where (as in ours) these formal items were stereotyped, Paul tends to elaborate them; and in his hands they become distinctively Christian.

The Greeting (1:1-2) In comparison with Paul's other letters, several elements of this greeting stand out: its comparative brevity, the fixed nature of the greeting proper (v. 2), and the inclusion of *overseers and deacons*. Several items call for comment.

The Writer(s) (1:1a) This is one of six letters where *Timothy,* who was well known in Philippi (see 2:20-22), is included in the greeting. Since the rest of the letter clearly originates from Paul alone (e.g., 1:12-26, 30), Timothy probably served as Paul's secretary. In the other letters where it appears in the greeting, Timothy's name is separated from Paul's, since Paul begins by identifying himself as "an apostle of Christ Jesus," and Timothy is not an apostle. But Timothy is a fellow servant (or slave), so here their names are linked: *Paul and Timothy, servants [slaves] of Christ Jesus*. Paul's reason for not identifying himself as an apostle in this case is most likely related to the matter of friendship (between "equals") noted in the introduction, which has no place in it for reminders of status.

The word translated *servants* is actually the Greek word for "slaves" and probably carries a double connotation. Gentile hearers would have instinctively understood the word to refer to those owned by, and subservient to, the master of a household. Although the institution of slavery in antiquity was a far cry from the racial slavery that blighted American society—and the English society that made it possible by the slave trade—the slave in the Roman Empire was still not a free person but "belonged to" another. At the same time, however, in the Greek translation of the Old Testament (the LXX), which would have been well known to the Philippians, this word was also used to translate the term "servant of Yahweh [the LORD]." "The slave of the Lord" thus carried a sense of distance from and dependence on God, while at the same time being a kind of honorific title for those in special service to God (e.g., Moses, 2 Kings 18:12; Joshua, Josh 24:29).

This double connotation is probably at work in Paul's present usage. He and Timothy are "slaves" *of Christ Jesus,* bound to him as slaves to a master, and also servants of the Lord (now *Christ Jesus!*) whose bond

1:1 On the significance of their being "God's holy people" *at Philippi* see my introduction. In writing *to all the saints at Philippi,* the first of five occurrences of *all* in verses 1-8, Paul is very likely (subtly, to be sure) also anticipating the repeated exhortations to unity found later in the letter (1:27; 2:1-4; 4:2-3). See Lightfoot 1881:83. For a discussion of the significance of using *the saints* to designate the New Testament people of God, especially to indicate their existence as an eschatological people who live the life of the future in the present ("already but not yet"), see Fee 1996:49-62.

is expressed in loving service on behalf of Christ for the Philippians—and others. This designation anticipates a significant moment later in this letter, where Christ himself is said to have taken *the very nature of a servant* (2:7). Elsewhere Paul uses this terminology to designate any and all who serve God as free bond-slaves—that is, as those who are free in Christ Jesus but have used that freedom to perform the duties of a slave (Gal 5:13) in the service of God and of his people. This is the closest thing to status one finds in our letter. And this is also the first of at least sixty-one mentions of Christ in the letter. Whatever else is said, everything has Christ as its cause and focus.

The Addressees (1:1b) *Saints* is one of several Old Testament terms used to designate Israel that was appropriated by New Testament writers for the people of God newly constituted by Christ and the Spirit. Its origins can be traced to the covenantal setting of Exodus 19:6, where God addresses Israel as his people, "a *holy* nation"—a people consecrated and subject to Yahweh and his service. Its New Testament usage most likely derives from Daniel 7:18, where God's end-time people, who receive the kingdom as an eternal inheritance, are called "the saints of the Most High." A preferable translation might be "God's holy people," which keeps both dimensions of the term intact—believers in Christ as constituting God's people, who are by that very fact also called to be his holy people, set apart by the Holy Spirit for God's purposes and distinguished as those who manifest his character in the world. Concern that the believers be God's holy people in Philippi will be picked up throughout Paul's letter (Phil 1:10-11; 2:14-15; 3:17-19; 4:8).

Their becoming "God's holy people" is the direct result of their relationship to Christ Jesus; they are *the saints in Christ Jesus.* Christ Jesus is responsible for their becoming the people of God. As the crucified and risen One, he also constitutes the present sphere of their new

---

For *episkopos (overseers)* see Paul's speech in Acts 20:28 where he urges the Ephesian elders to "give heed to . . . the flock, among whom [not 'over whom'] the Holy Spirit has placed you as *episkopoi,* so as to shepherd God's church" (my translation). Although there are titular implications in this usage, the accent is on function. In 1 Timothy 3 and Titus 1, although the concern is with character qualifications, even there they are described as those who "care for God's church" (see 1 Tim 3:5). For further discussion and bibliography see Fee 1995:68 nn. 49-50; see also the discussion of *apostolos* ("apostle") in this book's note on 2:25.

existence. They live as those who belong to Christ Jesus, as those whose lives are forever identified with Christ. This theme is thoroughgoing in Philippians, both in Paul's reflections on his own life (1:20-23; 3:7-11) and in his affirmations of and exhortations to the Philippians (1:27; 2:1, 5-11; 3:3; 4:7).

The most striking feature of this salutation is the addition of the phrase *with the overseers and deacons*. Surprisingly, this is the first designation of its kind in Paul's letters; even more surprisingly, after being thus singled out in the address, they are not hereafter mentioned or spoken to. As with the salutation itself, the letter in its entirety is always addressed to the whole community. Our difficulty from this distance is to determine who these people are and how they functioned in the community of faith. Nonetheless, some things seem clear enough.

First, exactly as one finds in the earliest (1 Thessalonians) and later (1 Timothy) letters, both references are plural. No evidence exists for a single leader as the head of the local assembly in the Pauline churches. The most probable reason for this relates to the role Paul himself played in his churches. Although he was not regularly present with them, they were his churches and owed their existence and obedience to him (cf. Phil 2:12).

Second, the language used for this addition, *together with* or "along with," is a sure giveaway as to the role of leaders in the Pauline churches. The community as a whole is addressed, and in most cases therefore the *overseers and deacons* are simply reckoned as being within the community. When they are singled out, as here, the leaders are not "over" the church but are addressed along with the rest, as a distinguishable part but clearly as part of the whole, not above or outside it.

Third, like all Paul's designations of church leaders, these terms first of all refer to people who function in these ways rather than hold an office. The noun *overseer* derives from a verb whose primary meaning is to "visit" in the sense of "looking after" or "caring for" someone. The people who bore this designation probably held the primary leadership roles in the local church and were responsible for caring for the people.

The word *deacon,* which means "servant," is most commonly used by Paul to designate those who serve others (Christ, Rom 15:8; government officials, Rom 13:4; Paul himself, 1 Cor 3:5; 2 Cor 3:6; his coworkers,

Col 1:7; 1 Thess 3:2). From our distance it is nearly impossible to know either what their function was or how they differed from the *overseers.* If the latter most likely gave general oversight to the congregation, *deacons* probably were distinguished by their actual deeds of service.

Why only in this letter are the *overseers and deacons* singled out in the salutation? The most likely clue is to be found in 4:2-3, where Euodia and Syntyche, who are probably among these leaders, apparently are not in full accord with each other. Thus both the *all* with which the address begins and the addition of *with the overseers and deacons* at the end anticipate the problem of friction that has arisen within this community, perhaps within the leadership itself.

The Greeting/Blessing (1:2) The greeting proper is a marvelous example of Paul's "turning into gospel" everything he sets his hand to. The traditional greeting in the Hellenistic world was *chairein*—the infinitive of the verb "to rejoice," but in salutations meaning simply "Greetings!" (see Acts 15:23; Jas 1:1). In Paul's hands this now becomes *charis (grace),* to which he adds the traditional Jewish greeting *shalom* (*peace,* in the sense of "wholeness" or "well-being"). Thus instead of offering the familiar "greetings," Paul salutes his sisters and brothers in Christ with "grace to you—and peace," reminiscent of the form of an ancient Jewish blessing.

In a profound sense this greeting nicely represents Paul's larger theological perspective. The sum total of God's activity toward his human creatures is found in the word *grace;* God has given himself to his people bountifully and mercifully in Christ. Nothing is deserved, nothing can be achieved. The sum total of those benefits as they are experienced by the recipients of God's grace is *peace,* God's shalom, both now and to come. The latter flows out of the former, and both together flow from *God our Father* and were made effective in our human history through *the Lord Jesus Christ.*

The collocation of the Father and Son in such texts as these must not be overlooked. In the theology of Paul, whose central concern is salvation in Christ, God the Father is understood to initiate such salvation, and his glory is its ultimate reason for being. Christ is the One through whom God's salvation has been effected in history. But texts such as this one, where Father and Son are simply joined by the conjunction *and* as equally the source of *grace and peace,* and many others as well, make it clear that in Paul's mind the Son is truly God and works in cooperation with the Father and the Spirit for the redemption of the people of God.

Although one hesitates to make too much of such relatively formal matters, the contemporary church fits into this salutation at several key points. Those in roles of primary leadership too easily slip into a self-understanding which pays lip service to their being *slaves/servants of Christ Jesus* but prefer the more honorable sense of this term found in the Old Testament to the paradigm either of Christ (in 2:6-8) or of Paul (2:17). Not only so, but the emphasis on *all* of God's holy people, *together with* the leaders, could use some regular dusting off so as to minimize the distance between clergy and people that too frequently exists in the church. *All* of us are *in Christ Jesus;* and all are in Christ Jesus in whatever "Philippi" God has placed us, since contemporary Western and westernized cultures are no more friends to grace than theirs was to these early believers. And finally, as for them, the key to life in Christ in our Philippi lies first of all in our common experience of *grace and peace . . . from God our Father* provided by Christ our Lord.

Prayer as Thanksgiving (1:3-8) In every truly Christian life the most obvious evidence of the experience of God's grace and peace is gratitude and joy (cf. 4:4, 6). Thus in his earliest letter, to a church that was experiencing severe trial, Paul concluded by exhorting, "Be joyful always; pray continually; give thanks in all circumstances, for this [all three of these] is God's will for you in Christ Jesus" (1 Thess 5:16-18). Our letter is the clear evidence, some twelve years or so later, that Paul was as good as his preaching.

It had long been Paul's habit to begin his letters with a thanksgiving and prayer report. This is not to be understood as thanksgiving and prayer in general, however, but it anticipates matters taken up in the

---

1:3-11 For a New Testament example of the standardized "prayer-wish" that begins most letters of friendship, see 3 John 2 ("Dear friend, I pray that you may enjoy good health and that all may go well with you, even as your soul is getting along well"); compare its absence from the "business letter" in Acts 15:23-29.

body of the letter. Here one often finds expressed both the immediate urgencies and the theological basis for much in the letter. Philippians is no exception.

Three matters make up most of our letter: (1) genuine gratitude for the Philippians' partnership with him in the gospel over many years, evidenced most recently by a material gift brought by Epaphroditus; (2) news about his present imprisonment and what he expects to come of it; and (c) an appeal for steadfastness and unity in light of some relational breakdowns, present opposition and the danger of false teaching.

These concerns predominate in Paul's thanksgiving and prayer. First, he is genuinely grateful for them; indeed *every time* he thinks about them in prayer, he both thanks God for them—and for their lifelong *partnership* with him *in the gospel*—and prays for them with great *joy, confident* that God will bring his own *good work* in them to full fruition (vv. 3-6). Second, Paul's present joy and confidence stem from his deep sense of personal relationship with them, evidenced both by their partnership with him in the gospel and his profound *affection* for them (vv. 7-8). They *share in God's grace with* him even in his present *chains.*

Finally, he reports the content of his prayer, whose concern is primarily for an increase in their *love* for one another, and thus that they be *filled with the fruit of righteousness* now and *blameless* at the coming of Christ (vv. 9-11). Thus through prayer and thanksgiving he anticipates the various concerns of the letter—their partnership with him in the gospel, his deep concern for them, and the need for love to replace internal bickering.

Thanksgiving—to God for His People (1:3-4) At this point in letters between friends, the writer usually inquires about her friend's present well-being, as in "I trust everything is finally going better for you, and that you have gotten over the bug that has been plaguing you." Ancient letters of friendship also began in this fashion, very often in a similar, somewhat standardized form, usually as a prayer-wish to the

1:3 The *you* is ambiguous enough in Greek that some scholars (e.g., Martin, O'Brien) think that Paul is thanking God for the Philippians' remembering him (with their gift); hence they would translate, "I thank my God for all your remembrance of me" (Moffatt). O'Brien (1991:58-61) presents the most significant case for this view, furthered by Peterman 1997:93-98. For the traditional view, based on Pauline usage and grammar, see Fee 1995:77-79.

gods (e.g., "before anything else I pray that you are well"). Like the greeting, in Paul's hands these kinds of conventions become transformed by the gospel.

Paul's various thanksgivings reveal some generally consistent patterns. First, they are always directed toward God on behalf of the people who are receiving the letter. Paul is first of all grateful for them, for the special gift of brothers and sisters whom God has brought into his life, not for "blessings" or material goods. Second, the thanksgiving occurs whenever his thoughts are focused on them in prayer *(every time I remember you)*. Third, for Paul prayer and thanksgiving blend; his thanksgiving for them always takes place in the context of his regular habit of praying for them *(in all my prayers . . . always)*.

What is different in our letter is the mention of making his prayer and thanksgiving *with joy*. Whatever else, the Philippians were for Paul a cause of great joy. The word order ("with joy the prayer making") gives this phrase special emphasis; indeed this is the first of sixteen occurrences of this word group *(joy)* in the letter. While this is not as dominant a motif as many suggest, it is a recurring motif and can scarcely be missed. The very awkwardness of the phrase in this case forces it upon the Philippians'—and our—attention.

Joy lies at the heart of the Christian experience of the gospel; it is the fruit of the Spirit in any truly Christian life, serving as primary evidence of the Spirit's presence (Rom 14:17; Gal 5:22). Precisely because this is so, joy transcends present circumstances; it is based altogether on the Spirit, God's way of being present with his people under the new covenant. Hence joy prevails for Paul even in prison; he will urge that it prevail for the Philippians as well in their present suffering in the face of opposition.

Here, then, is the paradigm of Pauline spirituality: thanksgiving and prayer, filled with joy, on behalf of *all* of God's people in Philippi. See further on 4:4-7.

Basis for Thanksgiving—The Past (1:5) Paul's thanksgiving is

1:5 For a helpful discussion of *koinōnia* see Hainz 1990. Several scholars (e.g., Hawthorne, Martin, Silva) take the "narrower" view, that the word refers exclusively to the Philippians' recent gift. But the usage in verse 7 and throughout the letter suggests a broader view, which includes their gift but is not limited to it.

not finished. Verses 3-4 focused on the Philippian believers themselves and Paul's joy in remembering them in prayer. He now indicates the basis of his joy, which serves as further reason for his thanksgiving: their *partnership (koinōnia)* in the furtherance of *the gospel.*

The precise nuance of ***koinōnia*** in this clause, however, is not easy to pin down. Usually translated into English as "fellowship," the word primarily refers to participating in something rather than sharing something in common with others. Its basic sense here, then, is "participation in the spread of the gospel," which in light of verse 7 very likely carries the further connotation of doing so in "partnership with Paul."

It does not take much reading of Paul's letters to recognize that *the gospel* is the singular passion of his life; that passion is the glue that holds this letter together. *The gospel,* especially in Philippians, for Paul refers primarily neither to a body of teaching nor to proclamation. Above all, the gospel has to do with Christ, both his person and his work. To preach Christ (vv. 15-16) is to preach the gospel, which is all about Christ; to preach the gospel is to proclaim God's good news of salvation that he has effected in Christ. Thus Paul's joy in prayer is prompted by their *partnership in [the furtherance of] the gospel.*

The present focus is on the Philippians' longtime association with Paul in the gospel, *from the first day until now.* According to the rest of the letter this took place in two ways: first by their sharing with him of their material means as he is imprisoned for the sake of the gospel (4:15-16); second by their proclaiming, and living in keeping with, the gospel in Philippi, where they are urged to "contend as one [person] for the faith of the gospel" (1:27) as they there "hold out the word of life" (2:16).

Basis for Thanksgiving—The Future (1:6) Paul is still not done with his thanksgiving. His mention of their participation in the gospel *from the first day until now* leads him to add, in a somewhat digressive way, that he is fully *confident* that what was true *from the first day* and is still true *now* will be true at the end as well. But this confidence has very little to do with them and everything to do with God, who both

1:6 Hawthorne (1983:29) also takes the narrower view, noted above (v. 5), for the *good work,* thus suggesting that Paul is expressing confidence that they will continue the grace of giving until the end.

began a good work, which is still in evidence, and will *carry it on to completion until the day of Christ.* Thus, having reminded them of his joy over their good past and present, Paul turns now to assure them of their certain future.

The *good work* that God has begun and will bring to full fruition may very well include their grace of giving, or perhaps their continued participation in the gospel in every way. More likely, however, it refers to God's *good work* of salvation itself, of creating a people for his name in Philippi. If so, the sentence anticipates 2:12-13, where Paul urges them to keep working out their common salvation in the way they live together as God's people in Philippi, since God is at work in them both to will and to do for the sake of his own good pleasure. Thus the concern is for their participation in the gospel in yet another sense, not so much their sharing it as their experiencing it and living it out in Philippi.

The day of Christ, on which God will bring his *work* in them *to completion,* points to the final consummation of salvation at Christ's (now second) coming. The reason for this otherwise digressive clause is probably related to another concern that surfaces at several points in the letter: that some of them have apparently begun to lose the basic future orientation that marks all truly Christian life. In 3:15-17 they are urged to follow Paul's example of desiring to know Christ above all (3:6-11) and eagerly to pursue the prize of knowing him fully at the end (vv. 12-14). Here Paul anticipates that exhortation by focusing on God's own commitment to bring them to *completion* on *the day of Christ.*

Believers in Christ are people of the future, a sure future that has already begun in the present. They are citizens of heaven (3:20) who live the life of heaven, the life of the future, in the present in whatever circumstances they find themselves. To lose this future orientation, and especially to lose the sense of "straining toward what is ahead, . . . toward the goal to win the prize for which God has called [us] heavenward" (3:13-14), is to lose too much. Thus their present gift, which also reminds Paul of their long association in the gospel, leads him to digress momentarily, to remind them that even in the midst of

1:7 *Phroneō* ("think of, be intent on, be careful about, set one's mind on, be disposed," Bauer), although not frequent in earlier letters, occurs ten times in Philippians, usually at critical moments (2:2 [2']; 2:5; 3:15 [2']; 3:19; 4:2; 4:10).

present difficulties, God has in Christ guaranteed their future as well as blessed their present situation in Philippi.

Basis for Confidence and Thanksgiving (1:7-8) Paul is still not finished with his thanksgiving, at least not with the (now convoluted) sentence that began as a thanksgiving. With the comparative conjunction "just as" (omitted from the NIV), he proceeds to offer justification for his confidence in verse 6 and to elaborate on his grounds for thanksgiving in verses 4-5.

It is, after all, Paul goes on, quite *right for me to feel this way about all of you*. The verb translated *feel* is especially prominent in Philippians. It has to do with having or developing a certain "mindset," including attitudes and dispositions. The NIV's *feel this way about all of you,* in the sense of having you in mind—being well disposed toward you—is good colloquial English for this idea. This is the proper verb to introduce the clause that follows and its companion in verse 8, a passage full of friendship motifs toward which this verb points; it also anticipates the kind of "mind" Paul will urge on them later in the letter (2:2-5; 4:2-3).

In giving the reason for his having them in mind in this way, Paul once more emphasizes their mutual relationship, one side of the three-way bond around which this letter finds focus. Certain realities—three are singled out—about that relationship call for such an attitude: his own deep affection for them (cf. vv. 3-4), their past partnership with him in the gospel (cf. v. 5) and the extension of that partnership to his imprisonment—and the defense of *the gospel*.

The basic reason for such affection is that (literally) "you all are participants together with me in the grace." But which grace? Many take it with the NIV to refer to God's saving grace, others to Paul's apostolic ministry. But in light of verse 29, where the verb of this noun occurs in conjunction with their mutual suffering for Christ, Paul very likely is referring to being "partners together in this grace," namely, in *defending and confirming* (= vindicating) *the gospel* in the face of suffering *(chains)*.

The gospel, as always, is the primary matter; both he and they have

For *I have you in my heart* the NRSV (cf. Hawthorne, NEB) has "because you hold me in your heart." But recent studies on word order with infinitives (Reed 1991; Porter 1993) seem decisive in support of the NIV and most commentators.

had a part in the defense and confirmation of the gospel. But the Philippians are also partners together with him (NIV *share*) in his present circumstances of being *in chains*. Here is the first mention of the suffering motif that will recur throughout the letter. Whether Paul was literally in chains or whether this is simply a metaphor for imprisonment cannot be known. In any case, the studied repetition of *chains* in verses 13, 14 and 17 indicates that he is smarting under the imprisonment.

But how do the Philippians *share in* this *grace with* Paul? Does this refer simply to their gift to him while he is presently in chains? Or does it possibly allude to what he will affirm in verse 30, that some of them are undergoing "the same struggle" as he in a nearly identical way in Philippi? One cannot be sure. Very likely the recent gift is more immediately in view; that, after all, is the immediate occasion of his thanksgiving.

Nonetheless, this may also refer to their own defense of the gospel in Philippi, especially in the face of hostility similar to what he has suffered. The hostility, after all, comes from the empire itself, of which both they and he are citizens, now in trouble because they hold allegiance to a citizenship in which Lord Christ holds sway even—especially—over lord Caesar.

The mild oath with which the thanksgiving finally concludes (v. 8) reveals the depth of feeling out of which the letter is written. The *affection* that one senses throughout the thanksgiving now spills out as open and unfeigned feelings toward the Philippians. At the same time, however, Paul is experiencing a measure of distress, because all is not right with them, and he can only sit in prison and pray. Pray he will, but now, having just noted their own love for him in Christ, he returns to the affirmation in verse 7 that he has them in his *heart*.

This oath also brings into focus once more the three-way bond between him and them and Christ that holds the letter together. For his part he longs for them, not simply to see them again (1:24-25; 2:24) but *for* them, his dearly beloved brothers and sisters in Christ (see 4:1). Whatever in fact was going on among them, reported to him by Epaphroditus, he wants them to know how strongly he feels toward them—toward *all of you*. Nonetheless, this relationship serves as only the second predicate on which the letter rests. The first predicate is their own relationship to Christ, which is the ultimate urgency of the letter.

Thus Paul's own deep longings for them come *with the affection of Christ Jesus* himself—almost certainly meaning "the love Christ has for you, which is also at work in me for you."

Such an uninhibited display of affection makes it clear that Paul was not an academic! He was, in fact, a passionate lover of Christ, which made him an equally passionate lover of Christ's people. Much can be learned here by those who have pastoral care of any kind, including parents for their children. Paul's emotion, after all, is simply the outflow of his theology and the spirituality that issues from such theology. His theology has to do with the gospel, which has God as its source and sustainer. Whatever else, those whom we love in Christ first of all belong to God. God has begun the *good work* in them that he has committed himself to concluding with eschatological glory. That good work is the result of *the affection of Christ Jesus,* through whom God has brought this "good news" on behalf of his people.

The net result in terms of pastoral care is thanksgiving and joy for the people themselves, for *all of* them, even those whose antics often seem to bring more grief than pleasure. They belong to God; it is ours to be grateful for what God has done, is doing and will continue to do in their lives. And all of this works much better if the caregiver also shares in *the affection of Christ Jesus,* by having a good measure of the same affection, predicated on being participants together in the gospel.

Prayer as Petition (1:9-11) Since Paul's thanksgiving for his Philippian friends takes place in the context of his praying for them (vv. 3-4), he now goes on to spell out the content of his prayer. Here are some specifics regarding the "good work" begun in them which he repeatedly prays God will bring "to completion" on "the day of Christ."

The prayer report is also a single sentence, whose overall concern and meaning seem clear enough. The connections between the various parts can be easily traced:

Paul prays (1) for their love to abound yet more and more;
  that (2) this be accompanied by full knowledge and moral insight,
    so that (3) they might approve those things that really matter,
      so that (4) they might be unsullied and blameless when Christ returns,

as (5) they are now full of the fruit of righteousness,
fruit that is (6) effected by Christ Jesus
and (7) for the glory and praise of God.

Items 1, 2, 3 and 5 thus give the "what" of his prayer; item 4 gives the "why"; and item 6 offers the means to the (ultimate) end expressed in item 7. The "what" begins on a familiar note, that their *love* grow still *more and more.* It ends on a similar note, that they bear *the fruit of righteousness.* The middle item (3), though a bit puzzling, is likewise concerned with behavior—that their knowledge (of God) and moral insight (into God's will) also increase so that they may test and approve what really counts. The whole, therefore, is singularly concerned with their behavior, with the ethical life of the believer in Christ.

Paul in part prays for the continuation of the very things for which he has just given thanks. This should surprise us none, since both reports reflect the same basic theological framework—present existence in Christ as both "already" and "not yet." This is where the "what" and the "why" join: Paul's prayer for them is that they might live the life of the future in the present, so that they might thereby be *blameless* at its consummation on *the day of Christ.* The concern is with present life in Christ; the orientation is toward its consummation—that they live for Christ now, and do so in light of his coming day.

What Paul Prays For (1:9) Paul's primary concern for the church in Philippi, as he will exhort them in 2:2, is that their *love may abound [yet] more and more. Love* is such a common word to us that it is easy to miss Paul's concern. Following the lead of the Septuagint, his use of *love* first of all points to the character of God, and to God's actions toward his people based on that character. God's love is demonstrated especially in his forbearance and kindness (1 Cor 13:4), manifested ultimately in the death of Christ for his enemies (Rom 5:6-8).

Thus the primary connotation of *love* is not "affection," as in the preceding phrase about Christ (Phil 1:8), but rather a sober kind of love that places high value on a person and actively seeks that person's

1:9 The word translated *abound (perisseuō)* is a favorite Pauline word (26 of 39 New Testament occurrences), basically meaning "to have in abundance" (as in 4:12; 4:18). It reflects his own understanding of the lavish nature of life in Christ, effected by the Spirit. Elsewhere he urges or affirms believers to "abound" in thanksgiving (2 Cor 4:15; 9:12; Col

benefit. This is what Paul now prays will *abound* (= be present in an abundant way) yet *more and more* among the Philippian believers. The rest of the prayer, after all, emphasizes love not as affection but as behavior, behavior that is both *pure* (stemming from right motives) and *blameless* (lacking offense).

The *more and more* indicates that Paul is not getting on them for something they lacked. His concern is rather that "selfish ambition and vain conceit" (2:3) not undermine what has long characterized them, to which 2 Corinthians 8:1-6 bears eloquent testimony. The problem is similar to that occasionally experienced by families, where love is sometimes more easily shown toward those on the outside, who are known very little and with whom one does not have constant association. But actively to love on the inside, to love those with whom one is in constant relationship and where one's own place in the sun is constantly being threatened—that can be another matter. Thus he prays that the *love* that has long characterized them will overflow still *more and more* toward one and all.

Paul also prays (item 2) for a similar increase *in knowledge and depth of insight.* Although this phrase grammatically modifies *that your love may abound more and more,* it nonetheless moves in a slightly new direction, so that Paul is in effect praying a second thing. Along with an ever-increasing love, he wants them to experience an ever-increasing *knowledge* (of God and his will) and moral *insight.*

The primary sense of the word translated *knowledge* is not so much "knowledge about" something as the kind of "full" or "innate" knowing that comes from experience or personal relationship. The second word denotes moral understanding based on experience, hence something close to "moral *insight.*" Very likely this phrase is something of an abbreviated equivalent to the similar phrase in the (roughly contemporary) prayer in Colossians 1:9 ("that by means of all of the Spirit's wisdom and insight you might be filled with the knowledge of God's will"—my translation).

2:7), hope (Rom 15:13), building up the church (1 Cor 14:12), the work of the Lord (1 Cor 15:58), and faith, speech, knowledge, earnestness, and the grace of giving (2 Cor 9:8). Here he desires that their love continue to "overflow abundantly" or "be present in abundance" toward each other.

Why Paul Prays for Them (1:10) The opening clause of the prayer is followed by two purpose clauses. One (item 3) expresses immediate purpose, why they need ever-increasing *knowledge* and moral *insight—so that you may be able to discern what is best.* The other (item 4) expresses his ultimate concern for them—so that they *may be pure and blameless until [better "for"] the day of Christ.*

For a truly Christian life, some things matter and others do not. In light of the term *fruit of righteousness* in verse 11 and the contrast in 3:1-11 between righteousness in terms of lawkeeping and that which is through faith in Christ, this petition probably anticipates the warning and personal testimony of that passage. Neither circumcision nor uncircumcision counts for a thing, Paul says elsewhere (1 Cor 7:19; Gal 5:6; 6:15). What counts, rather, is keeping the commandments of God (1 Cor 7:19), which in Galatians 5:6 is interpreted as "faith expressing itself through love." This is the kind of *insight* he prays for them to have, so that they will be able to continue to *discern what is best.*

The ultimate purpose for the preceding concerns, that they might *be pure and blameless* for *the day of Christ,* reflects the urgency already voiced in the thanksgiving that they be found complete at the coming of Christ. *Pure* most likely refers to purity (sincerity) of motive, in terms of relationships within the community. Likewise, the word translated *blameless* is not Paul's regular word for this idea. Ordinarily, as in 2:15 and 3:6, he uses a word denoting behavior that is without observable fault. But this word suggests being *blameless* in the sense of "not offending" or not causing someone else to stumble.

This choice of words probably reflects the present situation in Philippi. The behavior of some appears to have the latent possibility of mixed motives, or at least is a potential source of offense. Paul prays that they may stand *blameless* on *the day of Christ,* not having offended others through equivocal behavior.

The Ultimate Goal of the Prayer (1:11) Not one to leave his prayer hanging on what may sound like a negative note, Paul immediately qualifies his aspiration for them in verse 10 in two ways. First, by *pure*

1:11 The case for *righteousness* to mean "the gift of righteousness" can be found in O'Brien 1991:80-81. The phrase *fruit of righteousness* appears in Amos 6:12 and Proverbs 3:9 and 11:30, always denoting righteous behavior. For the grammar see Fee 1995:104.

and blameless until the day of Christ he means that he wants them to arrive at that day already *filled with the fruit of righteousness* (item 5), whose source, as always, is *through Christ Jesus* (item 6). Second, the ultimate goal of everything, especially *righteousness* expressed by their ever-increasing *love,* is that they might live *to the glory and praise of God* (item 7).

But by *the fruit of righteousness* does Paul intend "filled with fruit that comes from the righteousness Christ has provided," thus emphasizing the fruitfulness that has God's gift of right standing with himself as its source? Or does he intend "filled with fruit consisting of the righteousness that marks one who belongs to Christ," thus emphasizing the righteousness that, coming through Christ, has a new kind of content? Although my theological proclivities lie with the former, the Old Testament background of this phrase and the grammar of the sentence favor the latter.

In this letter the word *righteousness* occurs elsewhere only in 3:6 and 3:9. In contrast to "legalistic righteousness" (3:6), Paul says God has given him a different righteousness that expresses itself in particular by his adopting a cruciform lifestyle (3:9-11), like that of Christ himself (2:6-8). To be *filled with the fruit of righteousness* for Paul means to go the way of the cross, self-emptying so as to become servant of all in place of "selfish ambition" and, in that servanthood, humbling oneself to the point of dying for another in place of "vain conceit" (2:3-8). This is what it means for Paul to "know Christ." This is the righteousness that comes *through Jesus Christ.* All other righteousness, especially religious righteousness, is filth in comparison (3:8).

Such righteousness alone is *to the glory and praise of God* (item 7). Here is the ultimate goal of all things. Everything is to the single end that God will receive glory through the work he is doing in their lives. Love that reflects God's own love is the only righteousness that counts, the only righteousness that is to God's *glory* and to his *praise.*

This prayer is ever relevant for those who are caregivers in the church—pastors, leaders, teachers, parents and others. Most people

The word "cruciform" is used throughout this commentary to refer to living in a way that is in conformity to the cross, that is, in keeping with the God who in Christ sacrificed himself in death for the sake of those he loves.

entrusted to our spiritual nurture, like all of us, need love to overflow—not to mention the need to have *knowledge* of God and *insight* into his will also overflow so that they (we) may give themselves only to what really counts as believers in Christ. Who of them—of us—does not need to be filled with the kind of *righteousness* that characterizes God and that Christ has modeled? Thus we would do well to use these very words when we pray for those in our care.

There is paradigm here as well. Here is one who has a keen sense of priorities in Christ and who is concerned when those in his care grow slack in some areas. That this prayer anticipates a great deal of the burden of the letter itself tells us much about Paul in prayer. Before talking to the Philippians about some matters that need an increase, he talks to God about them—and tells them so. We could learn much here.

□ Paul's Affairs: Reflections on Imprisonment (1:12-26)

After opening with something like "I trust this letter finds you well," letters between friends most often begin by catching the friend up on the writer's present situation. The same was true of friendship letters in the Greco-Roman world, which appeared often with the very words Paul uses here. This material was usually brief and sometimes made up the whole of a (very brief) letter. In the present case, however, this section is quite long (vv. 12-26) and (as is typical for Paul) is thoroughly transformed by the gospel. What begins as a word to relieve the Philippians of anxiety (v. 12) evolves into a word about the current spread of the gospel (vv. 13-18), followed in turn by a reflection on Paul's desires and expectations regarding his forthcoming tribunal (vv. 18-26).

One can scarcely miss the focus of Paul's concern, here and always: Christ and the gospel. His present imprisonment has ultimately been to the advantage of the gospel, which is cause for joy (vv. 12-18); his singular longing regarding his trial is that Christ will be magnified,

---

1:12-26 On the nature of Roman imprisonment and how it would have affected Paul, see Rapske 1994.

1:12 Although a splendid idiomatic rendering of the Greek, the NIV's ***what has happened to me*** obscures a very important structural point for this letter. The Greek phrase ***ta kat' eme*** (see also Col 4:7; cf. Eph 6:21), whose equivalent occurs frequently in letters of

whether through life or death (vv. 19-20); if it were to result in death (execution), that means he finally reaches the goal of his life—Christ himself—and if choice were his, he would go this route (vv. 20-23); but most likely the outcome will be life (freedom), which will cause the Philippians' own boasting to abound in Christ Jesus (vv. 24-26).

There is nothing else quite like this passage in Paul's extant letters. Very likely, since his and their present suffering stems from the same source—the Roman Empire—he intends much of this to serve as paradigm. Here is how they too should respond in the context of their present difficulties.

The Present: Paul's Imprisonment Advances the Gospel (1:12-18)
Remarkably, Paul says little about himself personally in this opening reflection. The Philippians, of course, already know about his imprisonment, evidenced by their recent gift. Thus his present focus is not so much on himself—he probably expects Epaphroditus to fill them in on personal matters—as it is on how he views what has happened to him, very likely with an eye toward them and how they are handling their own adversity.

The passage has two closely related parts (vv. 12-14, 15-18a). Paul begins by turning the Philippians' attention immediately to the progress of the gospel, which his confinement has helped along in two ways: his captors and guards have been made aware of Christ (v. 13), and believers in Rome are more actively proclaiming Christ (v. 14).

Although this second matter is a cause for joy, it has not been without some personal wounds, which leads to the second part: a subparagraph flowing out of verse 14, in which he reflects on the twofold motivation—envy and goodwill—behind this renewed activity (v. 15). Verses 16-17 reiterate these in reverse order, in terms of love and selfish ambition directed toward him. But verse 18, where he expresses his response to this activity, is the obvious concern of the whole passage:

---

friendship, means literally "my circumstances/affairs." It is responded to at the beginning of the next section in verse 27 with "your circumstances/affairs" (NIV *about you*) and appears again twice at the beginning of the next section (2:19, "your affairs"; 2:23, "my affairs"). Not only is this the stuff of friendship letters, but in this case it seems clearly to be the structural key to chapters 1 and 2.

Christ is being proclaimed, and in that Paul rejoices. Although suffering, Paul is scarcely languishing in prison.

The Gospel Advances Both Inside and Outside Prison (1:12-14) Those who are fully alive because of the gospel, who in Paul's language have nothing yet possess everything (2 Cor 6:10), exist as a constant threat to those whose minds are set on merely earthly things. Leave Paul alone and he and his companions will be those who have turned the world upside down (Acts 17:6); put him in prison and he turns Caesar's elite upside down (Phil 1:13), not to mention Caesar's very household (4:22). To paraphrase Brutus, "Yon Paul has that lean and hungry look; he talks too much. Such men are dangerous." Here is a person not just making the best of his circumstances but actually turning them around for the glory of God. No wonder joy abounds.

The opening clause (v. 12) offers all kinds of clues as to the nature and structure of the letter. First, Paul begins with the exact words found in scores and scores of ancient letters, especially so-called family letters: *I want you to know, brothers [and sisters].* Second, *what has happened to me* ("my circumstances/affairs"), which also occurs frequently in these letters, serves as a key to the macro structure of Philippians, at least the first half (see 1:27 ["about you" = your affairs], 2:19 [your affairs] and 23 [my affairs]). This is exactly the stuff of letters of friendship in the Greco-Roman world.

Third, the word *advance* ("progress" in v. 25), otherwise rare in Paul's letters, frames the present set of reflections, thus serving as a microstructural key to verses 12-26. In verse 12 his imprisonment has served for the progress of the gospel; in verse 25 his expected release will serve to further their progress in the faith.

For Paul, of course, this is the language of evangelism. In a world of religious pluralism, where evangelism has become something of a dirty word, we must not give in to the temptation to downplay this dimension

---

1:13 On the word *praetorium,* translated "palace guard," as one of the cruxes of this letter regarding the place of Paul's imprisonment, see my introduction, p. 33.

1:14 The whole of this clause is filled with ambiguities regarding what modifies what, touched off by the first prepositional phrase, "in the Lord." Both Pauline usage elsewhere and the fact that all the modifiers, including this one, stand in the emphatic first position

of Paul's life in Christ. Evangelism was his "meat and potatoes" (or "rice," in the case of Asian Christians)—and not, as Christians are sometimes accused, because he was insecure or had a deep psychological need to be right and thus had to convert others so as to bolster his own convictions. Rather, he was a believer in the truest sense of that word: one who believed not only that the gospel is God's "message of truth" (Gal 2:5, 14) but that it contains the only good news for a fallen, broken world.

Paul himself is directly responsible for the advance of the gospel *throughout the whole palace guard and to everyone else* (Phil 1:13). *Palace guard* refers to the emperor's elite troops (his "green berets" or security police) stationed in Rome. They guarded Paul around the clock but would have given him access to visitors, to the writing of letters and to other routine affairs. Since they rotated on a basically four-hour shift, Paul would have had access to several—or many—of them, from whom eventually *the whole guard* came to know the reason for his bonds, that he was *in chains for Christ.*

It is not clear to whom *everyone else* refers—most likely another group of people outside the Praetorian Guard who had dealings with imperial affairs. Thus anyone in Rome who had occasion to know about Paul's confinement had also come to learn that it had to do with his being a propagator of the nascent Christian faith.

We should not miss Paul's obvious delight in this mild triumph regarding his arrest, the same kind we find at the end of the letter when he sends greetings from "all the saints, . . . especially those who belong to Caesar's household" (4:22). While this might be interpreted as a kind of one-upmanship, Paul's concern was to encourage the Philippians in their own current suffering, resulting in part from their lack of loyalty to the emperor. To the world—and especially to the citizens of a Roman colony—Caesar may be "lord"; but to Paul and to the believers in Philippi, only Jesus is Lord (2:11), and his lordship over Caesar is already making itself felt through the

(i.e., they precede the word[s] they modify rather than follow, as is more common in Greek), suggest that *in the Lord* modifies the participle "have become confident" (NIV *courageously*). The net result is a clause that should read (as will the revised NIV), "because of my chains, most of the brothers and sisters, becoming confident in the Lord, have dared all the more to speak the gospel message fearlessly."

penetration of the gospel into the heart of Roman political life.

At the same time, Paul is also indirectly responsible for the evangelism presently occurring outside prison (1:14). Again he emphasizes *my chains,* which have served as the immediate cause of newfound boldness among the brothers and sisters in Rome. Paul's reflection on this matter is remarkable indeed. Though he would surely prefer freedom so that he himself might evangelize, he recognizes that God has used his curtailment to prod others. The rejoicing that ensues (v. 18) must be taken seriously. Here is one for whom the gospel is bigger than his personal role in making it known.

Thus the majority of believers in Rome have found new confidence in the Lord (see note). *The Lord,* of course, is the risen Lord Jesus Christ, who is both the ground of their confidence and the content of *the word* which they have been emboldened to speak *more courageously and fearlessly.*

This probably reflects the situation in Rome in the early 60s, when Nero's madness was peaking and the church there had begun to fall under suspicion, as Nero's pogrom against them just a couple of years later bears witness. The present situation in Rome for the followers of Christ had perhaps (understandably) led them to be more quiescent than was usual for early Christians. For good reason, then, Paul joyfully explains to the Philippian believers that the net effect of his imprisonment has been to give their Roman brothers and sisters extraordinary courage to proclaim Christ, at the heart of the empire itself where storm clouds are brewing.

The Gospel Advances Despite Ill-Will (1:15-17) These surprising sentences follow hard on the heels of verse 14, directly modifying *most of the brothers [and sisters]* (literally, "some, on the one hand, . . . others, on the other hand"). They describe two kinds of evangelism, in terms of motivation, taking place in Rome in response to Paul's imprisonment. They are surprising in part because nothing in verse 14 prepared us for this, and in part because of Paul's description of the second group and his attitude toward them. The description itself

1:16-17 The KJV followed the majority—all very late—manuscripts in destroying Paul's chiasmus in favor of keeping the order of verse 15 (thus AB A′B′).

1:17 As one might well expect of such a (for us) cryptic reference to people who are trying

is set forth in a nearly perfect chiasmus (ABB′A′ pattern):

A Some preach Christ because of envy and rivalry (v. 15)
  B Others out of goodwill (v. 15)
  B′ The latter do so in love because they know my imprisonment is on behalf of the gospel (v. 16)
A′ The former proclaim Christ out of selfish ambition, not sincerely, supposing they are causing affliction in my bonds (v. 17)

The emphasis lies with the A/A′ clauses, with those who are trying to inflict suffering on Paul. But even though it smarts personally, Paul will have none of it—the supposed affliction, that is. Rather (v. 18), he rejoices because Christ is proclaimed on all sides; for him "to live is Christ" (v. 21), hence his ability to rejoice.

Evangelism is now expressed in terms of "preaching Christ." The pure motive of some who do so is *goodwill* and *love,* meaning love for Paul. They see that Paul can no longer be involved in preaching Christ publicly, so they have stepped in to pick up the slack. Among these we should probably number those whom Paul greets in Romans 16:3-16, many of whom he there applauds for their "hard work in the Lord."

Along with Paul himself, they understand his imprisonment to be appointed by God: *I am put here for the defense of the gospel,* words that echo verse 7 and anticipate the (apparent) tribunal referred to in verses 19-20. Thus these friends among the Roman house churches see their role as filling the gap—with regard to evangelism—for a wounded comrade in arms, as it were, who has been divinely appointed to defend the gospel at the highest level of the empire.

This surely reflects the heart of Paul's understanding of his ordeal. From the Roman point of view, Paul is on trial over a matter of *religio licita* (whether Christians are still under the banner of Judaism), or perhaps of *maiestas* ("treason"—because they proclaimed another than Caesar to be Lord?—see Acts 17:7). From Paul's own point of view, the gospel itself is on trial, and his imprisonment is a divinely appointed

to wound him, there has been a rather large amount of speculation among scholars in attempts to identify them; many of these conclusions differ considerably from the one presented here. See the helpful overview in O'Brien 1991:102-5.

defense of the gospel at the highest echelons.

That is exactly where the others have got it wrong. Their preaching of Christ is predicated on *envy and rivalry* and *selfish ambition,* aiming at gain for themselves in a personal battle against Paul. They are therefore preaching Christ, but *from false motives.* They suppose, incorrectly, that they will *stir up trouble* (*thlipsis;* cf. 4:14) *for me while I am in chains.* They think in terms of Paul, his imprisonment and his affliction; he thinks in terms of the gospel, for whose defense he has been appointed. Hence although they are probably something of an annoyance, they cannot really get at Paul; even their "impurity" (v. 18; NIV *false motives*), Paul recognizes, still advances the gospel!

Our dilemma is how to square his attitude toward these people with what he says elsewhere about those who oppose him and his gospel. The key probably lies with the two words translated *rivalry* and *selfish ambition (eris* and *eritheia),* especially since the latter term, which is infrequent in Paul's writings, appears again in 2:3, where he is urging a united mindset among the Philippians. The fact that these people are preaching Christ, but do so hoping both to afflict Paul and to gain personal advantage over him, means that they cannot be preaching a rival gospel—against which Paul inveighs so strongly in 3:1-3. Therefore they must be fellow believers, but those who have personal animosity toward the apostle.

The best guess as to who these people might be is to be found in Paul's letter to the Romans, where he is concerned about Jew and Gentile forming one people of God as they "follow Christ Jesus, so that with one heart and mouth you may glorify the God and Father of our Lord Jesus Christ" (Rom 15:5-6). That letter in effect tried to do two things: to get Jewish Christians to see how Christ brought an end to the law as a means of relating to God, and to get the Gentiles to moderate their behavior toward the Jewish believers on matters that did not count. Hence most of the letter is written from the perspective of his being an apostle to the Gentiles, trying to show that Christ and the Spirit have brought an end to the significance of Jewish boundary markers; yet the sections of exhortation, especially 14:1—15:13, are written from the perspective of the Gentiles with regard to their acceptance of Jews.

Despite Paul's insistence that the gospel is "for the Jew first" and his affirmations about Christ's being in continuity with things Jewish (Rom 9:3-5; 10:4; etc.), he also says enough things to make Jewish Christians anxious about his way of expressing the gospel. If so, then Romans was effective only in part. Our passage suggests that some of the Roman believers took considerable exception to Paul.

Even though Paul would disagree with these people's understanding of what Christ has accomplished, the difference between what Paul says of them here and what he says elsewhere can be attributed to two factors. First, in every other case (2 Cor 10—12; Gal; Phil 3) where Paul speaks strongly against Jewish Christian opponents, they are trying to convert his churches ("his" in the sense that he founded them and has apostolic responsibility toward them) to their way of understanding Christ. In the present case, of course, the church in Rome is not his own in either sense just noted. Second, the clear difference between this passage and the others is that here his opponents are evangelizing, proclaiming Christ to others (probably fellow Jews) who have not yet believed in him. The others are itinerants involved in "sheep stealing" pure and simple. For them Paul has only anathemas.

Very likely the reason for Paul's including these words here is related to a situation of internal unrest in Philippi. As Paul now writes to Philippi, he does so in light of the local situation in Rome. In 1:27 he exhorts the Philippians to contend for the gospel in one Spirit as one person; in 2:3 he urges that they "do nothing out of selfish ambition"; in 2:13 he reminds them that God is at work in them "to will and to act" for the sake of his goodwill; and in 2:21 he remembers again that some "look out for [their] own interests, not those of Jesus Christ." It seems reasonable to suppose that some strife on the local scene has heightened Paul's concern for the situation in Philippi. Thus with verses 15-17 he anticipates the exhortations of 1:27—2:16 and 4:2-3.

So What? (1:18a) Here is the evidence that verses 15-17 are something of an aside—probably for paradigmatic reasons. Paul began this paragraph by explaining that the net fallout of his imprisonment has been to *advance the gospel.* That, and that alone, is the cause of his joy: *Christ is preached. And because of this I rejoice.* His joy is not over his imprisonment as such; that kind of morbid "thanking God for all things" lies outside Paul's theological perspective. No, the pain is there, and some are indeed preaching Christ *from false [impure] motives.*

Paul's joy stems from his perspective—his ability to see every pirouette both for its own beauty and for its place in the whole dance. He had long desired to go to Rome, so that he might share with the Roman believers his understanding of the gospel and proclaim Christ to those who did not know him (Rom 1:11-14; cf. 15:23). Now he is there, although in circumstances not of his own choosing. But neither are these circumstances a cause for complaint, but for joy, because God in his own wisdom is carrying out his purposes, even through Paul's imprisonment. After all, some years earlier he had written of himself as "sorrowful, yet always rejoicing"—precisely because, although "having nothing," he yet possessed "everything" (2 Cor 6:10).

In Philippians 2:17-18 Paul will encourage the Philippians to rejoice with him, even if it means that his present circumstances are a form of libation, a sacrifice poured out to God on their behalf. Here he anticipates that exhortation to rejoice in the midst of difficulty, by offering himself as a pattern for them to follow.

It would be easy to dismiss this passage (vv. 12-18) as Paul's simply putting the best possible face on a bad situation. But that would be to miss too much. Paul can write things like this because, first, his theology is in good order. He has learned by the grace of God to see everything from the divine perspective. This is not wishful thinking but deep conviction—that God has worked out his own divine intentions through the death and resurrection of Christ, and that by his Spirit he is carrying them out in the world through the church, and therefore through both Paul and others.

It is not that Paul is too heavenly minded to be in touch with reality or that he sees things through rose-tinted glasses. Rather, he sees everything in light of the bigger picture; and in that bigger picture, fully emblazoned on our screen at Calvary, there is nothing that does not fit, even if it means suffering and death on the way to resurrection. Such theology dominates this letter in every part; we should not be surprised that it surfaces at the outset, even in this brief narrative.

Second, and related to the first, Paul is a man of a single passion: Christ and the gospel. Everything is to be seen and done in light of

Christ. For him both life and death mean Christ. His is the passion of the single-minded person who has been apprehended by Christ, as he will tell the Philippians in 3:12-14.

Third, Paul's passion for Christ has led him to an understanding of discipleship in which the disciple takes up a cross to follow his Lord. Discipleship, therefore, means to participate in the sufferings of Christ (3:10-11), to be ready to be poured out as a drink offering in ministry for the sake of others (2:17). Paul's imprisonment belongs to those trials for which "we were destined" (1 Thess 3:3) and thus come as no surprise.

Interestingly, these three theological realities are what also make for Paul's largeness of heart. True, he lacks the kind of "largeness" for which religious pluralists contend. Is that because such pluralists have not been apprehended by Christ and the gospel, as God's thing—his only thing—on behalf of our fallen world? Unfortunately, and ironically, such pluralism often has very little tolerance for the Pauls of this world! But in Paul's case it is his theological convictions that lead both to his theological narrowness, on the one hand, and to his large-heartedness within those convictions, on the other—precisely because he recognizes the gospel for what it is: God's thing, not his own. And that, it should be added, also stands quite over against many others who think of themselves as in Paul's train but whose passion for the gospel seems all too often a passion for their own "correct" view of things.

At stake for the Philippians—and for us, I would venture—is the admonition finally made explicit in 4:9: to put into practice for ourselves what we hear and see in Paul, as well as what we have learned and received by way of his teaching.

The Future: For Christ's Glory and the Good of the Philippians (1:18-26) From reflection on the present, which is a cause for joy, Paul now turns to assess the future, which is also cause for joy. The passage comes in three parts, held together by the anticipation of his (apparently) soon-expected trial (vv. 19-20). Verses 19-20 offer the reason for his continuing joy—his earnest expectation that Christ will be magnified whatever the outcome (*life* [= released] or *death* [= executed]). Even though he has no real choice in the matter, in verses 21-24 he ponders the options of *life* and *death*. Paul's clear preference is *death,* since that means to gain the final prize—Christ himself (cf. 3:12-14). But he expects the outcome to be *life*—since that is what is best for the Philippians. Verses 25-26 then offer the end result of his being given *life*—*your progress* (cf. v. 12) *and joy in the faith*.

Although this reflection is far more personal than verses 12-18, even here the focus is still on Christ and the gospel. By a fresh supply of *the Spirit of Jesus Christ* Paul expects his hope to be fulfilled, that *Christ will be exalted* whether Paul lives or dies; for to live means Christ and to die means to gain Christ. If he had a choice, he would choose death, because that would mean to be *with Christ;* but since he has no choice, life is the expected outcome, leading to his return to Philippi and their overflow of *joy in Christ Jesus*.

Most likely all of this is for the Philippians' sakes as well. As Paul's present joy is expressed in the face of conflict (some believers in Rome against him), so with his future joy, which will find expression in the face of external opposition—a point that will hopefully not be lost on the Philippians. For reasons not known to us, some of them have apparently lost their grip on future certainties (see on 1:6). Hence even this personal musing functions as paradigm. The future—the full realization of Christ—is a glorious prospect, Paul reassures them, even if it were to mean in his case to arrive there prematurely at the hands of others!

Again we see the three-way bond—between him, them and Christ—that informs every part of the letter. The present emphasis is on Paul's relationship with Christ *(to live is Christ;* hence his desire is to be *with Christ);* it concludes on the note of his relationship with them (they will glory in Christ *on account of* him when he comes to be *with* them), which has their relationship with Christ as its ultimate concern (their *progress and joy in the faith*).

1:19 The *this,* which is part of the Job citation, in Paul's sentence probably refers to "this whole affair (regarding my present circumstances)."

Some are anxious as to whether the Philippians would have heard the echo from Job. The chances are very good that they would have, given (a) the oral nature of the culture, which cultivated a far greater memory capacity than ours, and (b) the only Bible they had was the LXX, which they *heard* read over and over again (see my introduction, pp. 22-23). For a helpful discussion of the phenomenon of "intertextuality" in Paul, see Hays 1989, who in his introductory chapter uses this passage as a primary example.

All told this is one of the apostle's finer moments, a passage to which God's people have turned over and again to find strength and encouragement in times of difficulty. We all are the richer for it.

That Christ Be Exalted (1:18-20) With the clause *Yes, and I will continue to rejoice,* Paul begins a deliberate shift from the present to the future. The *for* with which verse 19 begins indicates that the (very complex) sentence that follows (vv. 19-20) offers the reason for continuing joy. The complexity of the sentence is due in part to Paul's beginning with a verbatim incorporation of a clause from Job 13:16 ("this will turn out for my deliverance") and in part to his piling up of prepositional phrases, the last of which ("according to my earnest expectation and hope") is then given content.

The following expanded translation is my own attempt to wade through the complexities and will serve as the basis for my comments: "for I know that through your prayers and God's supply of the Spirit of Jesus Christ 'this shall turn out [as with Job] to mean vindication for me,' which will also be in keeping with my earnest expectation and hope, namely, that in no way will I be brought to shame, but rather that with all openness/boldness—as always so now—Christ will be magnified in my 'body,' whether I am released or executed."

The quotation from Job controls Paul's own concerns. It is a classic piece of what literary critics call "intertextuality," the conscious echoing of fragments from an earlier text in a later one, refitting the borrowed language into the author's own setting. Job 13 contains one of Job's more poignant speeches, where he repudiates the perspective of his "comforters," who insist that his present situation is the result of hidden sin. Job knows better and pleads his cause with God, in whom he hopes and before whom he affirms his innocence. Indeed, the very hope of appearing before God in this way would be his "salvation," because the

---

A single article controls both nouns in the phrase *through your prayer* and the supply of *the Spirit of Jesus Christ,* thus indicating a very close (but not necessarily full cause-and-effect) relationship between them. See also Ephesians 6:18-20.

The word translated *help* in the NIV and others in fact never means that in any of its known uses in antiquity; rather it has to do with the "supply" or "provision" of something, as in Galatians 3:5, where the corresponding verb is used in an identical way, with the Spirit as the object supplied. See the full discussion in Fee 1995:132-34.

godless shall not come before God (Job 13:16). And "salvation" for Job means "I know I will be vindicated" (v. 18). So with Paul, but in quite different circumstances.

Our difficulties stem from the LXX translator's use of *sōtēria* ("salvation") to express what Job could expect from God were he to appear before him. In every other instance in Paul *sōtēria* denotes eschatological salvation, that is, God's final salvation of his people already brought present through Christ and the Spirit. But here it is controlled in part by its sense in Job, which has to do neither with final salvation nor with deliverance from prison (although Paul clearly expects the latter). Rather Paul's concern is altogether on Christ's being magnified, however the trial turns out. Christ's being thus magnified would be Paul's vindication (not to mention his gospel's). In its own way such vindication by God would thus mean "salvation" for him as well.

He expects this to happen through the combination of the Philippians' *prayers* for him and God's gracious fresh provision of *the Spirit of Jesus Christ.* Rather than *help given by the Spirit* (NIV), although it finally comes to that, the Spirit is what will be supplied in response to their prayers. The Spirit is further identified as the Spirit *of Jesus Christ,* one of three such instances in Paul (see Rom 8:9; Gal 4:6). Thus *Christ will be exalted* at Paul's trial through Paul's having been filled afresh with the Spirit of God, who is at the same time *the Spirit of Jesus Christ.*

The problem some have with this (how can one who has already received the Spirit receive him again?) is of our own theological making, not Paul's. Paul's concern lies with the ongoing, dynamically empowering work of the Spirit in his life (not to mention that of other believers; see Eph 5:18). Language fails him at this point, not because he had received the Spirit only partially at the beginning but because the Spirit was an experienced reality for him. Paul's language points to the freshness of the experienced reality, precisely so that Christ will be magnified through Paul at his trial. God thus supplies the Spirit to him

---

1:20 The basic meaning of *parrēsia* (NIV *sufficient courage*) is "outspokenness" or "plainness of speech" that "conceals nothing and passes over nothing" (Bauer); but it soon crossed over to mean "openness to the public," hence "publicly," and eventually took on the nuance of "bold speech," hence "confidence/boldness," of the kind that only the privileged would have before those in authority. Here it probably has to do with "openness" bordering on "bold speech."

who already has the Spirit in the sense of his receiving a fresh anointing of the Spirit so as to proclaim Christ more boldly still and so to magnify him.

Such vindication/salvation, Paul goes on (v. 20), is quite in keeping with what *I eagerly expect and hope,* which is then spelled out in the rest of the sentence. What follows also echoes the Old Testament, but in a less specific way. In biblical Greek "shame" has little to do with being *ashamed* (= inner feelings resulting in a red face) but with the utter disgrace that one will experience from failing to trust God—or more often, the disgrace that the humble who do trust will *not* experience, despite present appearances to the contrary. Paul's present usage appears to be echoing this motif from the Psalms, where the same words ("shame" and "be exalted") often stand together in the same passage (e.g., Ps 34:3-5; 35:26-27).

As verses 12-18 have made clear, Paul is experiencing no "shame" from being in prison; his present concern is that there will be no disgrace to the gospel when he finally stands before the Roman tribunal. Such disgrace, of course, is not what he expects, given their prayers and the supply of the Spirit of Christ. On the contrary, he expects the Spirit of Christ to "magnify Christ" with "all openness" (or boldness; NIV *sufficient courage*). This word suggests that in a very open and public way Christ will receive honor through Paul's bold defense of the gospel, however the trial turns out.

He wants this to happen *now as always.* This is the phrase that justifies our speaking of his apparently soon coming trial. Paul has always considered his life as in praise of Christ *(as always),* for which his rejoicing in verses 12-18 over the advance of the gospel resulting from his imprisonment offers a prime example. The *now* signifies that Paul, very well aware of his present situation, is looking forward to its resolution.

This hoped-for glorification of Christ will take place *in my body,*

Ordinarily Paul uses "in me" when he emphasizes that God will be glorified in him in some way. Thus some have suggested that *body* is intended to refer to the whole person. But that is indefensible in terms of Pauline usage (see Gundry 1976). His reason for using *body* in this case has to do with the context pure and simple; he is writing about what will happen to him physically, that is, whether his trial will result in (physical) life or (bodily) death. See the further emphasis in verses 22 and 24 (to continue to live "in the flesh").

referring to what happens to Paul physically. Depending on the results of the trial, the options are *life* and *death*. *Life* refers to being set free, *death* to his possible execution. Even though Paul expects a favorable outcome, there is always the possibility that it might go against him. That, of course, would hasten Paul's eschatological salvation/vindication before the heavenly tribunal. But for now, his singular hope is that Christ—and thus the gospel—will be vindicated through his life *or* death.

To Live—or Die—Is Christ (1:21) Having raised the possibility of execution, Paul sets out to explain his desire for Christ to be glorified even if the verdict were to go against him. Picking up on the final words of verse 20, he avows that since Christ is the singular passion of his life, he wins in either case, whether released or executed!

The striking words "to live, Christ *[Christos]*; to die, gain *[kerdos]*" epitomize Paul's life since Damascus. Once Paul was apprehended by Christ Jesus (3:12), Christ became the singular pursuit of his life. *Christ*—crucified, exalted Lord, present by the Spirit, coming King; *Christ,* the name that sums up for Paul the whole range of his new relationship to God: personal devotion, commitment, service, the gospel, ministry, communion, inspiration, everything. Much of what this means will be spelled out in his story in 3:4-14. Such singular focus does not make Paul otherworldly; rather, it gives heart and meaning to everything he is and does as a citizen of two worlds, his heavenly citizenship determining his earthly.

Thus if Paul is released as he expects, he will continue *(now as always)* in full pursuit of knowing Christ and making him known. Likewise, if he is executed, the goal of living has thus been reached: he will finally have gained Christ. The reason for this unusual way of putting it—the word *kerdos* ordinarily denotes "profit"—lies in the assonance *(Christos/kerdos)*; the sense lies in Paul's understanding death to be the ultimate "gaining" of his lifelong passion. This expresses not a death wish, nor dissatisfaction with life, nor desire to be done with troubles and trials; it is the forthright assessment of one whose immediate future is somewhat uncertain but whose ultimate future is both certain and to

1:23 It should be noted also that Paul belonged to a theological-spiritual milieu wherein his Lord could speak of God as "the God of the living, not of the dead," referring to Abraham, Isaac and Jacob (Mk 12:18-27 and parallels), and wherein Moses and Elijah appear

be desired. Death, after all, because it is "ours" in Christ Jesus (1 Cor 3:22), has lost its sting (1 Cor 15:55). Such a statement, of course, has meaning only for one to whom the first clause is a vibrant, living reality. Otherwise death is loss, or "gain" only in the sense of escape. Paul will pick up the metaphor of gain/profit again in 3:7-8 and there play it for all its worth.

Death Would Be to Paul's Advantage (1:22-23) Paul now begins a personal reflection on these two alternatives, whose point seems easy enough. If he had a real choice between the two, he would choose execution, for clear christological and eschatological reasons. But he gets there by a somewhat circuitous route.

Verse 22 is a clear follow-up to verse 21. Picking up on the first clause *(to live is Christ),* Paul assesses what its outcome will mean for him *in the body* (literally "flesh"), namely, *fruitful labor.* But rather than follow that up with a similar sentence ("if it means death"), he jumps ahead to reflect on what he might do if he in fact had a real choice in the matter. "I simply cannot say," he says; indeed, *I am torn between the two,* since it means *Christ* in either case.

The tension arises between Paul's "on earth" passion of serving Christ on behalf of others (= *fruitful labor*) and his personal desire finally to be with Christ "in heaven." After all, all of present life is given to "knowing Christ Jesus my Lord" (3:8) while at the same time pressing "toward the goal of winning the prize" of knowing him finally and completely (3:14).

Thus for Paul personally, *to depart and be with Christ . . . is better by far.* But what he understands by this is not fully clear, so this is a clause around which considerable theological ferment has boiled. At issue is the question of consciousness, for which in Paul we have no direct evidence one way or the other. On the one hand he uses the metaphor of sleep for Christians who have died; on the other hand the implication of a passage like this is that he expects to be consciously *with Christ*—since *depart* (= leave the body) and *remain in the body* and the strong feelings expressed in these sentences make very little sense otherwise.

---

with Jesus at the transfiguration. It seems most likely, therefore, that Paul expected to be *with the Lord* in full consciousness.

That such a view exists in some tension with belief in a future bodily resurrection is probably to be resolved in terms of the inherent tension between the "spatial" and "temporal" elements in Paul's eschatology. His present existence "in Christ" makes it unthinkable that he would ever—even at death—be in a "place" where he was not *with Christ.* Hence death means heaven now (the "spatial" dimension). At the same time, a person's death does not usher him or her into "timeless" existence; the bodily resurrection still awaits one "at the end" (the "temporal" dimension).

Ultimately this matter lies in the area of mystery. At issue is the interplay between time and eternity involved in the implied period of time between death and resurrection. From our human perspective, earthbound and therefore timebound as we are, we cannot imagine timeless existence; yet from the perspective of eternity/infinity these may very well be collapsed into a single "moment," as it were.

In any case, Paul understood death as a means into the Lord's immediate presence, which for him and countless thousands after him has been a comforting and encouraging prospect. Very likely he also expected such *gain* to include consciousness, and for most believers that too has been a matter of encouragement—although such a conclusion goes beyond the certain evidence we possess from Paul himself.

Life Is to Their Advantage (1:24-26) Although verse 24 is grammatically part of verse 23 *(remain* is in contrast to *depart),* with these words Paul first of all returns to what he began in verse 22 (to live in the body means *fruitful labor*). Paul clearly expects to *remain in the body,* precisely because that is *more necessary for you.* How so is what he takes up in the concluding sentence (vv. 25-26). In the end he yields to "divine necessity," which is also a way of saying that God's choice in this matter means that Paul's dilemma was purely hypothetical after all.

The final sentence (vv. 25-26) serves as the transition from "my affairs" (v. 12) to "your affairs" (v. 27). The sentence is in two clauses. In verse 25 Paul picks up his conviction from verse 24 and offers the first, more immediate reason for his release: it is for the Philippians' *progress and*

1:25 On the sense of *kauchēma* in Paul, see the helpful entry in the *Exegetical Dictionary*

joy in the faith. In verse 26 he offers the ultimate reason: that his release and coming to them will cause their "boasting" (NIV *joy*) *in Christ Jesus* to *overflow*.

The two words *progress* and *joy* together summarize his concerns for them in this letter. The first refers to the quality or character of their life in Christ, and especially to their "advancing," moving forward, in such; the second denotes the quality of their experience of it. And both of these are with regard to *the faith,* which may refer to their own faith in Christ, as in 2:17, but in this context more likely refers to the gospel itself, as in 1:27.

Such *progress* regarding *the faith* will manifest itself as their love for one another increases (1:10; 2:2), as in humility they consider the needs of others ahead of their own (2:3-4), as they "do everything without complaining or arguing" (2:14) and as they keep focused on the eschatological prize (3:14-21). This is what it means for them to "continue to work out [their] salvation with fear and trembling" (2:12).

If the first reason Paul is convinced that he *will continue with all of you* focuses on the Philippians themselves, the ultimate reason for all of this (his release and their progress) is expressed in terms of how it affects Christ (v. 26). Here the three-way bond that holds the letter together is in full evidence. Thus (literally) "your grounds for glorying will overflow in Christ Jesus in me." The occasion of Paul's coming to them again will cause their "glorying/boasting" to overflow, and all of this takes place *in Christ Jesus*. This is how Christ's being glorified *by life* (v. 20) is to find fulfillment.

The word *kauchēma* (NIV *joy*) is especially difficult to render into English. Although it can lean toward "joy," there is no reason to think it here means other than what it ordinarily means in Paul's writings, to "boast" or "glory" in someone. But "boast" is full of pejorative connotations in English—which it can also carry in Paul when one's boasting is wrongly placed. Paul's usage comes directly out of the Septuagint (LXX), especially from Jeremiah 9:23-24, where the truly wise person boasts not in wisdom, might or wealth but in the Lord, which is based on understanding and knowing God's character. "Boast," therefore, does

of the New Testament by Zmijewski (1991:276-79).

not mean to "brag about" or to "be conceited"; rather, it has to do first with putting one's full trust or confidence in something or someone and thus, second, in "glorying" in that something or someone. Hence a false "boast" (in the flesh; 3:3-6) lies at the heart of Paul's understanding of sin, whereas its opposite, "boasting/glorying in the Lord," is the ultimate evidence of genuine conversion. In cases such as this one, where the boast is "in" someone, the boast is still *in Christ*. What he has done in and for Paul serves both as the ground for the Philippians' glorying *in Christ* and the sphere in which such boasting overflows. In 2:16 they in turn will be Paul's "boast" on the day of the Lord.

Such an overflow of glorying on their part will be the direct result of the other bond—between him and them—that permeates the letter. In this case it finds expression in Paul's coming to be with them yet once more. Thus this sentence (vv. 25-26) looks beyond the present moment to the time of their joyful reunion; but there is also an "in the meantime" that concerns Paul very much, which is what he now turns to address in verse 27 (through to 2:18).

We should note, finally, that even though this larger section (vv. 18-26) begins and ends on the note of joy and of Christ's being glorified, verses 21-23 hold the key to everything, both to this letter and to Paul's life as a whole. Paul's saying *For to me, to live is Christ and to die is gain* puts everything into focus for us, as far as our understanding the apostle is concerned. It seems clear that this is what he also desires for the Philippians—and for us as well. Both our *progress* and that of the gospel depends on whether such a maxim characterizes our individual and corporate lives.

The Philippians' problem—and ours—is the strong tendency to speak thus but in effect to live otherwise. One wonders what the people of God might truly be like in our postmodern world if we were once again people of this singular passion. Too often for us it is "For me to live is Christ, plus other pursuits" (work, leisure, accumulating wealth, relationships, etc.). And if the truth were known, all too often the "plus factor" has become our primary passion: "For me to live is my work."

1:27—2:18 For a view that reads this section in terms of "disunity" within the church, and in turn the whole letter in light of the "disunity," see Peterlin 1995. While he has demonstrated that it is possible to read the letter in this way, he is less convincing that it

Both our progress and our joy regarding the gospel are altogether contingent on whether Christ is our primary, singular passion. This is surely an infinitely greater option than the self-gratification that dominates the culture within which this commentary has been written.

Moreover, to die is gain expresses, in relationship to Christ, the thoroughgoing eschatological orientation of Paul's existence. Here too the contemporary church has tended to lose too much. In a world that has lost its way, believers in Christ Jesus have the singular word of hope. We expect eventually *to depart and be with Christ*. For Paul this was a yearning; for us it is too often an addendum. The point to make, of course, is that such an orientation gives us both focus and perspective in a world gone mad.

□ The Philippians' Affairs: Exhortation to Steadfastness and Unity (1:27—2:18)

Nothing can frustrate the advance of the gospel more, both in a Christian community's effectiveness in their witness for Christ and in Christians' individual lives, than internal unrest among believers. The gospel is all about reconciliation, and unreconciled people do not advertise it well. Paul recognized this much more clearly than contemporary Christians seem to, and thus he devotes enormous energy to this matter in several of his letters (especially Rom and 1 Cor). Philippians is no exception. In now turning from his own circumstances (v. 12) to speak into the circumstances of his recipients (v. 27), he urges them to get their corporate act together (with a common mindset and mutual love) for the sake of the gospel in Philippi.

The previous section was mostly narrative; this one is mostly imperative. If 1:12-26 is the stuff of a letter of friendship, this is the stuff of a letter of exhortation (see introduction). Nonetheless the essential matter in both sections remains the same. Christ was the heart of the preceding narrative (vv. 21-23); the narrative of Christ's humiliation and exaltation (2:5-11) is the heart of this passage. Christ thus serves as the pattern for

is necessary to do so. The undeniable friendship motifs that surface throughout the letter, including in this section, tend to undercut this view.

the opening appeal—that the Philippian believers live "worthy of the gospel of Christ" (1:27—2:4)—and as the basis for the concluding appeals—that they live as "children of God without fault in a crooked and depraved generation, in which you shine like stars in the universe" (2:12-16).

Also laid out before us here is the evidence of opposition in Philippi (1:28), accompanied by suffering on their part (1:29-30; 2:17), plus the larger fact that their own community is not in full working order (1:27; 2:1-4, 12-16). For Paul, Christ is the obvious response to all of these concerns; hence he concludes once more on the note of rejoicing ("in the Lord" is implied; see on 3:1), urging them (2:18) to follow his own example in the face of opposition and suffering (1:18; 2:17).

The Appeal: In the Face of Opposition (1:27-30) Sometimes it is hard to say in a letter what one feels compelled to put to a close friend—like when writing to urge a ninety-one-year-old father to stop driving, for his sake and that of others. Without body language, voice inflections and facial expressions, the words might seem cold. Even though good friendships will endure such moments, confrontations and appeals always have the possibility of bringing some momentary tensions.

This is where Paul now is in his letter; and in his case there is the added burden that he has sometimes appeared to be more forceful when writing than in person (2 Cor 10:10). But speak into their situation he must, even though (perhaps especially because) they have partnered with him in the work of the gospel for these many years (see 1:5; 4:15-16). His friends are now in double jeopardy: there is some posturing going on among them that has all the potential of open conflict at the very time they are also facing strong opposition in Philippi.

All of these cards Paul lays on the table in this opening paragraph,

---

1:27 On the phrase *ta peri hymōn* ("about your affairs," NIV *about you*), see the note on 1:12 above.

For a discussion of the phrase "in one Spirit," see Fee 1995:163-66. Although most English translations and commentators see *in one spirit* to work as a doublet with *as one [person],* the only thing that favors such a view is the alleged doublet itself. This phrase *(en heni pneumati)* elsewhere in Paul's letters refers to the Holy Spirit. The Greek equivalent for something similar to the French *esprit de corps* is the one that follows, *mia psychē* (=

which in fact is one long, convoluted sentence in Greek. Its complexity is due in part to the friendship thing, as he makes transition from his hoped-for future coming (vv. 25-26) to present realities in Philippi, and in part to his attempt to say it carefully while putting it all in front of them. The various parts of the sentence can be easily traced (the numbers reflect the actual order of the sentence): (1) He starts (v. 27a) with an appeal to live *worthy of the gospel* in Philippi, using a metaphor that also contains an appeal to their civic pride, (3) followed (v. 27c) by a clause that spells out what that will mean for them, *contending* for the gospel in the unity of the Spirit while (4) not being intimidated by the opposition (v. 28a). Part of this is complicated (2) by his adding the presence/absence motif (v. 27b) as a way of transition from verses 25-26. (5) After an aside that spells out the eternal destiny of both sides (v. 28b), (6) he concludes with a theological explanation of Christian suffering (vv. 29-30).

The Appeal (1:27) The NIV's *whatever happens* translates the adverb "only," a word "lifted like a warning finger" (Barth 1962:45) to catch their attention about present realities. Paul expects to be released from his present imprisonment partly for the sake of his Philippian brothers and sisters' further "progress and joy" regarding "the faith." But in the meantime, while Paul is still "absent" from them, he wishes to hear the same kind of good report "about your affairs" (NIV *about you*) that he would hope to find had he been able to come now with Epaphroditus.

At issue is how the Philippians *conduct* themselves, meaning live out the gospel in Philippi. Pivotal to the present appeal is that instead of the ordinary Jewish metaphor "to walk [in the ways of the Lord]," Paul uses a political metaphor, which will appear again in 3:20-21. The people of Philippi took due pride in their having been made a Roman colony by Caesar Augustus, which brought the privileges and prestige of Roman

"one soul"), which occurs throughout Greek antiquity (in the New Testament in Acts 4:32) and is noted by Aristotle to be a common "proverbial" expression about friendship (*Nicomachean Ethics* 1163b). See also the notes on 2:2 and 2:20.

The unusual phrase *the faith of the gospel* probably means "the faith contained in the gospel," or possibly "the faith, that is, the gospel," in either case thus picking up the language *the faith* from verse 25.

citizenship. Paul now urges them to live out their citizenship *(conduct yourselves) in a manner*—and the sentence begins with these emphatic words—*worthy of the gospel of Christ*. What is intended by this wordplay is something like "Live in the Roman colony of Philippi as worthy citizens of your heavenly homeland." That, after all, is precisely the contrast made in 3:17-20, where "our citizenship is in heaven," in contrast to those whose minds are set on "earthly things."

The use of this metaphor is a brilliant stroke. Not only does it appeal to their own historic pride as Philippians, but now applied to their present setting, it urges concern both for the mission of the gospel in Philippi and especially for the welfare of the state, meaning in this case that they take seriously their "civic" responsibilities within the believing community. Their being of one mind and heart is at stake; disharmony will lead to their collective ruin.

How are they to bring this off? By standing *firm* in the one Spirit as they contend side by side as one person *for the faith of the gospel*. With these words, and in typical fashion, Paul switches metaphors, this time to an athletic contest, probably used metaphorically in turn to suggest a battle. The image is of people engaged in spiritual warfare (imagery that will hardly be lost on those who live in a military colony!), standing their ground firmly by the power of the Holy Spirit, who as the one Spirit is also the source of their unity (cf. 1 Cor 12:13), thus anticipating 2:1. Despite the frequency of its appearance in English translations, this phrase can scarcely mean *in one spirit* (NIV), as though it meant to have a common mind about something. Such an idiom with the word *spirit* is unknown in all of Greek literature. Paul himself uses this phrase elsewhere to refer to the Holy Spirit (1 Cor 12:9, 13; Eph 2:18), precisely in places, as here, where Christian unity is at stake.

They are urged thus to *stand firm in*/by the one Spirit so as to contend together as one person *for the faith of the gospel*. Here we are at the heart of things: their need to have harmony within the Christian community as they live out the gospel in Philippi. *The gospel* is the

---

1:28 For the view of the "opposition" offered here, see further Bockmuehl 1997:100-101, and especially two recent German works, Bormann 1995:217-24 and Pilhofer 1995:137-39. The view of some (e.g., Hendricksen 1962:87; Collange 1979:75; Hawthorne 1983:58), that

beginning and end of everything for Paul. Thus for them to live out their (heavenly) citizenship *in a manner worthy of the gospel* means for them to contend *for the faith of the gospel,* and to do so in the unity that only the Spirit brings. All the more so now because they are facing some kind of opposition that is resulting in suffering.

The Opposition (1:28) *Contending . . . for the faith of the gospel* immediately calls to mind the opposition. So Paul adds, *without being frightened in any way by those who oppose you.* The (somewhat rare) word translated *frightened,* used sometimes to refer to "spooking" horses, probably here carries the nuance "be intimidated" or "be thrown into consternation."

But what kind of opposition would possibly intimidate the Philippian believers? Although we cannot be certain, the best guess is related to the fact that Philippi was a Roman military colony, whose populace for very good historical reasons were devoted to the emperor (see introduction). In fact the cult of the emperor, whose "divine" titles were "lord" and "savior," apparently flourished in Philippi, so that every public event also served as an opportunity to proclaim "Caesar is lord"—in very much the same way as "The Star-Spangled Banner" or "O Canada!" is sung before public events in North America.

The problem for believers is obvious—and would easily arouse suspicions as well as hostility. For they were devoted to another Lord and Savior (Phil 3:20 is the only place this combination occurs in Paul's letters) and would find proclaiming Caesar as lord to be an impossible conflict of devotion. To top it all off, their Lord had in fact been crucified by the Roman "lord," thus branding him forever as an enemy of the state, of the insurrectionist type. Thus believers in Christ could scarcely be more out of touch with the sympathies of the local populace than in a place like Philippi. Hence Paul's concern that *those who oppose* them not intimidate or throw them into consternation.

This in part accounts for the constant focus on Christ in this letter. He who, following his crucifixion, currently reigns as Lord (2:9) will

they are the same as the "dogs" in 3:2, has almost nothing in its favor in the present context, since those people were Jewish Christian itinerants, who could scarcely be responsible for Christian suffering in Philippi where there was no Jewish colony.

someday return from heaven as Lord and Savior (3:20-21), before whom every knee will bow—including that of the current "lord Caesar," Nero himself, who will join with all others to confess that the only Lord is none other than Jesus Christ (2:10-11).

Paul's mention of the opposition now prompts him to insert a parenthetical moment, describing what their standing up to the opposition will mean, as by the Holy Spirit they form a united front in *contending for . . . the gospel* in Philippi. Such "Spiritual" boldness on their part will serve as a *sign* (perhaps "omen") *to them that they will be destroyed, but that you will be saved.*

How so, Paul does not say, but the answer probably lies with the Philippians' embracing the eschatological certainties just given in verses 21-24, which will give to them, as to Paul, uncommon boldness in proclaiming Christ in Philippi. Such people cannot be intimidated by anyone or anything, since they belong to the future with a kind of certainty that people whose lives are basically controlled by Fate could never understand—surely an "omen," Paul says, using the language of their own worldview, that they are headed for destruction.

At the same time, of course, such resolve and unity in the face of opposition will fall out as salvation for the Philippians. Although the grammar is a bit sticky here, most likely the word *saved* ("salvation") carries a sense very close to that in verse 19. Such salvation/vindication will not necessarily be manifest to the opponents, but it will become clear to the believers themselves. To drive this point of assurance home, Paul adds, "And this (their destruction and your salvation/vindication) comes from none other than God himself."

As always God is both the first and the last word. Salvation is at his initiative; it comes from him. Thus it is the first word. But in this sentence, in light of the Philippians' need for reassurance, it is the last word as well. Everything is from God; the Philippians can rest assured. Which is also a necessary word in light of the theological explanation of suffering that Paul is about to offer.

The Suffering—Theologically Explained (1:29-30) People who reflect an attitude that suggests "Oh boy, I get to suffer for Jesus" cause most of us to squirm. Somehow they haven't got it quite right; and they surely cannot appeal to Paul for such an attitude. Paul's attitude toward Christian suffering is altogether theological and christocentric at its core. It is based on Christ's teaching on discipleship, that servants are to be like their master, and on Paul's own understanding of present Christian existence as both "already" and "not yet."

The parenthetical nature of verse 28b makes the *for* with which this sentence begins a bit problematic. What ultimately triggers all of this is the mention of the opposition, filtered through Paul's knowledge of his readers' present, very real, situation. But the immediate reason for the *for* is the mention of their final salvation as from (NIV *by*) *God.* The God who saves you, who has thus *granted to you* (literally "graced you"!) *on behalf of Christ . . . to believe on him,* is the same God who has also graced you *to suffer for him.* So who needs such "gracing"? one might ask.

The clue again lies in the christocentric nature of Paul's understanding of everything. Literally he says, "To you has been graciously given on behalf of Christ . . . to suffer on his behalf." This emphasis must be understood in light of the Christ narrative to which Paul will appeal in 2:5-11. A crucified Lord produces disciples who themselves take up a cross as they follow him. We are thus to live *on behalf of Christ* in the same way Christ himself lived—and died—on behalf of this fallen, broken world. That is why salvation includes suffering *on behalf of Christ,* since those who oppose the Philippian believers as they proclaim the gospel of Christ are of a kind with those who crucified their Lord in the first place. And for believers, as for our Lord, the path to glorification leads through the suffering of the cross (= living "cruciform" [see note on 1:11]).

But Paul is not finished. He concludes by reminding his partners in the gospel that he and they are in this together as well; they are *going through the same struggle* they have seen him go through. His present accent falls on *the same,* meaning "of a kind with his," which causes a lot of things to fall into place, including both the length and the content of the preceding narrative about "my affairs" (vv. 12-26). Their present suffering on Christ's behalf has been equally brought on by those who oppose the gospel, very likely reflecting a common source as well, the Roman Empire.

In making this point, he reminds them that their *struggle* is identical to that which *you saw I had*. Among the recipients of this letter would be the jailer and his household and (perhaps) the young slave girl whose having been set free from Satan's tyranny had resulted in the first of Paul's sufferings on behalf of Christ that they had seen. In fact, not long after that initial stay in Philippi he wrote to another Macedonian congregation and referred to his Philippian experience in terms of suffering and being shamefully treated (1 Thess 2:2). The *struggle* was always there, and every time he came through Philippi they saw more of the same, which over time took on a variety of forms.

And so he reminds them that their present suffering is precisely of a kind with his current Roman imprisonment. They are partners in suffering for the gospel as well as in proclaiming it; and that reality—and resource—is what he will draw on as he now returns to the appeal that they stand firm in the one Spirit, contending side by side for the gospel (2:1-4).

Although our particulars differ considerably, the theological concerns that emerge in this paragraph are greatly needed in the church today, both in the Western church where the struggle in a post-Christian, postmodern world is immense, though the suffering is less so, and in churches in the emerging world, where suffering is often more prevalent but where sectarian strife all too often hampers the cause of the gospel.

One of the reasons most of us in the West do not know more about the content of verses 29-30 is that we have so poorly heeded the threefold exhortation that precedes: (1) to stand firm in the one Spirit (overall our pneumatology is especially weak); (2) to contend for the faith of the gospel as one person (*the faith of the gospel* has been watered down on all sides, by the blatant materialism that erodes the evangelical church as well as by a banal "liberalism," neither of which is worth contending for; and our sectarianism has more often resulted in in-house furor than in contending for the gospel in the face of pagan opposition); and (3) to do so without being intimidated in any way by the opposition (who tend to focus on our many weaknesses, so as to continually deflect our contending for the gospel of our crucified Savior per se).

The net result is that the content of Paul's explanation is something contemporary Christians hear reluctantly, either out of guilt that so many of us look so little like this or out of fear that it might someday really be true for us. The key is to return to Paul's emphasis, "for the sake of Christ." Our tendency is to focus on the suffering. What is needed is a radical paradigm shift toward Christ—and his apostle—as God's ultimate paradigm for us. Through "death on a cross" he not only "saved us" but modeled for us God's way of dealing with the opposition—loving them to death.

The Appeal Renewed: Unity Through Humility (2:1-4) Having acknowledged his friends' suffering by offering a christological reason for it, Paul now returns to the urgent matter at hand: the appeal in verse 27 that in the face of the opposition that is causing suffering, they stand firm in the one Spirit, contending for the gospel as a united body.

It is instructive to watch Paul deal with such matters, especially noting how he refrains from our own tendencies toward "saint-bashing" when the sins of others are clearer to us than our own. Again, their relationship to him as friends and his need to speak into their present situation combine to create another long and complex sentence. But the way the parts work is easy to see.

Verse 1 offers the basis of the appeal, which has to do (apparently) with their own trinitarian experience of God: Christ's comfort, God's love and their common sharing in the Spirit. But it is also based on their long-standing relationship with Paul, who has shared both the suffering (1:30) and these same graces with them, and now looks for tenderness and compassion from them.

The concern of the appeal is expressed in verse 2, where he piles up three phrases that all say essentially the same thing: that their community life should be characterized by unity of mind and love. Only thus can they complete Paul's own joy.

The content of the appeal (vv. 3-4) describes, first, those expressions of our human fallenness that altogether militate against unity within the household of faith, *selfish ambition* and *vain conceit;* and, second, those virtues necessary for it to happen, *love* and *humility,* which find concrete expression as God's people learn to live as Christ, to care for the needs of others as the matter of first priority—all of which will be gloriously displayed in the Christ narrative that follows.

The Basis of the Appeal (2:1) The NIV and other translations, following the unfortunate chapter division at this point, obscure the clear relationship of this paragraph with what has immediately preceded. Paul's sentence begins with a "therefore" (= "for this reason"), which is probably intended to pick up on all of 1:27-30. Thus although he is primarily resuming the appeal to unity, he does so now in light of the Philippians' suffering, in a struggle they have in common with Paul. "Therefore," he says in light of that—and to return to the matter at hand—"if there be any comfort in Christ, as indeed there is, . . . then complete my joy."

So how does one entreat friends to get back on track? By appealing to relationships, both divine and human. It may not always work, but this is certainly the primary way. Paul begins by appealing to the *encouragement* or "comfort" that *being* in (NIV *united with*) *Christ* can bring, as a direct response to their common experience of suffering for Christ in the preceding clause (1:29-30). But right at that point, before dictating a "then" clause, he adds three more "if" clauses, whose studied accumulation is part of the rhetorical effect.

The second clause, "if any solace of love," on its own is perfectly ambiguous. Does it refer to Christ's love (as NIV), or to Paul's and their shared love, or to God's love? While all of these can be shown to fit in context, most likely it refers to God's love for them, placed as it is between clear references to Christ and the Spirit, similar to the trinitarian grace in 2 Corinthians 13:14 (and with the same language).

While *fellowship with* is common coinage for the word ***koinōnia*** in the third clause, it is doubtful whether it ever means precisely that. The word has to do with "sharing in" or "participating in" something (usually

2:1 The fourfold repetition of *if* is almost certainly for rhetorical effect, in a situation where the letter will not be read privately but publicly. Although *if* ordinarily forms the protasis of a conditional sentence, in this case the protases do not so much express supposition as presupposition. Hence "if this be the case, as it certainly is."

Paraklēsis (NIV *encouragement*) in the first clause is a thoroughly ambiguous word in Greek whose meaning ranges from "exhortation" through "encouragement" to "comfort." Although the word in the next clause *(paramythion)* clearly and only means *comfort* or "solace," the close tie of the first clause to the preceding sentence suggests that the *encouragement* intended leans equally toward "comfort."

with someone else), which is almost certainly what is intended here (see 1:5). Paul's appeal is to their common sharing in the Spirit, thus picking up the language of 1:27.

Finally, he appeals, *if any tenderness and compassion*. This phrase brings into sharp focus the basic ambiguities of these clauses, in terms of the direction of the relationships implied. Is it God's love toward them (i.e., on the basis of the prior work of grace from their experience of the Trinity) that Paul appeals to, or the Philippians' common life in Christ that they have experienced together heretofore, or the relationship that they and Paul have together in the gracious work of God? While commentators tend to line up fairly evenly among the three options, my guess is that what Paul does is not quite as tidy as we would have it. Most likely the three-way bond between Christ, the Philippians and Paul that is central to this letter is once more in view.

At the beginning the focus is clearly on Christ—and the comfort that is theirs (the Philippians) by being in Christ. But as what immediately precedes (v. 30) makes clear, and the "therefore" implies, Christ's comfort is shared by him and them together. As Paul moves to the next two clauses, the primary focus again seems to be on the Philippians' experience of (presumably God's) love and their sharing in the Spirit; but again, he and they share these as well. When he reaches the fourth clause, however, which noticeably lacks a modifier, the direction shifts toward their relationship with him, thus leading directly to the imperative *make my joy complete*. While it is true that *tenderness and compassion* are regularly attributed to God, in Colossians 3:12, a letter written in close proximity to this one, the two words appear together to form the phrase "bowels of mercy" (= "heart of compassion," which the NIV reduces simply to "compas-

For a thorough and helpful discussion of the options and their ramifications for understanding the *if*-clauses—although I differ a bit with his conclusion and reason for it—see O'Brien 1991:167-76, who also includes data on the various scholars who take each option. Part of our difficulty here is probably related to the nature of dictation, in that what is written by way of dictation sometimes still carries the rhetorical effect of oral speech. In this kind of rhetoric, precision is a lesser concern than is the persuasive effect created by the accumulation of phrases. It is possible therefore (probable, I think) that the emphasis shifts as Paul warms up to his rhetoric.

sion") as an especially appropriate virtue for Christian community. Most likely it is to the Philippians' own "heart of compassion" toward him that Paul finally appeals.

Thus the basis of the appeal is first of all the Philippians' own relationship to the triune God, which he and they share together, and second, his and their relationship to each other, brought about by their common relationship to the Trinity.

The Concern of the Appeal (2:2) Only the deliberately blind could possibly miss what concerns Paul. Just as he rhetorically compounds the basis of his appeal, so here at least three times he repeats: be *like-minded;* have *the same love;* be *one in spirit* and of one mind. But how he gets there is a bit surprising, although by now certainly not unexpected. On the basis of your own—and our common—experience of the trinitarian God and of your well-known *tenderness and compassion,* then *make my joy complete* by getting your corporate life together. Again, this reflects the three-way bond between him, them and Christ that holds the entire letter together. Their unity in the Spirit, based on Christ's comfort, will bring Paul's joy over the advance of the gospel, already noted in 1:18, to full fruition. What is probably in view is his eschatological joy at their being together with him at the day of Christ (2:16).

The key word in the appeal, and indeed a key word in the letter, is the verb *phroneō* (see on 1:7), which is repeated in the first and third instances and has to do with the set of one's mind, how one is overall disposed toward something (cf. Rom 8:5-7)—thus (literally) "set your minds on the same thing"/"setting your minds on the one thing." This is the word that is picked up again in Philippians 2:5 ("have this same mindset, as Christ did") and in 4:2, where he reproduces the identical language of this first phrase in urging Euodia and Syntyche to the same mindset. The second occurrence (third phrase) is accompanied by the adjective *sympsychos* (= "together in soul"), thus joining mind and soul together, while picking up the phrase "one soul" from 1:27.

2:2 By translating *sympsychoi* as *one in spirit,* the NIV unwittingly supports the fact that *en heni pneumati* ("in one Spirit") in 1:27 refers to the Holy Spirit, not to a corporate mindset. What is perfectly natural for us in English would be quite unnatural to Greek speakers, and vice versa. That is, if "one in soul" is simply not our idiom so that (as here)

The middle phrase, *having the same love,* points back to the second clause in verse 1, "if any solace from [God's] love." The context suggests that Paul is first of all urging them to have *the same love* for one another that they already have experienced in God's love for them—and in theirs and his for each other. In 1:9 Paul told them he prays that their love might "abound more and more." Love, therefore, is not lacking in this community. At issue is the danger of its being eroded by internal friction. Thus they will fill Paul's joy to the full as they return to full and complete love for one another, which by definition means to care for another for her or his own sake. As someone well said: "Love begins when someone else's needs are more important than my own," which is precisely what Paul will urge in the elaboration that follows.

The Content of the Appeal (2:3-4) Whatever exactly Paul might mean by "having the same mindset," the rest of his sentence makes it abundantly clear that his concern is with the practical consequences of their life together as believers in Philippi. What he spells out is how *having the same love* (for one another) will take shape in their colony of heaven (see on 3:20) within this Roman colony at Philippi.

Although the NIV (and most translations) rightly turn these phrases into further imperatives, it is important to note that grammatically the first two *(nothing out of selfish ambition or vain conceit)* modify the final phrase in verse 2, "together in soul having minds set on the one thing." That is, to be *one in spirit* and of one mind eliminates altogether *selfish ambition* and *vain conceit* as options for one's mindset. It is also important to note that *selfish ambition* is precisely what Paul in 1:17 attributes to those who are trying to afflict him in his imprisonment, while *vain conceit* is conceptually related to their "envy and rivalry" (1:15). In fact, these words describe a mindset exactly the opposite of Christ's, who being in the form of God showed Godlikeness in "pouring himself out by becoming a slave/servant" (vv. 6-7). What exactly is going on in Philippi that calls for this appeal cannot be known, but these

---

it is translated *one in spirit,* then "one in spirit," which is perfectly natural to us, would to Greek speakers sound as "one in soul" does to us. In both 1:27 *(mia psychē)* and here Paul uses the normal idiom to refer to what we would naturally put as "one spirit."

attitudes that are already dividing the church in Rome over their relationship to Paul—even as they are evangelizing—must not be allowed a foot in the door in Philippi.

To the contrary, and again in clear anticipation of the story of Christ that follows, what *being like-minded* and *having the same love* calls for is *in humility consider* one another (NIV *others*) *better than yourselves. Humility* is a uniquely Christian virtue, which, like the message of a crucified Messiah, stands in utter contradiction to the values of the Greco-Roman world, which generally considered humility not a virtue but a shortcoming. Here Paul's roots are in the Old Testament—and in Christ. In the Old Testament the term indicates lowliness in the sense of "creatureliness," the truly humble showing themselves so by resting their case with God rather than trusting their own strength and machinations; and Jesus reveals "humbleness of heart" as something essential about God's character (Mt 11:29).

Humility is thus not to be confused with false modesty ("I'm no good") or with "milquetoast," that kind of abject servility that only repulses. Rather it has to do with a proper estimation of oneself, the stance of the creature before the Creator, utterly dependent and trusting. Here one is well aware both of one's weaknesses and of one's glory (we are in God's image, after all) but makes neither too much nor too little of either. True humility is therefore not self-focused at all but rather, as further defined by Paul, considers *others better than yourselves.*

As with humility, this last phrase does not mean that one should falsely consider others *better.* As Philippians 2:4 will clarify, we are so to consider others not in our estimation of them—which would only lead to the very vices Paul has just spoken against—but in our caring for them, putting them and their needs ahead of our own. Others in the community are not necessarily "better" than I am, but their needs and concerns "surpass" my own. After all, this is precisely how Christ's humility expressed itself, as Paul narrates in verse 8. This is how he

---

2:3 *Kenodoxia* (*vain conceit;* literally "empty glory": cf. Gal 5:26) is a compound denoting that kind of empty glory that only the self-blessed can bestow on themselves. This word occurs throughout the Greco-Roman world to describe those who think too highly of themselves—not those who appear to have grounds for "glory," but those whose "glory" seems baseless.

To translate *allēlōn* "others" (as the NIV) is to generalize what is clearly intended to be

elsewhere describes those whose behavior is genuinely Christian; they do not seek their own good, but the good of others (1 Cor 10:24). Here is the sure cure for *selfish ambition or vain conceit,* not to mention "complaining or arguing" (Phil 2:14).

The emphasis in verse 4, which thus spells out how verse 3b works, is on *each* and *others*. Here one finds a kind of tension between the individual and the community that occurs throughout Paul. As always in such passages, the accent rests on the community; it is only as a people of God together that God's people fulfill the divine purposes. But in the new covenant, persons become members of the people of God one at a time through faith in Christ. Therefore the concern is primarily with the community, but obedience must begin with the individual. *Each* one among them must have this care for the *others* among them. This emphasis is probably to remind some within the community who seem to be out of step with some others.

On its own merit this passage, read over and over again with prayerful hearts that are inclined toward obedience, could go a long way toward curing the ills that beset our Christian communities—including that most fragile of institutions, the Christian family, which after all forms the nucleus, or basic unit, of any larger Christian community. In the larger church community people can sometimes "get along" because they do not have to live with one another and they meet so seldom. But in the home it has to be worked out on a daily basis with those who are closest to us. The cure is the same for all: in humility before God, each of us putting the interests of others ahead of our own, rather than constantly looking at the other to supply our needs.

Happily, this passage, as wonderful as it is, does not stand on its own. Paul will now follow up with the sublimest of all New Testament passages, pointing to Christ's own story as the model of what he has urged in verses 3-4.

The Example of Christ (2:5-11) You probably know people who, like

local regarding the Christian community. This is one of Paul's favorite words to express relationships within the believing community. Everything is done with "one another" in view; see Fee 1995:188 n. 77.The word translated *better (hyperechontas)* can rightly mean that, but in its two further uses in this letter (3:8; 4:7) it clearly means something like "surpassing, going far beyond" something else. In light of verse 4 that seems to be the sense here as well.

the present author, when all else fails finally read the manual! That's what Paul is now up to, showing the Philippians "the manual." The ultimate paradigm of a genuinely Christian mindset is Christ himself, who is the premier manifestation of the character of God, which God is trying to reproduce in his people so that they might also thereby be truly human. Paul thus presents the essential matters of Christ's story—which he narrates in such exalted fashion, full of passion and poetry, that what serves as the centerpiece of our letter is in many ways the centerpiece of the entire New Testament. Not only does all of the present section (1:27—2:18) lead up to and flow out of this passage, but when Paul tells his own story in 3:4-14, as a further model for the Philippians to imitate, he clearly ties his narrative to this grandest of all narratives.

Understandably such a passage has elicited an enormous amount of scholarly attention, which will not detain us here (see the note for details). Although it is often set out in English translations as a hymn, there is no historical evidence that it was ever a hymn in the liturgical sense of having been sung in Christian churches, and in any case verses 9-11 are very much like argument (*therefore* . . . [in order] *that*), whose only poetic element comes from Paul's use of Isaiah 45:23 in verses 10-11. Two matters are important as we approach the passage: first, that in going through the passage we not miss the forest for the trees—that is, that we not get bogged down in the details so that we miss the grandeur of the whole; and second, that precisely because in some ways the passage can stand on its own (it is a complete narrative, after all), we not miss its very clear and essential ties to the present argument.

We begin with the former. After the appeal with which it begins (v. 5), the narrative itself presents what has historically been called "the mind of Christ" in two major parts, referred to as his "humiliation" (vv. 6-8) and "exaltation" (vv. 9-11). The story of his "humiliation" is likewise in two parts: verses 6-7, which tell us that as God he poured himself out

---

2:5-11 The scholarly issues regarding this passage are basically four: (1) whether or not Paul is citing a hymn; (2) if so, whether it is pre-Pauline; (3) if not by Paul, what its religious "background" is; (4) what role it serves in context. The literature is immense. For a quick read on most of these matters, see Bockmuehl 1997:115-26; cf. Fee 1995:192-94 nn. 1-6. For a more complete version see O'Brien 1991:186-202, 253-71.

2:5 A few scholars, notably Käsemann 1968 and Martin 1997, have argued that the point of the "Christ-hymn" in context is not to serve as a paradigm but is "kerygmatic," meaning

by taking the form of a slave/servant in his becoming human; verse 8, which tells us that as a human being he humbled himself, obediently going all the way to death on a cross. Part 2 (vv. 9-11) narrates the divine vindication of this self-emptying humbling of Christ: he has been exalted to the highest place and given the Name before whom every created being shall eventually offer obeisance. The glory of all this is that the self-emptying, humbling One never ceases to be God in his "humiliation"; indeed this is the full revelation of God's essential character—in the words of Graham Kendrick's wonderful hymn, "this is our God, the Servant-King."

But in telling the story in this way Paul clearly shapes the language to the context. In order to help the Philippians toward a common mindset (v. 2), he presents as a model the divine mindset (v. 5), graphically portrayed through Christ's incarnation and crucifixion. Instead of "empty glory" *(<u>keno</u>doxia),* Christ "emptied himself" *(heauton e<u>kenō</u>sen);* instead of "selfish ambition," he took "the form of a slave"; he did not *consider* his equality with God selfishly, just as they in humility are to "consider" the needs of others ahead of their own (a form of *hēgeomai* in each instance); as a human being he humbled himself (*etapeinōsen;* cf. *tapeinophrosynē* in v. 3); and all of this to God's glory (*doxan,* v. 11), over against the "empty glory" *(kenodoxia)* of selfish ambition. And beyond these clear linguistic ties are the conceptual ones: the whole narrative offers the highest expression of God's love (v. 1) urged on the Philippian believers (v. 2), not to mention that it is the ultimate example of not looking only to one's own interests but also to the interests of others (v. 4).

The Appeal—to the Mind of Christ (2:5) The transitional function of this sentence is a lot clearer in the Greek text than are some of its parts. Literally it reads: "This mindset have 'in you' which also 'in Christ Jesus.' " "This" points backward to verses 2-4; "which also" picks up

that the Philippians are to adopt in their relationships with each other what is already true of their being "in Christ" together, and that the "hymn" gives the soteriological basis for such an appeal. To get there, they read "in Christ" in this verse to refer to the Philippians' being "in Christ"; thus "become in your conduct and church relationships the type of persons who . . . have a place in [Christ's] body, the church" (Martin 1997:291). For a recent defense against criticisms of this view, see Martin 1997:xlvi-lv; for the most recent critique of it, independent of earlier debate, see Bockmuehl 1997:122-24; cf. Hurtado 1984.

"this" and points it forward to verses 6-8. What Paul says in effect is that "the attitude of mind I have been urging on you is exactly that of God himself, as it has been spelled out in the incarnation."

The phrase "in you" (obscured by the NIV's *your*) is nicely double-entendre here and elsewhere (e.g., 2:13). It primarily means "among you," that is, "in your community relationships." But the only way for that to happen, as noted in the commentary on verse 4, is for each one to assume the responsibility for such a disposition. Thus each is to have this mindset "in you" so that it will be fully manifested "among you." Since the second clause intentionally parallels the first (cf. "which also"), the phrase "in Christ Jesus" therefore parallels "in/among you" and looks to an attitude that can be found in Christ himself. The intended verb in the second clause is some form of "to be," either "was," pointing to the historical dimension of the story about to be narrated, or "is," pointing to the mindset that is always to be found in Christ and was historically demonstrated in the incarnation. Put together, the whole sentence means something like "In your relationships with one another, have the same attitude of mind Christ Jesus had/has."

As God He Emptied Himself (2:6-7) In displaying the mind of Christ, Paul begins with one of those sublime sentences whose essential intent and meaning seem clear as can be yet whose parts are full of mystery and wonder. The reason for this is simple enough; on the basis of what was known and came to be believed about Jesus' earthly life, Paul is trying to say something about what could not be observed yet came to be believed about Christ's prior existence as God. What is essential is this: In his prior existence as God, Christ demonstrated what equality with God meant, not by taking advantage of it for himself but by emptying himself, by taking the role of a slave/servant in becoming one of us. All of this, in the present context, is to portray the ultimate expression of "do nothing out of selfish ambition or vain conceit." What that "mind" entails is spelled out in the narrative that follows.

2:6 Some argue for an "Adam-Christ" analogy in verses 6-7, where Christ does the opposite of Adam in the Garden. This is an intriguing possibility; against it are the number of places the analogy does not work at all and the fact that there is not a single linguistic tie between this passage and the LXX of Genesis 2—3. Advocates include Murphy-O'Connor 1976, Hooker 1978 and Dunn 1980:174-81. See the overview in O'Brien 1991:263-68.

Some of those who argue for an Adam-Christ analogy at work also deny that

The details that need special attention are four: (1) Why does Paul say "in the form" of God (NIV margin) rather than simply say "as God"? (2) What does the word *harpagmos* mean (NIV *something to be grasped;* put above as "taking advantage of")? (3) What did it mean for Christ to "empty himself" (NIV *made himself nothing*)? (4) Why *in human likeness* rather than "in his humanity" or something similar? Other details of significance will be noted in the process of looking at each of these matters in turn.

First, the opening phrase, "who, being in the form *[morphē*] of God," expresses as presupposition what the rest of the sentence assumes: that it was the preexistent Christ who "emptied himself" at one point in our human history. Why then did Paul use *morphē*, which primarily refers to the "form" or "shape" something takes? The answer lies in what Paul is about in this sentence. His urgency is to say something about Christ's "mindset" in both expressions of his being, first as God and second in his humanity. But in the transition from Christ's "being God" to his "becoming human," Paul expresses by way of metaphor the essential "shape" of that humanity: Christ "took on the 'form' of a slave." Since *morphē* can denote "form" or "shape" in terms of both the external features by which something is recognized and the characteristics and qualities that are essential to it, it was precisely the right word to characterize both the reality (his being God) and the metaphor (his taking on the role of a slave). On the basis of Christ's resurrection and ascension, his earliest followers had come to believe that the One whom they had known as truly human had himself known prior existence in the "form" of God—not meaning that he was "like God but really not" but that he was characterized by what was essential to being God. This understanding (correctly) lies behind the NIV's *in very nature God.*

Second, in order to highlight the astonishing nature of the incarnation, Paul resorts to a typical "not/but" contrast. Reading such a sentence straight through without the "but" clause always helps to get at what is

preexistence is intended by Paul. This has been especially advocated by Dunn 1980; for an overview with bibliography for and against, see Fee 1995:203 n. 41.

For a recent discussion of *morphē* see O'Brien 1991:207-11 and the literature there cited; for an overview of the *harpagmos* debate see Wright 1986. The two works that have been most influential in moving toward consensus are by C. F. D. Moule (1970) and Roy Hoover (1971).

essential; in this case, "who, being in the form of God, . . . made himself nothing by taking the form of a servant/slave." That is glory indeed; but to heighten the glory Paul emphasizes two realities: first, that "being in the form of God" means being equal with God; second, that in Christ's "being in the form of God/being equal with God" he displayed a mindset precisely the opposite of "selfish ambition" and empty glory (v. 3). To accent this second point he uses an extremely rare (negative) word, *harpagmos,* which depicts the opposite of "in humility consider others better than yourselves" (v. 3).

Harpagmos is a noun formed from a verb that means to "to seize, steal [hence the KJV's 'robbery'], snatch, take away." Although its meaning has been much debated, there is a growing consensus that its probable sense leans toward something like either "a matter of grasping or seizing" or "something grasped for one's own personal advantage." In the first option the emphasis lies on the verbal side of the noun, on the idea of "seizing" as such. Thus Christ did not consider "equality with God" to consist of being "grasping" or "selfish"; rather he rejected this popular view of kingly power by pouring himself out for the sake of others. The alternative, which is probably preferable, is to see the word as a synonym of its cognate *harpagma* ("booty" or "prey"), which in idioms similar to Paul's denotes something like "a matter to be seized upon" in the sense of "taking advantage of" it ("he did not think he needed to take advantage of this equality with God," Bockmuehl 1997:114).

In either case, the clause comes out very much at the same point. Equality with God is something that was inherent to Christ in his preexistence; but he did not consider Godlikeness to consist in "grasping" or "seizing" or as "grasping it to his own advantage," which would be the normal expectation of lordly power—and the nadir of selfishness.

Third, Christ's selflessness for the sake of others expressed itself in his emptying himself by taking the "form" of a slave. Historically, far too much has been made of the verb "emptied himself," as though in becoming incarnate he literally "emptied himself" of something. How-

2:7 Paul's use of the metaphor "emptied himself" has led to the creation of an enormous literature on the meaning of *kenōsis,* the doctrine of Christ's "self-emptying," including debate over what he emptied himself of. For a useful discussion, see Feinberg 1980. On

ever, just as *harpagmos* requires no object for Christ to "seize" but rather points to what is the opposite of God's character, so Christ did not empty himself of anything; he simply "emptied himself," poured himself out, as it were. In keeping with Paul's ordinary usage, this is metaphor, pure and simple. What modifies it is expressed in the phrase that follows; he "poured himself out by taking on the 'form' of a slave."

Elsewhere this verb regularly means to become powerless or to be emptied of significance (hence the NIV's *made himself nothing;* cf. KJV, "made himself of no reputation"). Here it stands in direct antithesis to the "empty glory" of verse 3 and functions in the same way as the metaphorical "he became poor" in 2 Corinthians 8:9. Thus, as in the "not" side of this clause (v. 6b), we are still dealing with the character of God as revealed in the mindset and resulting activity of the Son of God. The concern is with divine selflessness: God is not an acquisitive being, grasping and seizing, but self-giving for the sake of others.

That this is Paul's intent is made certain by the two explanatory participial phrases that follow. The first explains the nature of Christ's emptying himself, how it was expressed in our human history: "by taking on the 'form' of a slave" (NIV *taking the very nature of a servant*). From Paul's perspective this is how divine love manifests itself in its most characteristic and profuse expression. Christ entered our history not as *kyrios* ("Lord"), a name he acquires at his vindication (vv. 9-11), but as *doulos* ("slave"; see on 1:1), a person without advantages, rights or privileges, but in servanthood to all. All of this, surely, with an eye to verses 3-4. It is further important to note that crucifixion was reserved by the Romans either for insurrectionists or for recalcitrant slaves.

The second participial phrase simultaneously clarifies the first by elaboration and concludes the present sentence by paving the way for the next (v. 8). Together these two phrases give definition to Christ's "impoverishment." The phrase "in the form of a slave" comes first for rhetorical reasons—to sharpen the contrast with "in the form of God" and to set out the true nature of his incarnation. It thus reflects the "quality" of his incarnation. The second phrase indicates its "factual"

the discussion of "form of a slave," especially whether it is intended to reflect Isaiah 53, see O'Brien 1991:218-24.

side. Thus Christ came "in the form of a slave," that is, by *being made in human likeness.*

This leads, fourth, to the troubling word *likeness (homoiōma),* which is most likely used because of Paul's belief (in common with the rest of the early church) that in becoming human Christ did not cease to be divine. This word allows for the ambiguity, emphasizing that he is similar to our humanity in some respects and dissimilar in others. The similarity lies with his full humanity; in his incarnation he was "like" in the sense of "the same as." The dissimilarity lies with his never ceasing to be "equal with God"; while "like" us in being fully identified with us, he was not "human" only. He was God living out a truly human life, all of which is safeguarded by this expression.

Thus, to put the sentence all together, in Christ Jesus God has shown his true nature; this is what it means for Christ to be "equal with God"—to pour himself out for the sake of others and to do so by taking the role of a slave. Hereby he not only reveals the character of God but also reveals what it means for us to be created in God's image, to bear his likeness and have his "mindset." It means taking the role of the slave for the sake of others—the contours of which are delineated in the next sentence.

As a Man He Humbled Himself (2:8) Apart from the absence of the "not/but" contrast, this sentence is formally very much like the preceding one. It begins (1) with a participle emphasizing Christ's present "mode" of being, in this case "as a human being," followed (2) by the main clause *(he humbled himself),* followed (3) by a similar participial modifier, again spelling out how he did so *(became obedient to death),* which in turn (4) is brought to rhetorical climax by specifying the kind of death *(even death on a cross).* Thus the two sentences in their essential parts are parallel:

Being in the form of God,
  he emptied himself
    by taking on the form of a slave,
      by coming in the likeness of human beings.
Being found in human appearance,

2:8 On the question of Jesus' death by crucifixion, its Roman background and its theological

he humbled himself
by becoming obedient to the point of death,
death, that is, on a cross.

But in contrast to the preceding sentence, full of mystery and metaphors as it is, this sentence is straightforward and literal. It tells how the divine self-emptying One showed the same mindset in his humanity.

The word *found* expresses the divine reality from our human perspective, while *appearance* puts the idea of *likeness* in a slightly different way, referring to the external qualities of something that make it recognizable. Christ Jesus, who came in the *likeness* of human beings (both similar and dissimilar to us), "appeared" in a way that was clearly recognizable as human. Together the two phrases accent the reality of his humanity, just as the first two phrases in verse 6 accent his deity.

As with true deity, true humanity is expressed in his humbling himself, picking up the language of verse 3. The obedience that characterized his entire human life found its definitive expression in his *death on a cross*. The emphasis on *obedient to death* points to his readiness, as one of us, to choose the path that led to a death "destined for our glory before time began" (1 Cor 2:7). Which is quite in keeping with him who, as God, impoverished himself by taking on the role of a slave.

The potency of the final phrase, *death on a cross,* lies in the repetition of *death* back to back: "to death, death, that is, on a cross." At the same time it combines with "in the 'form' of God" (Phil 2:6) to frame the narrative to this point with the sharpest imaginable contrast: God on a cross. Here is the very heart of Pauline theology, both his understanding of God's being and his understanding of what God is doing in our fallen world. Here is where the One who is equal with God has most fully revealed the truth about God: that God is love and that his love expresses itself in self-sacrifice—cruel, humiliating *death on a cross*—for the sake of those he loves. The divine weakness (death at the hands of his creatures, his enemies) is the divine scandal (the cross was reserved for slaves and insurrectionists).

No one in Philippi, we must remind ourselves, used the cross as a symbol for their faith; there were no gold crosses embossed on Bibles

significance, see Hengel 1977; for a brief but helpful overview see Green 1993.

or worn as pendants around the neck or lighted on the steeple of the local church. The cross was God's—and thus their—scandal, God's contradiction to human wisdom and power: that the One they worshiped as Lord should have been crucified as a state criminal at the hands of one of "lord" Caesar's proconsuls; that the Almighty should appear in human dress, and that he should do so in this way, as a messiah who died by crucifixion. Likewise, this is the scandal of Pauline ethics: that the God who did it this way "gifts" us to "suffer for his sake" in this way as well (see 1:29).

How radically different is God's view of our being fully human from the bland and shallow "beautiful people" Western culture exhibits to sell us on ourselves. Having abandoned both God and the one true Human, Christ Jesus, our culture fawns on—and takes advice from (!)—any and every celebrity, empty-headed as he or she might be, who appears on a television talk show. What fools we mortals be, whose truth about ourselves is finally to be found in the one truly human life that inhabited our planet.

Divine Vindication of the Example (2:9-11) The "mind of Christ" as example for the Philippian community has now been narrated (vv. 6-8). But neither the narrative nor Paul's present concern about the Philippians' "affairs" is finished. So he concludes with this final sentence, whose function is twofold: to assert that God's yes to Jesus' life and death has been punctuated with the ultimate exclamation point, and thereby to reassure the Philippians that their now exalted Lord is sovereign over the entire universe—including the "lord" of the Empire, Caesar himself.

For a suffering community that has been repeatedly reminded of Christ's preeminent role in everything—both present and future—here is the necessary concluding word. Believers in Christ are both "already" and "not yet." Already they know and own him as Lord of all; not yet have they seen all things made subject to him. Here, then, they are reminded of who, and whose, they are: glad followers of him who is King of kings and Lord of lords, before whom at God's final wrap-up every knee shall bow to pay him the homage due his name.

What the sentence affirms is not reward but the divine vindication of the self-emptying, humble obedience that led Christ to the cross. As a yes to this expression of *equality with God,* God the Father *exalted him to the highest place and gave him the name that is above every name.* Although expressed as a twofold action, most likely the two verbs point to a single reality: that God highly exalted Christ by gracing him with "the Name." Both parts of the sentence, however, raise issues that call for closer examination.

First, in asserting that God has "highly exalted" Christ, Paul uses a compound of the ordinary verb for "exalt" with the preposition *hyper,* whose basic meaning is "above." That might seem to suggest exaltation to a higher position than Christ held previously. But Paul virtually holds copyright to *hyper* compounds in the New Testament, and in the vast majority of cases they magnify or express excess, not position. Therefore for God to "highly exalt" Christ almost certainly means that God "exalted him to the highest possible degree."

But what does Paul intend by *the name that is above every name?* There is something to be said for *the name* as referring to Christ's earthly name, Jesus. That, after all, is what is picked up in the next phrase, *at the name of Jesus.* If so, then Paul does not mean that he has now been given that name but that in highly exalting him, God has bestowed on *the name of Jesus* a significance excelling that of all other names.

More likely, however, especially in light of how the rest of the sentence unfolds, Paul is making a kind of twofold wordplay. First, *the name* as "that which is above every name" unmistakably echoes the Old Testament use of "the Name" to refer to God and his character. To honor God is to honor his name above all. At his exaltation the *name above . . . every name* has been bestowed on Jesus. But not in its Hebrew form YHWH does Jesus receive the name, but by way of the Septuagint (LXX), in its Greek form *kyrios* ("Lord").

The fact that the LXX consistently translated the divine name as *kyrios* is substantial evidence that the habit of substituting *adonai* (Hebrew "lord") for Yahweh, which continues to this day in the Jewish community, goes back before the third century B.C.E. But this also makes for the happy situation that the earliest believers could use God's title, *Lord,* which also became God's "name" in the LXX, as their primary designation for Jesus. In so doing they expressed his equality with God but also avoided calling him Yahweh, which is reserved for God the Father.

The result of the exaltation of Jesus is expressed in two coordinate clauses taken directly from the LXX of Isaiah 45:23, both of which stress that the whole creation shall offer him homage and worship, presumably at his coming. Thus the narrative covers the whole gamut: It begins in eternity past with Christ's "being in the 'form' of God," then focuses on his incarnation, and finally expresses his exaltation as something already achieved (v. 9), thus presupposing resurrection and ascension; now it concludes by pointing to the final future event when all created beings shall own his lordship.

First, *at the name of Jesus,* the Lord, *every knee should bow.* "Bowing the knee" is a common idiom for doing homage, sometimes in prayer, but always in recognition of the authority of the god or person before whom one is kneeling. What Paul does is full of import: for the "to me" of Isaiah 45:23, which refers to Yahweh, he substitutes *at the name of Jesus.* In this stirring oracle (Is 45:18-24) Yahweh, Israel's Savior, is declared to be God alone, over all that he has created and thus over all other gods and nations. In verses 22-24 Yahweh, while offering salvation to all but receiving obeisance in any case, declares that "before me every knee will bow." Paul now asserts that at Christ's exaltation God has transferred this right to obeisance to the Son; he is the Lord to whom *every knee* shall eventually *bow.*

Also in keeping with Isaiah (cf. 45:18), but now interrupting the language of the quotation itself, Paul purposely throws the net of Christ's sovereignty over the whole of created beings: *[those] in heaven* refers to all heavenly beings, angels and demons; *[those] on earth* refers to all those who are living on earth when Christ comes, including those who are currently causing suffering in Philippi; and *[those] under the earth* probably refers to "the dead," who also shall be raised to acknowledge his lordship over all.

Second, *every tongue* (of every person on bended knee) shall express homage in the language of the confessing—but currently suffering—church: "The Lord is Jesus Christ." This confession, which comes by the Spirit (1 Cor 12:3), is the line of demarcation between believer and nonbeliever (Rom 10:9). And here lies the ultimate triumph and irony in the passage. Those responsible for the suffering in Philippi proclaim that "the lord is Caesar." But at the end, when all creation beholds the risen Jesus, both they and their "lord Caesar" will join with all others to declare that *Kyrios* is none other than the Jesus whom the Romans crucified and whom Christians worship. But the confession will not then constitute conversion, but final acknowledgment that "God has made this Jesus, whom you crucified, both Lord and Christ" (Acts 2:36).

One can scarcely miss the christological implications. In the Jewish synagogue the appellation *Lord* had long before been substituted for God's "name" (YHWH). The early believers had now transferred that "name" *(Lord)* to the risen Jesus. Thus, Paul says, in raising Jesus from the dead, God has *exalted him to the highest place* and bestowed on him God's own *name*—in the Hebrew sense of "the Name," referring to his investiture with God's power and authority. At the same time, Paul's monotheism is kept intact by the final phrase, *to the glory of God the Father.* Thus this final sentence begins with God's exalting Christ by bestowing on him *the name* and concludes on the same theological note, that all of this is to God the Father's own *glory.*

The grandeur of this passage can easily cause one to forget why it is here. Paul's reason is singular: to focus on Christ himself, and thus to point to him as the ultimate model of the self-sacrificing love to which he is calling the Philippians—and us. Here we have spelled out before us in living color both the "what" and the "why" of Paul's affirmation "For to me, to live is Christ." In Jesus Christ the true nature of the living God has been revealed ultimately and finally. God is not a grasping, self-centered being. He is most truly known through the One whose equality with God found expression in his pouring himself out in sacrificial love by taking the lowest place, the role of a slave, and whose love for his human creatures found consummate expression in his death on the cross. That this is God's own nature and doing has been attested for all time by Christ Jesus's divine vindication; he has been exalted by God to the highest place by having been given the Name: the Lord is none other than Jesus Christ. This is why for Paul "to live is Christ." Any faith that falls short of this is simply not the Christian faith.

But Paul's concern in all this is, in the words of the poet, "'Tis the way the Master went, should not the servant tread it still?" That Christ serves for us as a paradigm for Christian life reinforces a significant aspect of Paul's gospel, namely that there is no genuine life in Christ that is not at the same time, by the power of the Holy Spirit, being regularly transformed into the likeness of Christ. A gospel of grace that omits obedience is not Pauline in any sense; obedience, after all, is precisely the point made in the application that follows (v. 12).

The specific behavioral concern of this passage is of greatest urgency for Paul. Unity in Christ was the absolutely necessary evidence of the gospel at work in his communities. Redemption that does not redeem, that does not cause a Philemon to accept the runaway slave Onesimus back as a brother in Christ, is merely soft mush. Redemption that does not issue in forgiveness, that does not crush "complaining" against and "arguing" with one another in the Christian community (v. 14), mocks this narrative.

In the final analysis, this passage stands at the heart of Paul's understanding of God. Christ serves as pattern, to be sure; but he does so as the One who most truly expresses God's nature. That this is what God is like is the underlying Pauline point; and since God is in the process of re-creating us in his image, this becomes the heart of the present appeal. Thus we are not called upon simply to "imitate God" by what we do but to have his very mind, the mind of Christ, developed in us, so that we too bear God's image in our attitudes and relationships within the Christian community—and beyond.

Application and Final Appeal (2:12-18) From heaven back to earth; from the worship of the Son and glory of the Father back to Philippi with its suffering and threats of disunity. Thus Paul returns to his present concern—obedience expressed through a common mindset, for the sake of Christ and the gospel—by applying what he has just written to the Philippians' situation. But the return is not with a thud; rather, this is the reason for telling the story of Christ in the first place: as the model and means for them to *continue to work out [their] salvation* for the sake of (not *according to*) God's *good purpose*.

2:12 The language *fear and trembling* comes to Paul from the Old Testament, where it is used primarily of the dread that pagans experience at the presence of the living God (e.g., Ex 15:16; Is 19:16), which then becomes dread of God's people because of the wonders God performs for them (e.g., Deut 2:25; 11:25). Paul alone uses it in the New Testament (1 Cor 3:2; 2 Cor 7:15; Eph 6:5), and only of believers, although with varied nuances.

There has been considerable, and probably unnecessary, debate over whether *salvation*

The application is in three sentences, which together form a single appeal with a threefold concern: (1) that they return to their common cause, partly (2) for the sake of the gospel in the world and partly also (3) for Paul's sake, and thus for their mutual joy. The first sentence (vv. 12-13) speaks generally, urging that they show their "obedience" by getting their corporate act together *(work out your salvation)*. And lest he be misunderstood, Paul adds an encouraging theological word: God has committed himself to effecting their "obedience" for his own good pleasure. The second sentence (vv. 14-16) gives specifics: *complaining* and *arguing* must cease, for the sake of the *crooked and depraved* Philippi in which they *shine like stars* as they *hold* fast *the word of life*. This sentence concludes on the note of Paul's own ministry among them, which leads to the final sentence (vv. 17-18), where he returns to the theme of his suffering, their faith, and his and their mutual joy.

With these final words the appeal begun in 1:27 comes full circle, serving to bracket the section in two ways. The appeal began by urging them to walk worthy of the gospel whether Paul is present or absent. In verses 12-16 Paul now returns on that theme, at the same time responding to the specific concerns expressed in 2:1-4. Second, the opening appeal was put in the context of (his and their) present suffering (1:29-30); the present appeal ends by urging mutual rejoicing in mutual suffering (2:17-18). This leads directly to verses 19-30, in which he goes on to "what's next" regarding his and their circumstances—that he expects to hear further about "their affairs," now in light of the present letter, after they have learned further about "his affairs," and both from the same source, Timothy.

General Application—Obedience for God's Sake (2:12-13) With another complex sentence Paul comes back to the concern of 1:27—2:4. The complexity is created by his trying to cover a great deal of ground in a single sentence. His concern is that they "obey" now (cf. v. 8), just as they have always done. But before giving definition to obedience,

in this passage refers to the individual believer or the community of believers. For strong recent advocacy of individual salvation see O'Brien 1991:276-80 and Silva 1992:135-39, but they are basically (correctly so) critiquing a view that waters down the term *salvation* somewhat to be more sociological (as, e.g., in Hawthorne 1983:98-99). Unfortunately, their rebuttals tend to place more emphasis on the individual than the context seems to warrant.

he interrupts himself by placing the appeal within the "presence/absence" friendship motif (cf. 1:27). The content of the appeal is then expressed with a deliberate echo of "your salvation which is from God" (1:28). These echoes not only make the sentence complex, they also create some difficulty for English readers. The verb Paul uses means "to accomplish" or "to carry out," which is not easy to translate here without creating the impression that salvation is of our own doing. And to top it off, it is easy for us to read the imperative individualistically, rather than, as with verse 4, as a call to individually *work out* our common salvation in our life together.

The momentary "presence/absence" digression deliberately reminds them of the earlier appeal in 1:27. Along with the affectionate vocative (literally, "my beloved ones") and the reminder of their excellent history in this regard *(as . . . always),* this motif places the appeal to obedience within the context of their long-term friendship and common affection. But obedience to whom, Paul or God, since elsewhere Paul goes either way? In context it most likely means obedience to his earlier appeal in 1:27—2:4. But that automatically means obedience to Christ, the only kind of obedience to his own words that Paul could care anything about. In his view faith in Christ is ultimately expressed as obedience to Christ, not in the sense of following the rules but of being devoted completely to him. This appeal, after all, closely follows the twofold reminder of Christ's own obedience that led to the cross and of his present status as Lord of all.

Obedience in this case takes the form of *work out your own salvation,* meaning "in your relationships with one another live out the salvation Christ has brought you." This is therefore not a text dealing with individual salvation but an ethical text dealing with the outworking of salvation in the believing community for the sake of the world. That they must comply with this injunction at the individual level is assumed, and that their final salvation will be realized personally and individually is a truth that does not need stating, because that is not at issue here. The present concern is with their being God's people in Philippi, as 2:15 makes certain.

The phrase *with fear and trembling* indicates how important this matter is for Paul. One does not live out the gospel casually or lightly, especially in light of verses 6-11, but as those who know what it means to stand in awe of the living God. Nothing of cringing or lack of confidence is implied. Rather, the gospel is God's thing, and the God who has saved his people is an awesome God. Thus working out the salvation that God has given them should be done with a sense of "holy awe and wonder" before the God with whom they—and we—have to do.

By putting his appeal this way—urging the Philippians to *work out your salvation with fear and trembling*—Paul recognizes that he may have painted himself into something of a corner regarding his essential theology. So he immediately puts it in the context of God's action. For, he explains, God is the one who empowers you in this regard. They are indeed to "work at" it *(katergazesthe);* they are able to do so because God himself is "at work" *(energōn)* in and among them. This does not mean that God is "doing it for them," but that God supplies the working power. Happily for us, God is on the side of his people. Not only does he have our concern at heart, but he actively works in our behalf for the sake of his own good pleasure. The rest of the sentence gives us the "where, what and why" of that empowering.

The "where" is *in*/among *you*. As in 1:6 and 2:5, when using this phrase in a corporate context Paul primarily means "among you." For that to happen it must begin *in you,* that is, in the resolve of each of them to see to it that God's purposes are accomplished in their community.

The "what" is loaded with theology. God empowers both our "doing" (*energeō,* the verb just used to describe God's "working") and the "willing" that lies behind the doing. Christian ethics has nothing to do with rules that regulate conduct. Rather, it begins with a mind that is transformed by the Spirit, so as not to be conformed to this age but to the character of God, knowing God's will, what is good and pleasing and perfect to him (Rom 12:1-2). We are not those who have been begrudgingly caught by God, so that we obey basically out of fear and trembling over what might happen if we were to do otherwise. Rather, being Christ's means to be converted in the true sense of that word, to have our lives invaded by God's Holy Spirit, who creates in us a new desire toward God that prompts godly behavior in the first place.

But Christian ethics lies not just in the "willing." In Romans 7:18, in his description of life before and outside of Christ looked at from the perspective of life in the Spirit, Paul described pre-Christian life with these same verbs. "To will," he said, was present with him; but without the Spirit, "carrying out *[katergazesthai]* the good" does not happen. As a believer, however, Paul will have none of that (i.e., of our not being able to carry out the good that we will). Hence he urges the Philippians to "work it out" precisely because God (by his Spirit) is present with us both *to will and to act* on the good God has prompted us to will.

The "why" (*according to his good purpose,* NIV) is ambiguous. The word *eudokia (good purpose)* occurred in 1:15 as the motivation for those who preach Christ out of love and "goodwill" toward Paul. In light of what is about to be urged (v. 14), that meaning could prevail here as well; that is, God is at work in them both to will and to do what promotes goodwill in the community. More likely, however, given the emphasis of the present sentence, Paul intends God's own *eudokia*—in which case this word probably leans toward "good pleasure," in the sense that God does this for his people because it pleases him so to do. In any case, the preposition *hyper* should bear its regular sense, "for the sake of." This does not mean that God, despite verse 6, is a self-gratifying being after all. Rather, all that God does he does for his pleasure; but since God is wholly good, what pleases him is not capricious but what is wholly good for those he loves. God's pleasure is pure love; it delights God to delight his people.

Thus with verse 13 Paul puts the imperative into theological perspective. What follows is to be understood as flowing directly out of this word; what pleases God in this instance, of course, is that the Philippians cease the in-fighting that is currently going on among some of them.

Specific Application—Harmony for the World's and Paul's Sake (2:14-16) In moving from the general appeal to its specific application, Paul has clearly "quit preachin' and gone to meddlin'." *Complaining* and *arguing* are the sins that breed disunity and thus blur the effect of the gospel in Philippi. They are to *do everything without*

2:14-18 See Fee 1995:241-43 for a discussion of the unusually high incidence of Old Testa-

indulging these attitudes, which reflect "selfish ambition" and "vain conceit" rather than the humility that puts the concerns of others ahead of one's own (v. 3).

The first word, *gongysmos,* was used once before by Paul, in 1 Corinthians 10:10, alluding to Israel's grumbling/murmuring against God and Moses in the desert (Ex 16; Num 14; 16—17). There is every reason to believe that the word carries some of these echoes here as well, since the next part of the sentence clearly echoes Israel's experience in the desert. Like Israel, the Philippians are to stop their "grumbling," which in their case has taken the form of *arguing* or disputing with one another. Most likely this is the telltale word, for which "grumbling" offers a biblical frame of reference.

The clause that makes up Philippians 2:15-16 presents the reason for the prohibition. Their conduct is to be *blameless,* so that they might be recognized for who they are, the *children of God.* The arena is pagan Philippi, now described in the language of Deuteronomy 32:5: *a crooked and depraved generation.* But being *blameless* is the penultimate concern. The ultimate concerns are two: the gospel in Philippi, and their own successful arrival at the end, expressed in terms of their being Paul's *boast on the day of Christ.* Each of these phrases needs brief explanation.

That you might become blameless and pure repeats a concern from Paul's prayer (Phil 1:10), although with different words. *The day of Christ* is still in view, but the emphasis now is on present conduct. *Become blameless* is the exact language used by God to begin the renewal of the covenant with Abraham (Gen 17:1 LXX). The word refers to conduct with which one (probably God in this case) can "find no fault," while *pure* is directed more toward the heart, not in the sense of "clean" but of "innocent."

With *children of God without fault* Paul begins his echo of Deuteronomy 32:5 (LXX). *Children of God* is especially appropriate for those being urged to "obey." Moses states that Israel "no longer" has the right to this designation, to which the Septuagint translator added "being blameworthy" *(mōmēta),* a term from the sacrificial system (= "full of

ment echoes in this passage and its possible role in the "story of Israel" in Paul's theology.

blemishes"). Paul picks up this adjective, negates it (*a-mōma* = "without fault") and adds "in the midst of" before continuing the rest of the "quotation." He thus converts the whole phrase into its opposite with regard to the Philippians. Over against Israel, they *are* God's children; by refraining from internal bickering they will be *without fault.*

By adding the preposition "in the midst of," Paul also transforms the next words of Deuteronomy 32:5 into their opposite. Originally *a crooked and depraved generation* described "blameworthy" Israel; here pagan Philippi receives the epithet. In the context of 1:27—2:18, the term probably points to the opposition mentioned in 1:28, the pagan populace of Philippi, who took their devotion to Caesar as lord seriously and found those who advocated another Lord more than just a little nettlesome.

To describe the believers' role in Philippi, Paul uses language from the final apocalyptic vision of Daniel (12:1-4): among whom *you shine like stars in the* world (NIV *universe*). The qualifier *as you hold out [on to] the word of life* brings us face to face with the inherent ambiguity of the final part of this sentence, which also reflects one of the repeated ambiguities of the New Testament: that the people of God are to *shine* in the world over against its darkness, while simultaneously they are to illumine that darkness. The verb *epechontes* means "hold on to" (NIV mg) but not in a defensive posture (as in "hold the fort, for I am coming"). Although the believers' role in Philippi puts them in strong contrast (hence in opposition) to the paganism of Philippi, by holding fast *the word of life* (= "the message that brings life") they are to offer the life that Christ provides to those who are dying.

The eschatological context of Daniel 12:3, whose language Paul has just echoed, apparently prompts him to conclude his (now long) sentence on a similar eschatological note, one of many that permeate the letter. Although the concern is with the Christians' perseverance, the emphasis is once more on his and their relationship. By successfully holding fast the word of life in Philippi, they will be Paul's *boast on the day of Christ* (see Phil 1:6, 10), language that recalls their "boasting" in 1:26. These final phrases, therefore, are also transitional. Just as he

---

2:15 While the phrase *en kosmō* can mean *in the universe,* Paul's point is that they shine

brought them into the picture in 1:25-26 (at the conclusion of "my affairs"), he now uses some of the same language to bring himself back into the picture at the conclusion of "your affairs."

Thus Paul concludes his prohibition (2:14) with the sheer glory that he and they will experience together in the presence of Christ—they because of his ministry among them that brought them to that glory; he because his "glorying" in them, as he and they are in Christ's presence together, is but another way of expressing his "boast in the Lord" (1 Cor 1:31; 2 Cor 10:17).

The final appended phrase, *that I did not run or labor for nothing,* is vintage Paul. The two verbs, taken from the games and from manual labor respectively, are among his favorite images for ministry. Life in Christ has the features of a race, with the prize awaiting those who finish (see 3:14). More often in Paul, ministry involves *labor;* one "works hard in the Lord," just as the tentmaker does in the shop. Paul has invested his whole Christian life in seeing that others also obtain the prize for such running or realize the fruit of such labor. Hence at issue for him is not his own personal "prize"; that prize will consist primarily in having his "beloved" Philippians (and others) there with him (cf. 4:1).

Thus, based on their longtime friendship, this clause serves as a final incentive for them to "obey" by "working out their salvation" while he is "absent" from them. In this letter it is included especially for those whose vision of their certain future has diminished in some way. But could Paul's efforts really be in vain? On the basis of what he says here (vv. 17-18) and elsewhere, the answer seems to be twofold. On the one hand, such an expression as this makes sense only if the potential to have labored in vain really exists; on the other hand, Paul has such confidence in God regarding his converts that it would be unthinkable to him that such a potential would ever be realized. Which leads us to the final sentences in this present section.

Mutual Suffering and Joy (2:17-18) Paul concludes this long section regarding the Philippians' "affairs" on the note of suffering with which it began (1:29-30), punctuated in this case with rejoicing, thus recalling 1:18 (and 2:2). The key to how Paul gets here from verse 16

---

as stars "in the world," indeed in a specific corner of the world.

lies in his bringing himself—and his relationship with them—back into the picture in that verse. Although the *but* with which these final sentences begin signals a new sentence, it also stands in clear contrast to the "not in vain" at the end of verse 16. But what follows is so abrupt, and the metaphor so unusual, that the connection is not immediately obvious.

The form of the sentence is conditional, in this case expressing a real, not suppositional, condition. Thus (literally): "But if indeed I am being poured out like a drink offering in connection with the sacrifice and service of your faith, I rejoice." The metaphor itself is taken from the Jewish sacrificial system. Pictured is the burnt offering (*thysia,* "sacrifice"), the service itself *(leitourgia)* and the drink offering poured out at the sanctuary *(spendō)* in connection with (not "on" in Jewish ritual) the sacrifice (cf. Num 28:1-7). In 2 Timothy 4:6 Paul uses the metaphor of "being poured out like a drink offering" to point to his expected imminent death. But that is unlikely the intent here, since he is so "confident in the Lord" that he will be released (Phil 2:24; cf. 1:24-26)—not to mention that in 1:30 he has emphasized that he and the Philippians are undergoing "the same struggle," and their dying as the result of suffering is simply not in view in this letter.

Most likely, then, the whole clause is a metaphor for the present suffering that both he and they are experiencing at the hand of the Empire. He pictures his imprisonment as the *drink offering* that goes along with their "burnt offering," their present struggle in Philippi. That also means that the opening conjunction *(ei kai)* is not to be taken as concessive ("even though") but as intensive, "if indeed this is happening" (as the case really is). Given the return to this imagery in conjunction with their gift in 4:18, one is also tempted to see their "service of faith" (NIV *service coming from your faith*) as going beyond their present suffering and including their gift to him, which not only continued their commitment of friendship but was undertaken under their difficult present circumstances.

If this is how we are to understand the *if* part of the clause, then what of the connection with verse 16? The logic seems to be that rather than Paul's having run in vain, which in fact is unthinkable, his present suffering, which is also on their behalf in the midst of their own suffering, presents the real picture of their relationship. What is missing is an implied middle step. Thus the whole would go something like "I expect you to be my grounds for boasting at the day of Christ, evidence that I have not labored in vain. (And presently my labor includes imprisonment, as yours does suffering in Philippi.) But if indeed my present struggle represents a kind of drink offering to go along with your own suffering on behalf of the gospel, then I rejoice."

The "then" part of the sentence deliberately recalls 1:18. Even in the midst of what appear to be untoward circumstances, one's relationship with God does not change. At this point several matters about this theme in Philippians need to be noted. First, "joy" is primarily a verb in Philippians; it is something one does, not how one feels (as in the NIV's *am glad*). Second, as the reiteration of the imperative in 3:1 and 4:4 makes clear, "rejoicing" is not related to one's circumstances but is "in the Lord," as in the scores of Old Testament texts (especially in the Psalter) that Paul is echoing. That is, "rejoicing in the Lord" is part and parcel of Christian life and is quite unrelated to the present lay of the land. Indeed, this present text is very much reminiscent of the conclusion of Habakkuk's lament (3:17-18):

Though the fig tree does not bud
  and there are no grapes on the vines,
though the olive crop fails
  and the fields produce no food,
though there are no sheep in the pen
  and no cattle in the stalls,
yet I will rejoice in the LORD,
  I will be joyful in God my Savior.

This is not "sour grapes," nor making the best of a bad situation, nor "delight in feeling bad"; this has to do with true faith, and thus perspective, based as it is on the unshakable foundation of the work of Christ, both past and future.

Since Paul is so completely at home in the world of Scripture, as God's very Word, and since he really believes that "to live is Christ, to die is gain," he simply expresses this confidence in a thoroughly biblical way. Despite the constant "room service" he is provided (see 1:13), it is not the Rome Hilton, in a room with a view, where he currently finds himself. Yet his perspective is the right one, so "I rejoice," on my own as it were, but since we are in this thing together, *I . . . rejoice with all of you* as well. Which, of course, invites them to rejoice in the Lord by presuming that they are already doing so!

But just in case, he invites them to reciprocate: "In the same way you also rejoice (on your own, as it were), and then join me in rejoicing together" (see v. 19). To this point every mention of "joy," except in 1:25, has had to do with Paul. With this imperative in verse 18 a subtle, but noticeable, shift toward them takes place. What began in 1:25 as concern for their "progress and joy in the faith" is now put into the form of an imperative, an imperative that will recur at further points in the rest of the letter; significantly, its first occurrence is totally intertwined with Paul's joy and is found in the context of rejoicing in the midst of suffering and opposition.

Here, then, is the most likely reason for this otherwise unusual conclusion to the long appeal of 1:27—2:18. Paul has already modeled joy in the face of opposition and suffering (1:18); his concern for the Philippians is with both their "progress" and their "joy" regarding the gospel. Now, in anticipation of the renewal of their joy at the coming of Epaphroditus (2:28) and the imperative to "rejoice in the Lord (always)" that frames the final exhortation (3:1; 4:4), Paul begins by linking that imperative to his own joy, both in the context of present suffering and in the mutuality of that suffering.

Two significant theological points emerge here. First, we must not lose sight of the fact that everything else that is said is brought to bear on the opening imperative: *Do everything without complaining or arguing*. Because most of us are good at such behavior, it is easy to dismiss this as "mundane"; but the very fact that Paul spends so much energy giving biblical and theological support to it suggests otherwise. This is spoken in the context of their—and our—being God's children in a fallen, twisted world. Our corporate behavior, especially as that is reflected in our attitudes toward one another, goes a long way toward determining how effectively we *hold out the word of life* in such a world. Thus evangelism is the bottom line, and internal bickering among the people of God is thoroughly counterproductive activity.

Second, Paul's use of the story of Israel (in this case its failure) as his way of including the Philippians as God's people—indeed, as the true continuity of his people—says much about our own place in God's story. Again, the concern is with our behavior—with our succeeding where Israel failed. The underlying theology in all of this is God's own character, as that is now reflected in his children who bear his likeness as we live out the life of the future in the present age. Only as we reflect God's own likeness will our evangelism be worth anything at all, in terms of its aim and in terms of success.

□ What's Next Regarding Paul's and Their Affairs (2:19-30)

After the heights of the preceding section, it is easy to skim past these "everyday" matters to get on to the next "good stuff" (usually 3:3-21). But that would be to miss too much. Letters between friends have not changed all that much over the centuries. Besides words about the writer's and recipients' respective situations ("my affairs/your affairs"), they very often included information about the movements of intermediaries, which is what Paul is up to now.

The section is in two parts. First (2:19-24), Paul hopes to send Timothy as soon as the outcome of his imprisonment has been resolved, which he expects to go in his favor. Thus he is confident in the Lord that he himself will come *soon,* but after he has heard back from Timothy (v. 19). Meanwhile, second (vv. 25-30), he has sent the now-recovered Epaphroditus on ahead with this letter. He owes that to them out of friendship—between him and them, and between them and Epaphroditus. It also gives him opportunity to send this letter in advance.

But why send Timothy at all, given Epaphroditus's return and Paul's own hope to come as soon as possible? And why this order of the two paragraphs, since they are chronologically in reverse? And why "commend" to the Philippians two such well-known brothers? Answers to these questions could tell us a lot about the reasons for the letter.

What Paul has written so far does not imply a desperate situation in Philippi. Yet it is serious enough to warrant the sending of both Epaphroditus with this "prearrival" letter and Timothy, who is to find out about "your affairs" and return, before Paul comes himself. Thus even though Timothy will come later chronologically, his paragraph comes first logically, with its repetition of the phrase "your affairs" (see

vv. 19, 20; cf. 1:27) and "my affairs" (v. 23; cf. 1:12), plus echoes of "one's own interests" from 2:4.

Commendation of the bearer of a letter was a frequent component of first-century letters. Both the length and the language of these two "commendations" (Timothy is not even bearing a letter) suggest that these men also serve as exemplary paradigms for the two central concerns that emerged in 1:27—2:4. Timothy models serving the gospel by caring for the needs of others; Epaphroditus models the suffering that accompanies serving the gospel.

Timothy and Paul to Come Later (2:19-24) True friendship, especially between Christians, can have a fragile side. On the one hand, one of the reasons for friendship is personal, the need to have someone close with whom to share joys, sorrows and everyday events. On the other hand, the goal of all truly Christian friendship is growth in Christ on the part of both parties. And that's the fragile part: how to be gently honest with a friend without jeopardizing the relationship. That's where Paul now is in his relationship with the Philippians. He intends to send Timothy to find out whether this letter will have done any good; but he wants to do so without implying that he is really just checking up on them.

Verse 19 sets out the basic datum and its reason—a proposed visit by Timothy, with the hope of cheering Paul by (further) *news* about "your affairs" (NIV *about you;* see commentary on 1:27), presumably whether his letter has had any effect. Since this needs explanation, verses 20-22 offer a twofold justification for the sending of Timothy, which turns out to be only partly justification for doing so at all, and mostly justification for sending Timothy in particular. But the explanation gets away from Paul a bit, so in verses 23-24 he returns to the basic datum—the sending of Timothy—but with two additional pieces of information: Timothy is to be sent as soon as Paul has some sense about "his own affairs" (NIV *how things go with me*); and he himself will come

---

2:19 Although the word translated "soon" *(tacheōs)* ordinarily means "quickly" in the sense of "without delay," it can hardly have that meaning here; it is even more problematic in 2:24. But that usage offers the clue to this one, since there it can only mean "without delay once things are settled."

as soon as possible. These pick up items from 1:19-20 and 24-26.

But it is not possible even here for the apostle to speak without expressing concern for the gospel. So along with the basic issue of his and their relationship, and his concern about them, the explanatory "commendation" of Timothy (vv. 20-22) has the gospel as its underlying current, becoming explicit at the end of verse 22.

The Plan—to Send Timothy Soon (2:19) Having brought himself back into the picture in verses 16-18, Paul now returns to where the narrative left off in 1:26; it assumes the presence/absence motif (1:27; 2:12). Not able to come himself, he hopes *to send Timothy to you soon,* meaning "without delay" once the present delay regarding his future is resolved. His reason for it is primarily personal, *that I [for my part] may be cheered when I receive news about* "your affairs." Since the outcome of his trial is still future, he hopes to do this (*I hope* is repeated in v. 23), a hope qualified as *in the Lord Jesus,* emphasizing the grounds for it (as well as offering a proviso for something future that is simply in the Lord's hands; Bockmuehl 1997:165). *Hope,* therefore, should not to be watered down to our idiom "I hope so" (when we have very little confidence about something). This qualifier, plus "I am persuaded in the Lord" when referring to his own coming in verse 24, indicates that hope moves much closer to certainty.

The reason for sending Timothy is expressed in terms quite the reverse of Paul's ordinary reason for sending one of his coworkers to a church. In most cases it is for their sakes—to straighten something out or to bring something started to completion. But here it is expressly for his own sake, that "I for my part" *may be cheered* by good news about them. What will cheer Paul will be to "learn about your affairs," probably having not so much to do with their affairs in general as with those addressed in 1:27—2:18. This, after all, is a primary reason for the letter. This way of putting it also implies that he expects Timothy to return before he himself comes, which makes the *soon* in Paul's case problematic (see commentary on v. 24).

The NIV (correctly) translates *kagō* "I also"; but that probably does not mean that it assumes their being cheered by news of him is equal reason for sending Timothy (after all, Epaphroditus will carry that news). Rather it means something like "I for my part," implying by assumption that they will already have been cheered by news of him.

The Commendation of Timothy (2:20-22) What happens next catches us off guard. Not only is Timothy not the bearer of the present letter, but he is also well known to the Philippians (see comment on 1:1); yet Paul proceeds to "commend" him. Moreover, and significantly, the commendation does not speak first about their own long-term knowledge of him but about Paul's having *no one else like him* (literally, "of like soul" = like-minded). This sounds so much like the appeal in verses 2-4, one must assume it to be intentional—and for their sakes.

But "like-souled" to whom? Although the phrase is ambiguous as it stands, most likely Paul means "like-minded to me," rather than no one else's being like-minded to Timothy. Thus with a slight wordplay on being *cheered* (literally "good souled"), Paul emphasizes that the primary reason for Timothy's coming is that he carries Paul's own deep concerns at heart. When he arrives, therefore, they can count on it: "he will genuinely show concern for your affairs" (repeating from v. 19), especially with regard to their standing firm in the one Spirit in the face of opposition in Philippi (1:27-30). Paul thus begins with the reasons from his perspective that only Timothy will do; he will go on in 2:22 to the reason from their perspective. But before that he takes a broadside at some people who do not have Timothy's (thus his own) mindset.

With an explanatory *for,* Paul contrasts Timothy's like-minded concern for the Philippians' *welfare* with the mindset of others who are looking out for their own interests, *not those of Christ Jesus.* That they stand in direct contrast to Timothy, with language reminiscent of verse 4, indicates that "looking out for the interests of Christ Jesus" equals "looking also to the interests of others." This is what the preceding section was all about, Paul's own seeking the interests of Christ Jesus, by appealing to the Philippians to work out—among themselves and in

---

2:20 The NIV divests this sentence of much of its punch and purpose by generalizing Paul's future tense, "he will show genuine concern for your affairs," into *who takes a genuine interest in your welfare.* Some recent commentators (O'Brien 1991:319; Silva 1992:155-56), while recognizing the future, consider the present tense adequate for conveying Paul's meaning into English. But that seems unlikely. While the generalized present would have been true of Timothy, Paul's point is case specific: when he comes to you, you can count on him to "show genuine concern for your situation."

The word *isopsychon* ("like-souled") echoes the *sympsychon* ("together-souled") in 2:2. These two words, along with *eupsychō* ("well-souled"; thus "refreshed") in verse 19, occur

Philippi—the salvation that Christ has brought them.

But we are poorly prepared for this sentence. Verses 20 (Paul's reasons from his perspective for sending Timothy) and 22 (Paul's reasons from their perspective) make perfectly good sense. So why this interruption, and who are these people, especially since Paul's brush sweeps so widely: *everyone* is like this? We begin with the *everyone* (or "all"), which can only refer to people in Rome, not Philippi, and probably means something like "the whole lot of them." But "the whole lot of whom," since he hardly intends to indict every believer in Rome? The form of the contrast, including *I have no one* "like-minded" in verse 20, at first blush sounds as if he intended to contrast Timothy with other coworkers who might be available for such duty. But Paul does not say that; and the content of the sentence makes such a view even difficult to imagine. Given what we know of Paul elsewhere and the high regard with which he holds those who travel with him, and that in 4:21 he sends greetings from "the brothers who are with me," it seems highly unlikely that he should here slander them with this kind of barrage. And in any case, in light of the next verse it also seems unlikely that he would have even considered sending anyone else.

The contrast, therefore, is not between Timothy and other coworkers who could make this trip but are too self-serving to send, but between Timothy's character qualifications and those of some other people who came to mind as Paul was dictating. These people are condemned precisely because they lack the two essential qualities noted of Timothy in verse 20: (1) like-mindedness with Paul, which expresses itself in (2) *genuine* concern for others and thus exemplifies the character of the gospel that was presented in 2:3-4. Probably, then, this aside looks in two directions at once. What prompts it are people like those already

---

only here in the New Testament and are rarely found in other extant Greek literature. This is what suggests an echo of 2:2 here and a bit of wordplay with 2:19.

2:21 Some have considered this sentence to reflect the situation Paul describes in 2 Timothy 4:10-12, especially referring to people like "Demas who abandoned [Paul], having loved this present world" (my translation); but that is dependent on one's reconstruction of the history behind the Pastoral Epistles. What makes the equation difficult is that Paul is there writing *to* Timothy, apparently informing him of something that had more recently taken place. Here Timothy is *with* Paul; and Philippians 4:21 indicates that he is not there alone.

mentioned in 1:15 and 17, who preach Christ but "not purely/sincerely," and who therefore are not truly doing so for Christ's sake. But as verse 20 has already hinted, Timothy is being set forth as yet another model of one who "thinks like Christ" and is therefore being singled out for the benefit of some in Philippi who are otherwise-minded (2:3-4). That it is intended in part for Philippi seems verified by Paul's language, which is the clue to much. Such people, he says, "seek" (NIV *look out for*) their own *interests;* Paul has already appealed to the Philippians to do nothing out of self-interest but rather in humility to regard the needs of others as having precedence over their own (2:3-4).

From his denunciation of the self-seeking, Paul returns to the commendation of Timothy, reminding the Philippians of their own knowledge of him: *you know that Timothy has proved himself.* The word "proven character" (NIV *proved himself*) has been coined from the verb "to put to the test." Because of long associations with Timothy, they know his worth, that his character has been put to the test and thus he *has proved himself.*

But as with other matters in this letter, Paul's interest in Timothy's "proven character" is not with his character in general but in particular by the way *he has served with me in the work of the gospel.* As the Philippians well know, that relationship is like that of *a son with his father,* the apprentice son who exhibits the mind and concerns of his father, alongside whom he has served for so many years. The reminder is similar to that in 1 Corinthians 4:17, "like father, like son": You can count on Timothy's being among you as a *son* who looks and acts just like me. *He has served with me in the work of the gospel* sounds very much like what Paul had earlier thanked God for with regard to the Philippians (in 1:5). Thus, like the content of the two preceding verses, this is expressed in terms that recall earlier moments in the letter and therefore is very likely intended also to reinforce the paradigm.

Would that all of us were like Timothy, putting the interests of others as the matter of first importance! Here again the way of humility, taking the lower road by way of the cross, is on full display; and here alone, as the gospel affects the people of God in this way at the core of our beings, can we expect truly to count for the gospel in a world that lives the opposite, not only as a matter of course but for the most part as its primary value. One must "look out for number one," after all. Agreed, as long as the cross dictates that "number one" is one's neighbor and not oneself.

The Plan Resumed—Timothy Soon, Paul Later (2:23-24) With a resumptive *therefore* Paul returns to the basic datum of verse 19, that he hopes to send Timothy. But now, instead of *soon,* he qualifies with a clause that indicates why Timothy is coming later and has not accompanied Epaphroditus. As soon as Paul has any inkling as to the outcome of the trial, he will send Timothy to fill them in further on "my affairs." Thus Timothy's reason for coming is twofold: in the first instance (v. 19) for Paul's sake, to see how the letter has affected them; and now for their sakes, to be encouraged and brought up to speed about the outcome of Paul's imprisonment.

Having indicated the second reason for Timothy's coming—to report on "my affairs"—Paul concludes this brief look into the expected future by repeating what he told them in 1:24-26, this time even more emphatically: *I myself will come soon.* Here is the certain evidence that the adverb "quickly" does not mean "right away," as it ordinarily does, but "quickly" in the sense of "at once after I see how things go with me."

In 1:24 this persuasion was expressed in terms of necessity ("more necessary for you"), implying divine necessity that had their "progress . . . in the faith" as its ultimate concern. Now he expresses that persuasion in the strongest kind of language: *I am confident in the Lord* (cf. 1:14). It is hard to make it plainer, given that the outcome is still in the future, that he fully expects to be released and therefore that the talk about death in 1:21-23 was a yearning, not an anticipation of the near future. Which in turn also indicates that the metaphor in 2:17 is unlikely to be a reflection on martyrdom, but a reference to his present suffering.

Epaphroditus to Come Now (2:25-30) From his plans to hear about their affairs (now in response to this letter) and to come himself as soon as possible, Paul turns to the more immediate matter at hand—the return of Epaphroditus, who is also the bearer of the letter. The paragraph is in two parts (vv. 25-27; 28-30), both of which (a) begin on the same note (Paul's having sent Epaphroditus), (b) mention Epaphroditus as the Philippians' "minister to my needs" and (c) note that Epaphroditus's illness brought him very near to death. What is being explained in both parts are the reasons for sending Epaphroditus now and not waiting for the outcome of Paul's trial.

The first part gives the reason from Epaphroditus's perspective: his own deep longing for the community back home in light of their knowing about his illness (v. 26). Verses 28-30 then give the reason for sending him from the Philippians' perspective: their own joy in seeing him again, which will lessen Paul's present sorrow to some degree (v. 28).

But the whole should especially be read from Paul's perspective, which helps to explain what (for us) is the most striking about the paragraph—that it takes the form of commendation, the kind of thing that regularly appears in letters from the Greco-Roman period to introduce the bearer of the letter to the one(s) addressed. Why such a commendation in this letter? Most likely it is another reflection of the "mutual affection" dimension of friendship, which pours forth regularly in this letter. This profusion of commendation is part of that affection. Paul has received the Philippians' gift from Epaphroditus (cf. 4:18); now in sending him back he commends him to them as one of their own, and in honoring Epaphroditus, Paul honors them. That Epaphroditus should have risked his life on their behalf is reason enough for Paul to urge them to receive him back with joy. That God has spared him so that he could come back at all is all the more reason for joy—on everyone's part.

Given the paradigmatic role of every preceding narrative to this point, that may well be so again. If so, the paradigm here moves toward the

2:25-30 Some of the language of this passage ("necessity," v. 25; "the more eager," v. 28, understood as "sooner than expected"), plus its length, has given rise to a variety of hypotheses regarding Epaphroditus's mission to Paul and his relationship with the church. Most common is the "two mission" approach: that Epaphroditus was sent to Rome both with the gift of money and with the commission to attend Paul for as long as he was needed (first proposed by Michael 1928:118-29, and picked up by several commentators [e.g., Beare, Gnilka, Hawthorne, Silva] and by J. L. White 1972:145); thus he is accused of "leaving his post" (White). Others see Paul as walking a fine line between "parties" in Philippi, since Epaphroditus belongs to one of these parties (e.g., Mayer 1987; O'Brien 1991:341). But none of these is necessary (see note on 2:28 below); and all of them seem to assume that one cannot simply take what Paul says at face value.

"suffering" theme in this letter. Epaphroditus models one who was ready to risk his life and thus to suffer for the sake of Christ on behalf of others. What makes one think so in this case is the unique phrase "unto death" (v. 30; NIV *almost died*), used elsewhere in Paul's letters only in 2:8 to refer to Christ's death on the cross.

Epaphroditus: Their Messenger, Paul's Brother (2:25) It is difficult for most of us to enter into the worldview of the first century, especially regarding matters like communication and medicine. By way of telephone, fax or e-mail we can be in instant communication with people almost anywhere on the globe; and we are so used to the results of medical science that they now cease to amaze us. In our world most people expect to live through even the most dreaded of diseases, not realizing how recent such a worldview is. In the Greco-Roman world people expected to die of disease or illness and were amazed by recovery; and the only way one could find out about a friend from afar was through courier—and then only if someone happened to be going that way.

So one rightly wonders how the Philippians responded to seeing Epaphroditus again. Apparently he had suffered a kind of illness that ordinarily issued in death. That much they knew, but of the outcome they knew nothing. And that is why Paul thought it *necessary to send back to you Epaphroditus,* and to do so as soon as he was strong enough to travel, rather than to wait until news of Paul's situation had been resolved. But before elaborating those reasons, the very mention of his now-recovered friend causes Paul to burst into accolades. Here is one who ministered to Paul at the risk of his own life (vv. 29-30), and Paul cannot help himself. With three epithets he describes Epaphroditus's

---

2:25 *Leitourgos* (NIV *to take care of*) is the personal noun for the priest who performs the sacral duties (*leitourgia,* vv. 17 and 30) in the sacrificial system. Some see this as supporting the "two mission" view noted above; but the use of the noun in 4:18 to refer specifically to the Philippians' gift makes that a difficult position to maintain.

That Paul should call Epaphroditus "your apostle" (NIV *messenger*) is clear indication that the term served primarily to describe a function rather than an "office," even as late as this letter. Which makes the whole concept of "apostleship" in Paul a tenuous one. He clearly also used it in a semitechnical way to refer to himself and others who were "sent" by Christ to found churches; but he never uses it in the later, more fully technical sense of, for example, "the Twelve Apostles" (who in Paul are simply "the Twelve," 1 Cor 15:5).

relationship to himself; with two more reminds the Philippians that his service to Paul was on their behalf.

First, he is *my brother,* the fundamental term of relationship within the believing community; he is to Paul what the rest of the Philippian Christians are as well. Second, he is Paul's "coworker" (NIV *fellow worker*), Paul's most common term for those who have labored with him in the gospel in some way, including Euodia and Syntyche and others in Philippi (4:3). But in this case, third, he further defines Epaphroditus's role with a military metaphor; he is also *my . . . fellow soldier.* Whatever may have evoked this uncommon (for Paul) metaphor (his being surrounded by the Praetorian Guard, 1:13? or the fact that Roman Philippi originated as a military colony?), it images Epaphroditus as a wounded comrade-in-arms who is being sent home for rest. Since Epaphroditus was almost certainly present at the dictation of the letter, these words are probably in part for his sake; but they are surely for the community's sake as well, to emphasize the role their messenger has played on Paul's behalf.

Paul further designates Epaphroditus as *your messenger* (apostle) and ministrant to *my needs*. First, he was their "apostle," sent on behalf of the congregation to perform a given task. That task is then expressed with a sacrificial metaphor: he offered priestly service (to God, it is implied) on their behalf for Paul's needs. This is the first certain mention of their gift to Paul (although see comment on 1:5 and 2:17). Paul's present point is clear: in a culture where prisoners were not cared for by the state but had to depend on friends or relatives for food and other necessities, this is no small thing the Philippians have done. This present word about Epaphroditus anticipates the full acknowledgment in 4:10-20.

Epaphroditus's Concern for Them (2:26) The mention of Epaphroditus's role in the church's ministry to Paul brings Paul to the first reason for sending him back now. Epaphroditus is full of concern for "the folks back home"; he *longs for all of you* (cf. 1:8)—a longing not just to see them again but to relieve their distress over his illness.

2:26 This passing reference to their having heard that Epaphroditus was ill has had a considerable role in the framing of a hypothesis that Ephesus was the place of Paul's imprisonment (see introduction, pp. 33-34). It is presumed—with confidence that far

Epaphroditus's concern is perfectly understandable. He knows as they do that he could have died from his illness, but they do not yet know he has recovered.

How the Philippians had learned of Epaphroditus's illness cannot now be known. It is usually assumed that he took ill in Rome and that a courier, going by way of Philippi, carried the news to them. But another scenario seems more promising. Given that Epaphroditus was probably carrying a considerable sum of money, it is altogether unlikely that he was traveling alone (cf. 2 Cor 11:9, where the same Philippian service to Paul is brought by "brothers," plural). Very likely Epaphroditus took ill on the way to Rome, and one of his traveling companions returned to Philippi with that news (which is how Epaphroditus knew they knew) while another (or others) stayed with him as he continued on his way to Rome, even though doing so put his life at great risk (Phil 2:30). This view is favored in particular by the way Paul phrases verse 30: *risking his life* in order that he might fulfill his mission on behalf of Philippi.

God's Mercy on Epaphroditus (2:27) With an emphatic *indeed,* Paul goes on to bear witness to the severe nature of the illness and then to the wideness of God's mercy—both to Epaphroditus and to himself. We have no way of knowing the nature of the illness; what Paul underscores is how serious it was, enough to bring Epaphroditus to death's door. The repetition of this motif in verse 30 further indicates its great seriousness.

But the other side of reality, which the Philippians would now be experiencing with Epaphroditus's arrival, is that *God had mercy on him*—a clause probably read much too nonchalantly by those of us who have the benefits of modern medical science. How *God had mercy on him* we do not know (perhaps by "gift of healing"?); the phrase probably does not mean simply that in God's good mercy Epaphroditus got better, but that God had a direct hand in it. Paul's emphasis in any case rests altogether on the *mercy* of God evidenced by Epaphroditus's recovery, which stresses not so much generosity toward the undeserving—although that is always true as well—but the experience of mercy itself.

exceeds the data—that there were five communications to and fro between the church and the place of Paul's imprisonment (see, e.g., Collange 1979:119). But that is both unlikely and unnecessary.

This is indicated by the final addendum, *not on him only but also on me, to spare me sorrow upon sorrow,* a phrase that once again presupposes Paul's close relationship with this community. They know well his affection for them; the concluding plaintive note simply underscores it.

But what is the first level of *sorrow* on which additional sorrow would have been piled? Probably it alludes to the recurring motif of suffering, of Paul's continually being poured out as a drink offering (v. 17), especially in his present imprisonment. This little phrase should also be kept in mind when in this letter we repeatedly hear Paul speak of rejoicing. Joy does not mean the absence of sorrow but the capacity to rejoice in the midst of it. Paul's gratitude in the present case is for mercy, that he has not had sorrow of this kind—the loss of a longtime and dear brother in the Lord—added to the sorrow he already knows.

As usual, therefore, Paul can hardly speak without reflecting on everything from a theological perspective. The God he serves is full of mercy, both in healing the sick and in sparing the heavy-laden from further sorrow. Note too that Paul simply would not understand the denial of grief that some express today when they rejoice over the death of a loved one. No, death is still an enemy—ours and God's (1 Cor 15:25-26)—and grief is the normal response; but it is sorrow expressed in the context of hope (1 Thess 4:13).

Joy Back Home (2:28) With an inferential *therefore* Paul returns to the opening words of verse 25, "I sent him," now qualified in light of verses 27-28 with *all the more eager.* Thus Paul offers the reciprocal side of Epaphroditus's distress over their knowledge of his illness: "that you may see him again and rejoice" (NIV *be glad;* see comment on 2:17), expressing here a gladsome, spontaneous delight in seeing their brother again, and especially in seeing him alive and well. Whether Paul intended "see him again and rejoice" or "see him and again rejoice" is ambiguous. Pauline usage clearly favors the latter, since this adverb almost always precedes the verb it modifies. Paul therefore probably intended that in seeing him they would "rejoice again," which is quite in

2:28 *Spoudaioterōs* (NIV *the more eager*) is another word used to support the "two mission" view. Although the word group *spoud-* can carry the sense of "haste," nowhere else does it do so in Paul; rather he always uses it to reflect some nuance of "eagerness, earnestness,

keeping with the repetition of this imperative in the letter. But one cannot be sure that this is how the Philippians would have understood it, since *again* also seems to go naturally with the participle "seeing." In either case, Epaphroditus's return will be cause for renewing their joy.

Not only so. Just as Paul added a word of personal relief at the mercy of God in sparing Epaphroditus, so here he adds a similar word, "and I for my part may have less sorrow" (NIV *anxiety*). God's mercy on Epaphroditus meant that Paul was not given extra sorrow; his anticipation of the Philippians' joy in seeing Epaphroditus again, along with their relief from anxiety over him, will also have the effect of lessening Paul's ongoing grief (related to his imprisonment).

The Commendation Itself (2:29-30) With another inferential "therefore" Paul comes at last to the commendation proper. Since Paul has sent Epaphroditus back for the triple reasons given (for Epaphroditus's, theirs and Paul's sakes), "therefore," he concludes, *welcome him in the Lord with* all *joy, and honor [people] like him.* Having given the reasons for their welcoming him back with joy, Paul now concludes by urging them to do so (not all imperatives in Paul are correcting something that has gone wrong!).

Welcome him . . . with [all] joy repeats what he said in the preceding clause as to the purpose of his sending Epaphroditus home. But it does so with the typical (for this letter especially) qualifier *in the Lord.* The nuance of this phrase is again not easy to pin down, but most likely it is similar to Paul's "hope in the Lord" (v. 19) and "confident in the Lord" (v. 24) in the preceding paragraph. Everything that believers do is *in the Lord* in some way or another. Their common existence, theirs and Epaphroditus's, is predicated on the fact that together they are *in the Lord,* meaning they belong to him.

Moreover, Paul adds, they should hold people like Epaphroditus in *honor.* Although this plural (literally "such people") may indicate, as suggested above, that others are traveling with Epaphroditus and that in this final word they too are included, more likely this simply reflects a standard idiom. When Epaphroditus is held up for *honor* of this kind, he

---

diligence" (Bauer). Since that makes perfectly good sense here, it becomes an expedient for a point of view to translate it otherwise.

belongs to the larger category of "such people" who deserve esteem. Thus the two phrases together indicate the kind of reception Epaphroditus deserves upon his return, the kind of esteem in which the Philippians should hold him for what he has done. Such honor is not drawing glory away from God, but is that properly given to one of God's own who nearly "poured out his life" on behalf of a brother for Christ's sake.

With a final causal clause (v. 30) Paul repeats, but also elaborates, the two basic reasons the Philippians should esteem Epaphroditus highly on his return home: first, *he almost died for the work of Christ,* which is then elaborated, *risking his life to make up for the help you could not give me.* What is added to what was already said in verse 27—which we could have guessed at but without certain evidence—is that his coming so close to death was the direct result of engaging in *the work of Christ.* The grammar of the sentence indicates that this refers to Epaphroditus's bringing the Philippians' gift to Paul in Rome; and since Paul's imprisonment is directly related to *the work of Christ,* any gift brought to him by fellow believers in this way would be seen as participating in the gospel, as 1:5 suggests.

The next qualifier intensifies *he almost died for the work of Christ.* By completing his mission in the midst of severe illness, Epaphroditus put his own life in jeopardy. At least that is what the grammar implies. The main clause says *he almost died for the work of Christ,* which is now modified by an aorist (in this case past) participle followed by a purpose clause, which goes with the participle, not the main clause. Thus, *he almost died for the sake of Christ,* by "having risked his life in order to complete . . . your service to me." The clear implication is that there is "a causal connexion between the bringing of the gift and the risking of his life" (Mackay 1960:169). This is the phrase that gives credence to the view noted above (v. 26), that he most likely took ill en route to Rome but pressed on anyway to fulfill his commitment to the church and Paul, and thus exposed himself to the very real possibility of death.

The final purpose clause gives the reason for Epaphroditus's so

---

2:30 *Paraboleusamenos* (literally "having risked") occurs here for the first time in known literature, but an inscription noted by Adolf Deissmann (1927:88) suggests that it was not

risking his life, while at the same time offers the believers in Philippi their ultimate reason for holding him in high *honor:* he was willing to risk his life so that he might make up *for the help you could not give me.* But it is doubtful whether Paul intended to sound quite so pejorative. This combination of the verb "make up for" and the noun "lacking" is used in a similar context in 1 Corinthians 16:17 to refer to "making up for the absence of the rest." That is almost surely the intent here. Thus the clause begins "he has made up for your lack" in the sense of "your absence." Paul's absence from Philippi has created a gap in his life, and Epaphroditus has filled that to a degree.

Having made that point, Paul then returns to the sacrificial imagery of verse 25. With a genitive qualifier he indicates that by the "lack" of their presence, neither could they minister to his needs as they would have liked; but now Epaphroditus has done so in their behalf. As in verse 25 he expresses their gift to him through Epaphroditus in terms of performing the duties of a priest in his behalf. Very much in keeping with 4:10, he thus acknowledges that their "lack" was not in the willing but in the opportunity. Though stated very awkwardly, the sense of the sentence goes something like this: "so that he might make up for your absence and thus minister to my needs as you have not had opportunity to do recently."

Thus Paul concludes this brief narrative of proposed travel plans, a narrative full of warmth and pathos, victory and trepidation. His affection for the Philippians spills over through his expressions of affection for Epaphroditus, their "ministrant" to his human needs. At the same time the passage echoes with notes of gratitude and joy: gratitude to God for his mercy in healing a brother, joy renewed as they see him again. Paul hints at his sorrows but does not elaborate; instead the passage is full of affection and honor for one who dared to risk his life for the work of Christ in bringing him material aid. His ultimate concern is that the Philippians themselves appreciate Epaphroditus for what he has done in their behalf for Paul's sake. If Epaphroditus also serves to model one who was willing to suffer for the sake of Christ, that note, while not played loudly, neither is played

coined by Paul. Most likely it is a term associated with gambling, here used metaphorically.

so softly that it cannot be heard. Here is very personal material, which includes theological moments because Paul seems incapable of doing anything otherwise.

□ The Philippians' Affairs—Again (3:1—4:3)

Now that the basic matters are in hand—reporting on his own situation, appealing to the Philippians to get theirs in better order, and informing them as to what's next—Paul returns once more to their "affairs." But here both the way Paul begins and the content of the section have made it difficult for later readers to see how things fit together—a problem abetted by the variety of paragraphing options for verses 1-2 in our English translations.

Paul begins with what appears to be a concluding word (v. 1a); but this is followed by a sentence indicating that he is about to repeat things they have heard before (v. 1b), and then by a severe denunciation of some people (v. 2) who the following sentences (vv. 3-6) imply are Jewish Christian itinerants promoting the circumcision of Gentiles. After telling his own story in response (vv. 4-14) and encouraging the Philippians to follow his example in contrast to some who do not (vv. 15-21), he concludes (4:1-3) with language and ideas that recall the opening appeal in 1:27 and 2:2. This is then followed (4:4) with a repetition of the call to rejoice in the Lord with which the whole began.

Various hypotheses have been offered to explain how all this fits (or doesn't fit) in the letter: that an editor has "sewn together" two or more letters of Paul to the Philippians, or that Paul started to conclude his letter, was interrupted or put it aside for awhile, and then took off on a totally new tack before returning to his interrupted conclusion. But such views tend to focus on verses 2-6 in such a way as to neglect the remarkable verbal and conceptual ties the rest of this section has with what has preceded.

Indeed, the correspondences are so striking that it should cause us to read verses 2-4(6) as related in some way to the rest, even if we cannot be sure of that relationship. The correspondences include

---

3:1—4:3 On the issue of the integrity of Philippians see the introduction, pp. 23-24; for a

□ Paul's description of his Christian life as one long yearning to gain/know Christ (vv. 7-10; cf. 1:21-23)
□ his description of "knowing Christ" (vv. 10-11) in terms that echo the heart of Christ's story (2:6-8), followed by his own confidence in attaining the eschatological prize (vv. 12-14) just as Christ's vindication followed his suffering and death (2:9-11)
□ his appeal (vv. 15-16) that the Philippians adopt his own mindset on these matters (life that is cruciform, while pressing on toward the sure future), the latter being a repeated motif in chapters 1—2
□ his second appeal (vv. 17-21) that they follow his example in contrast to some enemies of the cross whose minds are set on earthly things and thus will miss the final glory of heavenly citizenship (cf. 1:27; 2:2, 9-11)
□ his final appeal (4:1) that they thus stand firm (echoing 1:27)
□ which all concludes by a very specific appeal to two women leaders (4:2-3) in the precise language of the more general appeal in 2:2

These correspondences, in which Paul's own story echoes that of Christ and equally serves as an example of the mindset the Philippians are to pursue, are too many and too exact to allow all of this to be simply digressive. What this suggests further is (1) that *to loipon* in 3:1 (NIV *finally*) means "as for what remains to be said," thus introducing a concluding section of the letter (cf. 1 Thess 4:1; 2 Thess 3:1), not a conclusion per se; (2) that the appeal to "rejoice in the Lord" serves to frame the whole section, as the context in which the warning of verse 2 and the various repeated appeals are to be understood; (3) that the warning against the "Judaizers" in verses 1b-6 (9) should be understood as related in some way to the appeal to having Christ's mindset; which in turn (4) is most likely also related in some way to the friction between the two women that is responsible for much of the content of this letter.

How these are related to the whole is more speculative. Very likely one of these women was urging that the community go the way of the Judaizers—either because securing oneself with God by visible forms of religious observance has for some reason a very strong appeal even

helpful overview of the issues pro and con see O'Brien 1991:10-18 or Bockmuehl 1997:20-25; cf. Garland 1985.

to Christian believers (cf. Galatians) or because Judaism, even though despised for its exclusive monotheism, had been given legal standing in the Empire, while the followers of the crucified Nazarene were becoming more and more suspect (see Tellbe 1994).

The key to how this section begins lies in the area of Greco-Roman friendship, where to be friends meant automatically to have enemies in common (see introduction). Pilate, for example, could not be "a friend of Caesar" and at the same time not consider Jesus as an enemy who was a potential threat to Caesar (Jn 19:12). The problem for Paul is all the more striking if one of his own friends (Euodia or Syntyche) in Philippi is leaning toward a view that is opprobrious to him.

At Issue: The Circumcision of Gentiles (3:1-4) What would you do if a longtime member—and leader—of your community, who over many years had faithfully resisted the attractions of "rules" as a way of identifying God's people, had finally begun to play the devil's advocate for such a view—and was apparently being persuaded by it in the process? And to top it all off she and another leader are carrying on open disputes about the issue in the context of the community.

We cannot be sure of this scenario, of course, but Paul's way of going at the issue is remarkable indeed. He chooses to capitalize on the anticipated rejoicing in Philippi over the return of Epaphroditus (2:28-29) and thus to return to the imperative by which he concluded his earlier appeal (2:17-18). Only this time he expresses it in the language of the Psalter: *Rejoice in the Lord;* and when all has been said about the present dispute, he will say it again: "Rejoice in the Lord always. I will say it again, Rejoice!" (4:4). This may seem like a strange framing device within which to speak to a controversial matter; but for Paul it is the only way. Not only does he focus them again on *the Lord,* but he does so in the language of both the laments and the praise psalms, so as to set their focus above themselves and their sufferings by active participation in singing and praise to Christ.

Rejoice in the Lord thus serves as the context in which he will warn them of the *same things* (= same people) yet once more, the memory of which brings forth the one moment of impassioned rhetoric in this letter: literally, "Beware the dogs; beware the evil workers; beware the mutilation." What these people are about is made clear by the sharp contrast with *we* in verse 3. The true circumcision "serves" (in the new temple, is implied) by means of the Spirit of God, thus "boasting" in Christ and putting no confidence in the flesh. These final contrasts, between "serving" by the Spirit and trusting in "the flesh," serve as the springboard for Paul's personal testimony—exhibit A supporting the validity of verses 2-3.

Given the frequency with which Paul speaks to this issue in his letters, one must assume that the arguments of the Judaizing faction had a surface attractiveness to many, despite the (literally) painful consequences if Gentiles were to submit. But Paul appeals not to the physical pain but to historical and theological realities. Moreover, despite the emotive language of verse 2, there is little hint either here or elsewhere in the letter that such people are actually present in Philippi at the time of this writing. After all, Paul's primary response takes the form of personal narrative, not argumentation as such; and not once does he threaten the Philippians with the consequences of such action. His main thrust is altogether positive, setting life in Christ in stark contrast to what he had formerly known as a Torah-observant Jew. This suggests that the emotive language is more a reflection of Paul's own distaste for such people, after many years of struggle against them, than a direct attack against anyone currently in Philippi.

The Framework—Rejoice in the Lord (3:1) We have already noted that the adverbial phrase *to loipon* that begins this section means something like "as for the rest [of what needs to be said]." A new section is further indicated by the vocative *brothers [and sisters],* one of four occurrences in this section (3:13, 17; 4:1). The first and last of these are also accompanied by the familiar *my,* probably stressing their relationship as friends.

This is the sixth occurrence of the verb *rejoice* in the letter. It was noted earlier (on 2:17) that for Paul "joy" is primarily a verb, something we do rather than how we feel. The verb itself means to verbalize with praise and singing. Echoing a repeated refrain from the Psalter (e.g., Ps 32:11; 35:9; and many others; cf. Hab 3:18), Paul thus gives this motif perspective. We are to *rejoice in the Lord.* As with the psalmists, the Lord who saves is both the basis and focus of rejoicing. The phrase *in the*

Lord refers to the ground (or sphere) of our present existence (cf. Phil 2:19, 24) and thus points to our basic relationship with Christ. This in itself should eliminate all attraction to mere religion. Knowing Christ makes trash even of blameless Torah observance; it is unthinkable that under the pressure of present sufferings the Philippians should lose their joy in Christ by yielding to such observance.

In the context of rejoicing in the Lord, Paul begins his warning by noting that what he is about to say he has said many times before (cf. v. 18). That he should have done so in Philippi, where the Jewish contingent was so small it could not even form a synagogue, only underscores the potential threat these itinerants were to every church Paul had established among the Gentiles. Since Philippi straddled the Egnatian Way, the east-west turnpike through Macedonia, this church was always in danger of the Judaizers' showing up with their subversive teaching. So using this letter to warn the Philippians one more timeis "not onerous" (NIV *no trouble*) to Paul; *it is a safeguard for you.*

The Warning (3:2) The very thought of his and their common enemies causes Paul to come out with guns blazing—with rhetoric (including assonance) that is impossible to capture in English. The threefold repetition of *blepete* (*watch out for;* "beware") followed by the thrice-repeated definite article and three words beginning with *k* nearly spits out: *blepete tous kynas; blepete tous kakous ergatas; blepete tēn katatomēn.* Although we are hardly prepared for this outburst, such people have dogged Paul all the years of his Christian ministry (see Gal 2:1-14). So the warning addressed to the Philippians turns out to be full of invective and sarcasm against (apparently) Jewish Christians who promote circumcision among Gentile believers. Each of the words is intended to score rhetorical points.

First, *watch out for those dogs.* This metaphor is full of "bite," since dogs were zoological low life, scavengers that were generally detested by Greco-Roman society and considered unclean by Jews, who sometimes used "dog" to designate Gentiles. Paul thus reverses the epithet;

3:1 Some have seen verse 1b as referring to *rejoice in the Lord,* but that seems nearly impossible, since *the same things* is plural, not singular, which would be the natural expression if Paul intended to point to the preceding imperative. Moreover, one can imagine any number of adjectives that might serve as reasons for him to repeat the imperative to

by trying to make Gentiles "clean" through circumcision, the Judaizers are unclean *dogs*.

Second, they are *evildoers*. The clue to this usage lies in its position between "dogs" and "the mutilation." Since both of these terms express reversals, it is arguable that this one does as well. If so, then the irony derives from the Psalter's repeated designation of the wicked as "those who work iniquity." In trying to make Gentiles submit to Torah observance, Judaizers (and their contemporary counterparts, the legalists) do not work "righteousness" at all but evil, just as those in the Psalter work iniquity because they have rejected God's righteousness.

Third, and changing from the masculine plural to a pejorative description of the Judaizers' activity, Paul warns, "Beware the mutilation," an ironic reference to Gentile circumcision. The Greek word for circumcision is *peritomē* (= "to cut around"); *katatomē*, used here, denotes "cutting to pieces," hence "mutilate." This wordplay, especially the emphatic *For it is we who are the circumcision* (v. 3), makes it certain this is the primary issue between Paul and them. This is the most "cutting" epithet of all, the ultimate derogation of circumcision, since the cognate verb occurs in Leviticus 21:5 (LXX) prohibiting priests (who serve God) from cutting their flesh as pagan priests did (cf. 1 Kings 18:28).

We miss too much, however, if we think of this language as merely expressing a personal pique. At issue for Paul is Christian existence itself. As with the exhortations in Philippians 1:27—2:18, living the gospel in Philippi is what is at stake. This is why he speaks of such repetition as not "burdensome" for him, even though being reminded again of the Judaizers' activities appears to be irksome.

The Contrast (3:3-4) As immediate response to the ironic use of "mutilation," Paul asserts: "For we [not they] are the circumcision [hence you do not need literal circumcision], who serve by the Spirit of God and boast in Christ Jesus, and who put no confidence in the flesh." This, not verse 2, is the principal sentence in the present appeal, full of

---

rejoice, but *a safeguard for you* is not one of them, whereas it fits perfectly with the warning and exhortation that follows.

3:2 On the issue of Paul's "opponents" in this verse, see the Introduction; for a helpful overview and critique of alternative positions see O'Brien 1991:26-35.

theological grist that is going to be milled by means of Paul's own story in verses 4-14.

The emphatic *we*—not they—by which the sentence begins reflects Paul's regular habit in the middle of an argument to shift from the second or third person to the inclusive first-person plural whenever the point shifts to some gospel reality that includes him as well as his readers (cf. vv. 15-16 and 20-21 below). Thus *it is we*—you and us, Gentiles and Jews together—*who are the* true *circumcision,* which Paul elsewhere calls "circumcision of the heart, by the Spirit" (Rom 2:29, echoing Deut 30:6). Paul knows nothing of a "new" Israel; for him the one people of God are now newly constituted—quite in keeping with Old Testament promises—on the basis of Christ and the Spirit.

Paul first describes the true circumcision as *we who [minister] by the Spirit of God.* His use of the crucial verb *latreuō* (NIV *worship*) is determined by the LXX, where it most often denotes levitical service or ministry in the sacrificial system. Here it stands in ironic contrast to Philippians 3:2: mutilated priests could not serve in the former temple; the true circumcision now serve Christ in the new temple by means of the Spirit. As the rest of the sentence makes clear, what Paul has in view is neither congregational worship nor internal "spiritual" service (personal piety) over against external rite, but two ways of existing: *in the flesh,* meaning life centered in the creature as over against God, and *by the Spirit,* as people of the future for whom all life in the present is now service and devotion to God.

"Serve" thus still refers to "righteousness" (vv. 6, 9) but now especially has to do with reflecting God's likeness and character in how we live (i.e., looking out for the interests of others, 2:3-4, as modeled by him who revealed Godlikeness in emptying himself by taking on the form of a slave, 2:5-7). Such ministry, effected by God's own indwelling Spirit, is a million miles removed from religious observance. In turning Torah (or Scripture in any form) into laws to be observed, God's people turn them into mere human regulations, missing their intent as revelation of God's likeness to be lived out among God's people. Hence the need for

3:3 A major textual variation occurs in this sentence, between "serve by the Spirit of God"

a circumcision of the heart, effected by the Spirit, to replace that of the *flesh*.

The basis of such life in the Spirit is Christ himself, expressed in terms of "boasting/glorying" *in Christ Jesus* (see 1:26). This seems to be a clear echo of Jeremiah 9:23-26, where the Lord says that the truly wise will boast in the Lord (thus not put confidence in such "flesh" matters as wisdom, strength, wealth), in a context where "the whole house of Israel" is judged as being "uncircumcised in heart." This seems all the more pertinent here, since Jeremiah says that true boasting in the Lord means to "understand and know me," in the sense of knowing God's true character—which is exactly the point Paul will pick up in Philippians 3:8-11. As in Jeremiah, "boasting" here carries the nuance of putting one's full trust and confidence in Christ, and thus to *glory* in him. Although the Spirit functions as Paul's primary contrast both to "works of law" and to *the flesh,* in this letter he can scarcely bring himself to speak of Christian existence without mentioning Christ. In the personal narrative that follows, this is the theme to which he returns in grand style.

Finally, and now in contrast both to boasting *in Christ Jesus* and to serving *by the Spirit of God,* he adds the telling blow: *who put no confidence in the flesh*. This clause is full of irony, Paul's way of moving from the specific expression of Torah observance (the circumcision of the flesh) to what he recognizes as the theological implications of Gentiles' yielding to circumcision. It reflects the similar argument in Galatians 3:2-3, where "flesh" refers first to the actual flesh cut away in circumcision but at the same time is the primary descriptive word for life before and outside of Christ. As in that passage, *Spirit* and *flesh* are overlapping realities that describe existence in the "already/not yet." One lives either "according to the Spirit" or "according to the flesh." These are mutually incompatible kinds of existence; to be in the one and then to revert to the former is spiritual suicide. And this is where the Judaizers have gone astray; they reject boasting *in the Lord* in favor of *confidence in the flesh*. But there is no real future in the past, which

(so NIV) and "serve God in spirit" (so Moffatt) or "by the Spirit." See Fee 1995:288 n. 10, for arguments that favor the NIV.

Christ and the Spirit have brought to an end.

As a final addendum to the description in Philippians 3:3, but also as a lead-in to the personal word that follows, Paul appends *though I myself have reasons for such confidence*—although he actually says it a little more starkly: "though I myself have confidence even in the flesh." What this means will be clarified in the following sentence (vv. 4b-6). We who serve *by the Spirit,* Paul says, who boast *in Christ Jesus,* have thus abandoned altogether putting *confidence in the flesh*—which by implication is what the Judaizers are bringing Gentiles to by urging circumcision. But, he now concedes, if they want to play that game, then I win there as well, since I excel on their turf, "having [grounds for] confidence even in the flesh." Again "flesh" refers first to the rite of circumcision but now carries all the theological overtones of trying to have grounds for boasting before God in human achievement, the ultimate self-centered expression of life. And with that he turns to offer, first, the evidence for such a bold statement (vv. 4b-6) and, second, the zero net worth of such achievement in light of having come to know Christ and being found in him (vv. 7-9).

The Example of Paul (3:4-14) Despite the subjective element, there is nothing like telling one's own story to silence what are merely arguments on the other side. This is what Paul is now up to; but it is also more. As verse 15-16 make clear (note the crucial verb *phroneō,* "have this mindset"), he intends his story to be an example for the Philippians to follow, just as he did the story of Christ in 2:5-11. In his case, three crucial matters are being modeled: first, picking up the final clause of verses 3-4a, he sets his former and present life in contrast to what the "evil workers" are trying to achieve (vv. 4b-6[7]); but, second, the middle part (vv. 7-11) reminds us of earlier moments in the letter (especially his "motto" in 1:21 and the story of Christ in 2:6-8), calling us to knowing Christ as our ultimate concern and thus to live cruciform; he concludes, third, by returning to the recurring theme of vigorous pursuit of the final prize (vv. 12-14), which in light of verses 20-21 is an obviously primary

3:4 Both V. C. Pfitzner (1967:142) and Ralph P. Martin (1980:123) consider verses 4-6 to reflect a "self-defense" against the accusation of opponents, rather than as a negative model

concern in this letter as well (see 1:6, 10, 22-23; 2:16).

Thus he tells his (possibly) faltering and (apparently) feuding Philippian sisters and brothers that the future does not lie in embracing the past (vv. 4-6); rather, it lies altogether in knowing Christ *now,* even as that means knowing "the participation in his sufferings" (vv. 7-11); and such present "knowing" of Christ means that a certain prospect still lies in the future, where also lies the ultimate prize of knowing Christ forever (vv. 12-14).

For many of us, especially those from deeply religious but essentially "observant" backgrounds, this must become our story as well, or the gospel for which Paul eventually gave his life comes to naught. The same is true for the many whose past is not religious but in "the flesh" in the form of every kind of *un*righteousness. And we may not choose the parts of the story we like and leave out the rest. For *the surpassing [worth] of knowing Christ Jesus my Lord,* I not only must abandon every attempt to gain an advantage with God on the basis of giftings and achievements. But I must also be prepared to discover anew that truly *knowing Christ* means simultaneously knowing *the power of his resurrection* (the part I like) and *sharing in his sufferings* (the part I like less) so as to be conformed to the likeness of Christ's own *death* (2:8) and thus to gain the *resurrection.*

Rejecting His Religious Past (3:4-6) Paul's encounter with the risen Christ functioned like a divine audit in his life. For all of his hard work to have "credit" with God, Christ turned these "gains" into "losses," so that Paul might have profit of such surpassing worth that the former now looked like dung to him. This opening paragraph in his story illustrates what formerly had worth with a list of seven items, six of which indicate different ways in which he "excelled." He begins with circumcision (not surprisingly, given verses 2-3), then moves on to his membership in the ancient people of God, including his tribal origins; he is *a Hebrew of Hebrews,* which can be demonstrated in three observable ways, concluding with the declaration "blameless, according to the righteousness found in the law." His B.C. (before Christ) credentials

from which to argue for a cruciform lifestyle. See the critique in Fee 1995:303 n. 1.

are both noteworthy and impeccable.

Little is new here, except the final assertion of blamelessness as to the law. From a sociological point of view, Paul is reiterating items that indicate "status." But the final two (and very likely, therefore, his being a Pharisee as well) indicate "achievement"; so the interest is not simply in what was given to him by birth but in what he himself did so as rightly to be designated *a Hebrew of Hebrews*. All of this, he will go on, amounts to nothing more than "street filth" in comparison with knowing Christ. The Philippians' own future, therefore, does not lie in Paul's religious past.

Verse 4b basically reiterates the preceding addendum to verse 3. It is at once ironical and theological. Not only can Paul play the Judaizers' game (v. 4a), but "I can play it better than they can." His credentials with regard to Jewish identity and observances are impeccable; indeed, in comparison with their grounds for *confidence in the flesh, I have more*. In saying *If others think they have reasons to put confidence in the flesh,* Paul does not imply that Judaizers were present in Philippi. Rather, this is his way of giving perspective to any in Philippi who, because of present suffering, might be tempted to lean this way—thus his way of warning against Judaizing teaching for their safety (v. 1). What follows is a catalog of seven items that illustrate the foregoing assertion.

First, *circumcised on the eighth day*. For obvious contextual reasons, Paul leads with this particular item rather than with the next two. The Judaizers insist on Gentile circumcision; thus Paul, who through Christ and the Spirit belongs now to *the* circumcision, begins here: as a Jewish boy, born into a Jewish home, I was *circumcised on the eighth day;* that is, "I received circumcision long before any of you in Philippi had even heard about Christ and the gospel."

Second, *of the people of Israel*. Here is the crucial item. What the Judaizers hope to achieve by Gentile circumcision is to bring them into the privileges of belonging to God's ancient people, "Israel's race." Paul had been given this privilege by birth.

Third, *of the tribe of Benjamin*. The reason for this one is almost certainly for effect. Gentiles could become members only of Israel; Paul's membership was of a kind whereby he could trace his family origins. He belonged to the tribe of Benjamin, that favored tribe from which came Saul, Israel's first king, of whom he is namesake; the tribe blessed by Moses as "the beloved of the LORD . . . whom the LORD loves [and who] rests between his shoulders" (Deut 33:12), in whose territory sat the Holy City itself. They were also notable because they alone had joined Judah in loyalty to the Davidic covenant. It is not difficult to hear a ring of pride in this little reminder, which then calls for the next designation.

Fourth, *a Hebrew of Hebrews*. This is the "swing" term, summing up the preceding three and setting the stage for the final three. *Hebrews* appears to be a term Jews used of themselves, especially in the Diaspora in contrast to Gentiles. Paul was in every way a "Hebrew, born of pure Hebrew stock."

Fifth, *in regard to the law, a Pharisee*. This is in keeping with the data recorded in Acts 23:6-9 and 26:5 and with Paul's own word in Galatians 1:14, that he had advanced in Judaism far beyond his contemporaries, being "extremely zealous for the traditions of [his] ancestors." The reason for mentioning this feature of his history is at least threefold: (1) It defines his relationship to the law in a very specific way, as belonging to the Jewish sect devoted to its study and codification. (2) Any Jewish Christians who came to Philippi to promote circumcision on the part of Gentiles would most likely also belong to this sect (cf. Mt 23:15 and Acts 15:5). (3) It gives the framework for understanding the next two items.

Sixth, *as for zeal, persecuting the church*. Paul was not just your everyday, run-of-the-mill Pharisee. Emulating prophetic *zeal* for God, he had demonstrated his own most surely by his untiring dedication to stamping out the nascent Christian movement, probably related to his conviction that God had especially cursed Jesus by having him hanged (Gal 3:13; Deut 21:23). In their own way his Judaizing opponents are also persecuting the church; but Paul surpasses them even here. In light of his and the Philippians' present suffering for Christ, the fact that he himself once stood on the other side on this issue suggests a bit of irony as well. How easy it is for the religious to confuse zeal for their own cause with zeal for God, which explains both the bombing of abortion clinics and the confusion of "the American way of life" with the gospel.

Seventh, as for righteousness in the law, *faultless*. This brings the catalog to its climax. But it is also the item that has generated long debates among later readers, since it seems to contradict what Paul says elsewhere about his ability to keep the law (Rom 7:14-24). The key to the present usage lies at three points—the term *righteousness,* the qualifier "in the law" (NIV *legalistic*) and the word *faultless*—which together indicate that he is referring to Torah observance understood as observable conduct.

The key to the use of *faultless* lies with its sacrificial overtones (cf. Phil 2:15). Paul has no "blemishes" on his record as far as lawkeeping is concerned, which means that he scrupulously adhered to the Pharisaic interpretation of the law, with its finely honed regulations for sabbath observance, food laws and ritual cleanliness. This means further that *righteousness* in this context does not refer to right standing with God, but precisely as he qualifies it, that *righteousness* which is "in the law." Here he is probably referring especially to matters of "food and drink" and "the observance of days," since, along with circumcision, these are the items regularly singled out whenever discussion of Torah observance emerges in his letters.

Both the narrative that follows (vv. 8-9) and Romans 14:17 make it clear, however, that for Paul true *righteousness* goes infinitely beyond these matters; indeed, the kingdom of God has nothing at all to do with "food and drink" but with righteousness, peace and joy in the Holy Spirit. What makes the present kind of *righteousness* worthless is that it generates "confidence in the flesh"; it is "a righteousness of my own" (v. 9)—my own achievement, based on lawkeeping (v. 9), which stands in stark contrast to the "righteousness that comes from God" predicated on faith. But the concern for righteousness in the present passage is not first with "right standing" but with "right living" (see on 1:11).

Paul's point, of course, is not his sinlessness but his being without fault in the kind of righteousness the Judaizers are into by insisting on circumcision. This has nothing to do with righteousness at all, is his point. He has excelled here and found it empty and meaningless; hence he insists for the Philippians' benefit that there is "no future in it."

And there is still no future in it, even though pride of religion continues to persist in a whole variety of forms in contemporary

3:7-8 The three consecutive uses of the preposition *dia* ("because/on account of") in these two verses can possibly be prospective (*for the sake of* = gaining Christ is the goal of the loss); it is more likely retrospective ("because of" = the "cause" of loss is what Christ has

Christianity. There are those who still define righteousness in terms of "food and drink and the observance of days," who thus still maintain distinctions between "clean and unclean," although variously defined. To be able to claim that one does not indulge in such "sins" is a badge of honor in many circles. Likewise for those who define righteousness in terms of "church"—rites, sacraments, forms—rather than in terms of knowing Christ.

Paul has not given up his heritage, nor is he against "form" of various kinds. What for him is "refuse" is to put confidence in them, as if righteousness had anything to do with such. And if that seems too strong for some readers, at least that gives one an opportunity to sense the passion fellow Israelites would have felt toward Paul. Our problem in hearing this text lies with our ability to distance ourselves too easily from their passions, which Paul is treading on in this passage with characteristic single-mindedness. None of these things has anything at all to do with knowing Christ, he will go on to say.

Knowing Christ Now (3:7-11) Here is one of those passages to which we (gladly) turn again and again, so much so that it is easy for us to miss what Paul is up to in telling his story. Using the language of commerce ("gain/loss"), he puts his past, present and future into perspective. Everything has singularly to do with Christ, who functions for us all as the great divide. In "gaining Christ" his remarkable past now looks like *skybala* ("street filth/dung"; NIV *rubbish*). Nor does Paul dwell longingly on the past, as some Christian testimonies seem to. When our first son at age six discovered the bicycle, the toy trucks in the sandbox were history.

In revising the balance sheet in this way, Paul again writes an especially complex sentence (vv. 8-11), whose various parts and relationships are nonetheless discernible. The renunciation in verse 7 sets forth the leading themes of the whole—the "loss/gain" metaphor and its reason, "because of Christ." This is then elaborated in the long sentence of verses 8-11 in several ways: (1) the *loss* of *whatever was to my profit* (= vv. 4-6) is expanded to *everything,* which is now considered

done). In any case, there are no analogies for it to mean *compared to* in verse 8 (NIV), nor should one read *for the sake of* to mean "in behalf of."

skybala (v. 8); (2) "because of Christ" is expanded to *the surpassing [worth] of knowing Christ Jesus my Lord* (v. 8); (3) in the great reversal Christ is now Paul's *gain;* this means to *be found in him,* and thus to find true *righteousness* which is based on *faith,* vis-à-vis the "faultless" righteousness of verse 6 which is based on law and is nothing more than *a righteousness of my own* (v. 9); (4) the ultimate purpose of all this (repeating from v. 8) is *to know Christ,* now spelled out as simultaneously knowing *the power of his resurrection* and *sharing in his sufferings,* which has a cruciform lifestyle as its present goal and resurrection as its final goal (vv. 10-11).

Paul thus covers a lot of ground in this sentence-turned-paragraph. But the essential matters are two. (1) The theme of righteousness is triggered by the warning in verse 2: "faultless righteousness" found in or based on the law (vv. 6, 9) is utter trash in comparison with that "found in Christ," which comes from God and is based on faith. Paul thus moves subtly from behavioral righteousness, of a kind whereby one hopes to gain advantage with God (v. 6), to positional righteousness, which God gives through Christ and is available to faith alone. (2) "Knowing Christ" relationally is the aim of everything; it entails knowing both the (present) power of his resurrection and participation in his sufferings, thus being conformed to *his death* so as to realize the future *resurrection from the dead.*

As the narrative unfolds, the theme of *righteousness* gives way to that of *knowing Christ,* suggesting that the former exists primarily as grounds for the latter. This also suggests that the real emphasis of verses 1-4a is less on warning as such and more on the Philippians' "continually rejoicing in the Lord" because their experience of Christ and the Spirit has removed them forever from Torah observance. Because of *the righteousness that comes from God and is by faith,* we now know God through knowing Christ—which also means to embrace, not disavow, the attendant suffering.

3:7 In verse 7 Paul uses the perfect *hēgēmai* ("I have come to consider"; NIV *I now consider*); the two occurrences of the verb in verse 8 are present (= "I continue to consider"). The perfect in verse 7 implies that "on this side of things this is my considered view of them." Given the inclusion even of his birth and Jewishness, a simple affirmation, "what things were gain are now loss," would have been both imprecise and misleading.

1. *Renouncing false boasting (3:7).* With bold contrasts Paul renounces his former advantages, both "gifts" and "achievements," as grounds for boasting. *For the sake of Christ* (more likely "because of Christ"), Paul declares, *whatever was to my profit I now consider loss.* But this is said with flair. In two nicely balanced lines, "whatever things" and "these things" occupy the emphatic first position while the contrasting "gains" and "loss" occupy the emphatic final position. Thus:

Whatever things	were	for me	gains,
these very things	I consider	because of Christ	loss

"Gains" (plural) harks back to 1:21, "to die is [to] gain [Christ]." Paul now plays on the metaphor. His former gains are collectively a *loss* because of his ultimate gain, Christ himself.

Still in view is the warning against the Judaizers. While he cannot renounce—nor does he wish to—what was given to him by birth (circumcision, heritage and the like), he does renounce them as grounds for boasting. But as verse 9 makes clear, he is especially renouncing "righteousness that is in the law," even though his is "faultless."

2. *Knowing Christ now (3:8a).* With an emphatic "not only so, but what is more," Paul explains the "how so" of verse 7. He begins with a thesis sentence that reiterates verse 7b in grand and expansive language: *I consider everything a loss*—not just the advantages enumerated in verses 5-6 but "all things"—"because of" (not *compared to,* NIV) *the surpassing greatness of knowing Christ Jesus my Lord.* This is a reprise on the theme struck in 1:21, "for to me, to live is Christ." *Knowing Christ Jesus my Lord* so far surpasses all other things in value that their net worth is zero. Everything that others might consider to have value in the present age—religious advantages, status, material benefits, honor, comforts—these appear to Paul as total *loss* in light of Christ.

As verse 10 will clarify, *knowing Christ* does not mean to have head

3:8 Several scholars (e.g., Beare 1959; Koester 1962) have sought a Hellenistic (especially "gnostic") background for Paul's "knowing Christ." But given the clearly Jewish context of this passage, not to mention Paul's primary Old Testament background for such ideas, this view has not gained a significant following. For a helpful overview of the various backgrounds suggested see Koperski 1996:20-59.

knowledge about him but to know him personally and relationally. Paul has thus taken up the Old Testament theme of knowing God and applied it to Christ. It means to know him as child and parent know each other, or wife and husband—knowledge based on personal experience and intimate relationship—and thus to know Christ's character intimately. In Jeremiah 9:23-24 those who "boast" in the Lord (see comment on v. 3) do so precisely because they "understand and know me," which is then spelled out in terms of God's "kindness, justice and righteousness." It is this kind of knowing of Christ that Paul will spell out in verses 10-11, where he echoes the Christ story of 2:6-11.

But in the present expansive language *(the surpassing* worth *of knowing),* the object of *knowing* is not simply "Christ," nor even "Christ Jesus," but *Christ Jesus my Lord.* Here is both intimacy and devotion. Ordinarily Paul says "our Lord Jesus Christ"; only here does he reverse the order and substitute *my* for "our." The reason for such devotion and longing rings forth clearly in Galatians 2:20, "who loved me and gave himself for me." This is not simply coming to know the deity—it is that, of course—but knowing the One whose love has transformed the former persecutor of the church into Christ's "love slave," whose lifelong ambition is to know him in return, and to love him by loving his people. There is something unfortunate about a cerebral Christianity that "knows" but does not know in this way, as though without such knowing one could truly be in Paul's train.

Like a composer giving his theme yet another variation, Paul repeats once more: *for whose sake I have lost all things [and] consider them rubbish.* The first item is straight repetition. The second catches us by surprise; but it also helps us to see the depth of feeling Paul had for those who would "advantage" his Gentile converts with what is so utterly worthless. The word *skybala* is well attested as a vulgarity, referring to excrement (hence the KJV's "dung"); it is also well attested to denote "refuse," especially of the kind that was thrown out for dogs to forage through. Although it could possibly mean "dung" here, more likely Paul is taking a parting shot at the "dogs" in verse 2. "Street filth" might capture both the ambiguity and the vulgarity. It is hard to imagine a more pejorative epithet for status and achievement! Paul sees them as total loss, indeed as foul-smelling street garbage fit only for dogs.

3. *Being found in him (3:8b-9).* At this point Paul's sentence becomes a bit convoluted. In the form of two purpose clauses (vv. 8b-9, 10-11), he goes on to express the twofold goal/result of his having *lost all things*. The first is penultimate, his final word on "boasting in Christ Jesus" over against "confidence in the flesh" as that finds expression in the "faultless righteousness found in the law." The second is ultimate, returning to the theme of knowing Christ by spelling out what that means in our present "already/not yet" existence.

He begins by completing (and thus discarding) the commercial metaphor, *that I may gain Christ.* Thus verse 7 is turned on its head: what was gain is now considered loss because of true gain, Christ himself. Implied is that gaining Christ requires the loss of all former things; to be rich in Christ means to be rich in him alone, not in him plus other gains. On the other hand, neither is there any sense of calculation, as though Paul were setting about to gain eternal life and eventually settled on Christ as the means to that end. The "gain" comes first, and comes in such a way that the rest falls away as trash.

To *gain Christ* is immediately interpreted as being *found in him,* which is further interpreted as *not having a righteousness of my own*. To *be found in him* implies divine initiative, to have a God-given righteousness in contrast to the righteousness of verse 6, which served as grounds for self-confidence. As to when Paul expects this "gaining" and "being found" to take place, the answer lies with his "already but not yet" perspective (cf. vv. 10-11 that follow). The first point of reference is almost certainly future, looking to the "day of Christ" mentioned in 1:6, 10 and 2:16. This fits the future orientation both of the immediate context (vv. 11-14) and of the letter as a whole (see on 1:6). On the other hand, the participle, *having . . . righteousness,* is oriented toward the present. He expects to *gain Christ and be found in him* then precisely because he is already *in him* now.

Someone once described the further elaboration of being *found in him* as a "little meteorite from Romans that has fallen into this letter." It is also a piece of art: a (typical) "not/but" contrast of the two kinds of "righteousness," in three parts:

not having my own righteousness
  that comes from the law,

but that which is through faith in Christ

which is then repeated in another phrase with the same three parts, the first two "lines" serving as counterpoints to the former phrase, and ending again on the note of *faith:*

the righteousness

that comes from God,

which is based on faith

Although the contrast is clearly with verse 6, the intervening gain/loss metaphors have moved Paul from a focus on behavioral righteousness to positional righteousness, and thus back to verse 3 ("boasting in Christ Jesus and putting no confidence in the flesh"). The reason that even "faultless" Torah observance is rubbish is that it means *having a righteousness of my own*. Because it *comes from the law* (= "predicated on observance of the law"), it gives me grounds for "boasting in the flesh," in human achievement. Which is why it is no means to righteousness at all. It makes an end run around Christ Jesus and puts confidence in a symbol, mere flesh, rather than in the reality. One is thus righteous neither in the sense of being rightly related to God nor in the sense of living rightly as an expression of that relationship.

True "behavioral righteousness" will issue in a cruciform lifestyle (v. 10; see note on 1:11); to get there one must first receive *the righteousness that comes from God*. Truly Christian life "boasts in Christ Jesus," predicated on a relationship with God that comes *through faith in Christ*—which in Paul is always shorthand for "by grace through faith." Some think this phrase means "through Christ's own faithfulness" in our behalf, that is, through his faithful obedience that led to death (2:8); however, the contrasts in verse 3 (boasting in Christ versus confidence in the flesh) that this clause is bringing to conclusion, plus Paul's constant insistence that we must believe in (= have faith in = trust) Christ for our salvation (see 1:29), gives the nod to the traditional understanding in this case.

3:9 Two terms in this sentence—*righteousness* and *dia pisteōs Christou* (through faith in Christ)—have been hotly debated over the past twenty years, generating an enormous bibliography. Regarding *righteousness,* at issue is its precise sense (positional, behavioral, God's character, God's activity); for a useful discussion see Kertelge 1990:325-28 (and his

Thus Paul warns the Philippians once more against the Judaizers who would forever try to make them "religious." There is simply no future in it. But his greater concern is with their current behavior, in two directions: (a) that their love for one another may increase (1:9), as they learn in humility to consider the needs of others to be more important than their own (2:3-4)—just as Christ demonstrated by his death on the cross (2:6-8)—and (b) that they learn to "rejoice in the Lord" even in the midst of their present suffering (2:17-18; cf. 3:1, 10-11), so that, conformed to Christ in his death (v. 10), they might also be conformed to him in his resurrection (v. 21)—just as Paul models in his story.

4. *What knowing Christ means (3:10-11).* With a final purpose clause, Paul concludes his long sentence (from v. 8) by returning to the theme of *knowing Christ Jesus my Lord,* now offering the primary reason for rehearsing his story. In keeping with his Old Testament roots, *knowing Christ* is the ultimate goal of being in right relationship with God; and knowing Christ is both "already" and "not yet." Through the righteousness Christ has effected we know him now, both *the power of his resurrection* and *sharing in his sufferings;* the ultimate prize, to have present knowledge of him fully realized, awaits *resurrection* (and/or transformation; vv. 20-21). This, then, is the decisive word over against those who would bring the Philippians under the old covenant. Obedience under that covenant could issue in blameless Torah observance, but it lacked the necessary power to enable God's people truly to know him and thus bear his likeness by living cruciform *(becoming like him in his death),* which is true righteousness in the "right living" sense.

To understand the details of this remarkable passage, we need to note two things about its structure. First, Paul almost certainly does not intend that we know three things: Christ, the power of his resurrection and participation in his sufferings. Rather, the second two spell out what knowing Christ entails. Second, Paul follows that up with two further

bibliography); cf. Ziesler 1972. On the debate over *faith in Christ* see the overview and bibliography in Fee 1995:325 n. 44; for recent papers on either side (read at the same seminar) see Dunn 1991 (for the traditional view) and Hays 1991 (for the newer view).

clauses which pick up the first two in reverse order (thus creating a chiasmus, A B B′ A′), emphasizing in turn Christ's resurrection and sufferings and how Paul participates in both of them. Thus:

so that I may know him

A both the power of his resurrection

B and sharing in his sufferings

B′ being conformed to his death

A′ if somehow I might attain the resurrection from the dead

In turn these lines point to Christ's resurrection (line A), as the means whereby Paul is enabled to endure suffering (B), and to Paul's resurrection as the eschatological fruit of such suffering (A′), as the latter is a portrayal of the Crucified One (B′).

A. To *know Christ* begins with *the power of his resurrection,* the power that comes to believers on the basis of Christ's resurrection. This is the reality that radically altered the early Christians' understanding of present existence—as both "already" and "not yet." Paul's reasons for starting here are two, related to the concerns of the rest of the appeal. First, the primary focus in what follows is the future, hence the connection between the two A lines: the power inherent in Christ's resurrection guarantees our own resurrection. Second, Paul's urging the Philippians to "rejoice in the Lord" in the context of suffering (2:17-18) makes sense only in light of the resurrection of Christ. Without the power—and guarantee—inherent in Christ's resurrection, present suffering can be both harsh and senseless.

Paul is no triumphalist (all glory without pain), but neither does he know anything of the rather gloomy stoicism that is often exhibited in historic Christianity, where the lot of the believer is basically to "slug it out in the trenches" with little or no sense of Christ's presence and power. *The power of Christ's resurrection* was the greater reality for him. So certain was Paul that it had happened—accosted and claimed by the Risen Lord on the Damascus Road as he had been—and that Christ's resurrection guaranteed his own, that he could throw himself into the present with a kind of holy abandon, full of rejoicing and thanksgiving; and that not because he enjoyed suffering, but because Christ's resurrection had given him a unique perspective on present suffering (spelled out in the next two lines), as well as an empowering presence whereby the suffering was transformed into intimate fellowship with Christ himself.

B. Paul next speaks to one of his main concerns regarding the Philippians' "affairs," *sharing in his sufferings,* which must be read in light of 1:29-30 and 2:17-18. This is the simultaneous flip side of the first line; and here is where the example of Christ (2:6-8) and Paul's example meet—and press the Philippians toward having a single mindset in the midst of present difficulties.

With this word we come to the heart of Paul's understanding both of his relationship with Christ and of the nature of existence in the "already/not yet." Suffering on behalf of Christ is the ordinary lot of believers (1:29). With the present phrase we get some theological insight into what that means. First, Christ's resurrection and present exaltation is the direct result of his having suffered for us to the point of death on a cross (2:6-11); by analogy, the way to resurrection for his followers also leads down the path of suffering. Second, *sharing in his sufferings* is the clue to everything. While our sufferings do not have the saving significance of Christ's, they are nonetheless intimately related to his. Through our suffering the significance of Christ's death is manifested to the world, which is why in 1:29-30 Paul describes such suffering as "on behalf of Christ." Paul is here reflecting the teaching of our Lord, that those who follow Christ will likewise have to "bear the cross" on behalf of others.

Hence *knowing Christ* involves *sharing in his sufferings*—and is a cause for constant joy, not because suffering is enjoyable but because it is certain evidence of Paul's intimate relationship with his Lord. Now the opening words "rejoice in the Lord," which reiterate the same appeal in 2:18 in the context of suffering, fall into place. The grounds for joy in the Lord lie with knowing him, as we participate in his sufferings while awaiting our glorious future.

B'. With the next phrase, *becoming like him in his death,* several important matters converge. The combination "being conformed" *(symmorphizomenos)* and "death" recall the Christ narrative in 2:6-11 and offer the linguistic ties between Paul's story and the story of Christ. Thus Christ's sufferings are not "sufferings in general" but those sufferings that culminated in his death, which was for the sake of others; no other suffering is in conformity to his. Thus, as Christ's life and suffering serve as paradigms, so also does Paul's *becoming like Christ in his death.* Christian life is cruciform in character; God's people, even as they live presently through the power of Christ's resurrection, are as their Lord forever marked by the cross. The heavenly Lion, one must never forget, is a slain Lamb (Rev 5:5-6).

This phrase also serves as the transition between Paul's knowing the power of Christ's resurrection in the context of present suffering and his own future resurrection, noted next. Resurrection applies only to those who have first experienced "death." Moreover, the word for "being conformed" is picked up again as an adjective in verse 21, indicating once more the closest possible ties between death and resurrection, and especially the close relationship between our present suffering (by which we are being conformed into the likeness of his death) and our future resurrection (in which our present bodies "of humiliation" will be conformed into the likeness of his present resurrected, and therefore "glorified," body).

A′. Paul now moves from *knowing Christ* in the present to its full realization in the future, *and so, somehow, to attain to the resurrection from the dead.* The point of this final clause is easy enough: conformity to Christ's *death* in the present, made possible because of the power of Christ's *resurrection* in the present, will be followed by our own *resurrection from [among] the dead* at the end. But the way Paul says it is a bit puzzling: *somehow* seems to imply doubt.

The reason for this way of putting it seems to be twofold and interrelated. First, this hesitation is not to be understood as lack of confidence about his own—or their and our—future; rather, it emphasizes that the resurrection of believers is integrally tied to their first "being conformed to his death." Without "death" of this kind, there is no resurrection. This is another way of saying "we must go through many hardships to enter the kingdom of God" (Acts 14:22). But the future itself is not in doubt—everything in Paul, including verses 12-21 that follow, refutes such a notion. What is uncertain for him is whether his certain

3:11 Some have been willing to argue that Paul had real doubt about his future resurrection (e.g., Otto 1995, based on the misguided view that Paul expected martyrdom), but that flies full in the face of Paul's confidence expressed elsewhere, including 3:20-21. Most likely

future is to be realized by resurrection or by transformation (as implied in vv. 20-21). This matter is in God's hands, to which Paul gladly submits by this use of language.

Second, this is his way of moving toward the concern that the Philippians "stand firm" in the present (4:1; cf. 1:27) and especially not lose their clear focus on, and keen anticipation of, their certain future in Christ. Hence this last clause also serves as the direct lead-in to the final section of the narrative (vv. 12-14) and its final application (3:15—4:1). In whatever way the future is realized—through resurrection or transformation at the parousia (vv. 20-21)—the present involves knowing the power of Christ's resurrection as key to participating in Christ's sufferings. The final, complete knowing of Christ is "not yet"; neither he nor they have attained to it. Nonetheless, such a future prize is the one certain reality of present existence and is thus worth bending every effort to realize, which is what the end of the story (vv. 12-14) is all about.

Because this passage (vv. 7-11) is very popular and thus very easy to read apart from its context, it needs careful analysis; but when the analysis is over, we should return to the text and read it again and again. Here is quintessential Paul, and a quintessential expression of the New Testament view of Christian life. Such life means to be finished with one's religious past as having value before God or as a means of right relationship with God; it means to trust wholly in Christ as God's means to righteousness. But such "righteousness" has as its ultimate aim *the surpassing* worth *of knowing Christ Jesus my Lord;* and *knowing Christ* means to experience *the power of his resurrection* for present *sharing in his sufferings,* as those sufferings are in "conformity with his death." The final two clauses put it in perspective: to *know Christ* in the present means to be "conformed to his death," so that all of Christian life is stamped with the divine imprint of the cross as we live out the gospel in the present age and await the hope of resurrection.

Like 1:21 and 2:5-11, Paul's selective personal history here once again demonstrates how totally Christ-focused he is. For him Christian life is

---

Markus Bockmuehl (1997:217-18) has it right in suggesting that the issue is not certainty or uncertainty but the need to persevere, which is precisely what verses 12-14 pick up.

not simply a matter of salvation and ethics; it is ultimately a matter of knowing Christ. So too with resurrection; Paul's focus is not on "everlasting life" or anything else such. The goal of the resurrection, the prize for which Paul strains every effort in the present, is Christ himself.

If suffering and the temptation to become religious were causing the dimming of such vision for some in Philippi, in contemporary Western culture (and much of the rest of the world) the dimming is for different reasons, more often connected with values related to material gain. Paul's vision seems to have the better of it in every imaginable way; and a common return to "the surpassing worth of knowing Christ Jesus our Lord" could go a long way toward renewing the church for its task in the postmodern world. Our lives must be cruciform if they are to count for anything at all; but that reminder is preceded by an equally important one—the power of Christ's resurrection both enables us to live as those marked by the cross and guarantees our final glory.

Pursuing the Prize: Knowing Christ at the End (3:12-14) Despite the unfortunate section break (with title!) in the NIV, Paul does not now begin something new. Rather, with a striking change of metaphors his story takes a final turn, which simultaneously looks back to verses 4-8 (forgetting the past), embraces the present (he is not yet fully conformed to Christ's death, nor has he arrived at the goal, vv. 10-11) and emphasizes his present pursuit of the final goal. Knowing Christ now and attaining the resurrection combine to give purpose to Paul's life—his "running," to use his current metaphor. He has seen the future, and it is ours—full of the single reality that marks the present: Christ Jesus my Lord. And everything in Paul's present life is drawn to a future in which Christ is finally and fully known.

So strongly does Paul feel about this divine pull that makes him run full tilt toward it, that he says it twice (vv. 12 and 13-14). Both sentences are structured alike: the main subject and verb, *I press on,* is preceded by a disclaimer about "not having arrived," followed by a word about what he presses toward, which is further qualified by the divine initiative

3:12 The language of this verse has given a field day to those who would "mirror read" this passage in light of alleged false teachers in Philippi, who are also Paul's opponents in the church there (see Fee 1995:341 n. 15 for a sampling of views). The problem with all of these views—and finding consensus is well-nigh impossible—is that one must "mirror

(Christ has already "taken hold" of him; God has called him heavenward). The only additional item in the second sentence is the notation about disregarding (NIV *forgetting*) *what is behind*. It is the nature of such rhetoric that the second sentence reinforces or elaborates the first—and sometimes, as in this case, clarifies it as well.

There are some difficulties in interpretation, to be sure, mostly related to two phenomena: the first verb *(elabon,* "taken"; NIV *obtained)* has no object (the NIV supplies an interpretive *all this*); and Paul uses striking wordplays (first with *katalabō* [NIV *take hold of*], a compound of *elabon* which he milks for all it's worth; and second with cognates of *teleios* [= "reach one's goal"], which the NIV puts as *perfect* in verse 12 and *mature* in v. 15). This leads him to say some things in unusual ways, which are very difficult to transfer into English (it's like trying to tell a joke in a second language).

But kept in context, it all makes perfectly good sense. So far he has modeled for the Philippians that their own future does not lie in Paul's (now rejected) past (vv. 4-6) and that the "already/not yet" of the future lies singularly in *knowing Christ,* through whom we have been given present righteousness (vv. 7-11). Now he picks up the final ("not yet") thread from verse 11 and insists that the future is still future. He has not "already" gotten there, but he strains every muscle finally to do so. In context the "there," of course, is not heaven or reward as such but the final prize of knowing Christ even as Paul himself is known (1 Cor 13:12).

1. *Pursuing him who took hold of Paul (3:12).* The *not that* which begins this sentence is an idiom that qualifies something previously said so that readers will not draw the wrong inference. Along with the repeated adverb "[not] already" Paul thus offers a twin disclaimer—what not to infer about the already present future. The disclaimers emphasize that despite present realization of *the power of his resurrection* and *sharing in his sufferings,* Paul has not yet reached the final goal. He has not *already obtained* ("taken/received") it, nor has he *already* arrived at the goal (NIV *been made perfect*). He will proceed to play on both

read" with remarkable clairvoyance, since everything is based on Paul's disclaimers with nothing explicitly said in the letter to guide one's reconstruction. Here is a sure case of opposition's being found in the eye of the beholder, not in the text of Paul.

of these verbs, the first immediately, the second in verse 15.

In light of what he says in verse 13 about "disregarding what is past," the implied object of *obtained* might be "all things"; more likely it refers to what has more immediately preceded. It must be remembered that Paul is not writing a new "paragraph"; that is our invention. This sentence follows hard on the heels of the preceding clause (v. 11). What he has obviously not *obtained* is that which he is pressing on *to take hold of,* which verse 14 makes clear is the final goal. Thus he adds, *or have already* "arrived at my goal." There is a sense, of course, in which perfection does happen at the end; but the root *(telos)* of this verb *(teleioō)* has the primary sense of "goal" or "aim," before it takes on secondary senses of "perfect, complete, fulfill, mature." Nothing in context implies that perfection is an issue. Since that English word conjures up all kinds of wrong connotations here, and since everything in these final sentences indicates that the eschatological prize is what Paul is pursuing with such vigor, the verb here almost certainly carries its primary sense of "reach the goal."

Since Paul has not yet "arrived," he does what he wants the Philippians to do, *press on to take hold of* ("seize") *that for which Christ Jesus took hold of me*. With this wonderful wordplay he moves from not already "taking" to yet "taking hold of" the very thing/one who "took hold of" him. He will go on in the next sentence to elaborate what his own "taking hold of" means. In context the next phrase, *that for which Christ Jesus took hold of me,* points back at least to verses 8-9 (being *found in Christ* and thus having a *righteousness that comes from God*); but in terms of his own story, and especially the use of this strong verb, he probably intends them to hear echoes of the Damascus Road as well. A good dose of memory about one's beginnings in Christ can serve as the proper shot of adrenaline for the continuing race.

2. *Pursuing the final prize—knowing Christ fully (3:13-14)*. What could otherwise be ambiguous about verse 12—because of Paul's wordplays—is clarified by this sentence, now turning the verb "pursue" *(press on)* into a full-fledged metaphor from the games. The vocative "brothers [and sisters]" does not signal the beginning of something new but emphasizes what he is about to repeat. The disclaimer in this case picks up the immediately preceding language *(not . . . to have taken*

hold of it); but before picking up the verb *press on,* he recalls his singular passion to know Christ from verse 8 (cf. 1:21) in terms of *but one thing.* There is no *I do* in Paul's narrative; the language is terse and stark: his whole Christian life has been *one thing*—the pursuit of Christ.

The metaphor itself begins with a "not/but" contrast. Pictured first is the runner whose eyes are set on the goal in such a way that he "pays no attention to" (the runner had better not *forget*) *what is behind.* This imagery always brings to my mind the famous "miracle mile" (the first time two milers ran under four minutes in the same race) run in 1954 in my present hometown (Vancouver, B.C.) by Roger Bannister and John Landy. Landy had led all the way, but coming off the final turn toward the finish line he looked over his shoulder to find out where Bannister was, only to be passed on the other side and beaten to the wire. The picture of that event has always been for me commentary enough on Paul's metaphor. In context *what is behind* probably refers to verses 4-6, but it would also include all other matters that might impede his singular pursuit of Christ.

The flip side of the image is the runner's *straining toward what is ahead.* The picture is of coming down the home stretch, leaning forward, extending oneself to break the tape. It is generally hazardous to press metaphors, and this one can be pressed in all kinds of wrong directions. Paul's purpose—both his use of this metaphor and its intent—is singular; not "perfection" is in view, but perseverance. As Paul "runs" toward the Christ who has already taken hold of him, he does so in the same focused, full-tilt way a runner does who is intent on winning. To be sure, his using such a metaphor results is one of those small inconsistencies that are created by active minds as they move quickly from one point to another. He has just recalled Christ's having "taken hold of" him, so it is clear that he does not totally disregard the past. This is imagery, pure and simple, whose meaning will be given in what follows.

The "what" that Paul presses on toward continues the athletic imagery; it is to reach *the goal* and thus *win the prize.* But no mere "celery wreath" for Paul (the ordinary prize in the games). The *goal* is God's eschatological conclusion of things; the *prize* is Christ, which in context means the final realization of knowing him. This is what Paul would gladly die to gain (1:23); this is what his whole life is about; no other reward could have any meaning for him.

What draws him on is a combination of the past and the future: that *God has called me heavenward in Christ Jesus*. This has been said by a series of Greek genitives ("of" phrases), which intend the following relationships. First, God has *called* us to himself, which will culminate in glory; second, that call, which began at conversion, is *heavenward* in terms of its final goal; third, God's call found its historical and experiential location *in Christ Jesus;* and fourth, at the end of the race we will gain *the prize,* Christ himself, the tangible evidence that the goal of God's call has been reached.

Paul tends to see all of Christian life in terms of God's calling. It begins as a call into fellowship with his Son (1 Cor 1:9), thus a call to "be saints" (1 Cor 1:2) and thereby joined to his people who are destined for glory. The present usage is unusual in looking at our calling from the perspective of its completion rather than its beginnings. This has been the aim of God's call right along, to lift us *heavenward* to share in his eternal Presence.

Here, then, is the first note of what will be emphasized at the end of the appeal in verses 19-21: some, who are no longer walking in the way set forth by Paul, have their "minds set on earthly things," whereas Paul and the Philippians are among those whose "citizenship is [already] in heaven," from whence they await the coming of the Savior. Thus he turns immediately (vv. 15-17) to press on them the need to follow his example—with a "mature" mindset like that just described.

This singular and passionate focus on the future consummation, which Paul clearly intends as paradigmatic, often gets lost in the contemporary Western church—in an affluent age, who needs it? But Paul's voice needs to be heard anew. Part of being human is that by nature we are oriented to the future; in a day when most people have no real future to look forward to, here is a strikingly powerful Christian moment. The tragedy that attends this rather thoroughgoing loss of genuine hope is that our culture is now trying to make the present eternal. North Americans are probably the most death-denying culture in the history of the race. How else can one explain cosmetic surgery's having become a multimillion-dollar industry?

In the midst of such banal hopelessness, the believer in Christ, who recognizes Christ as the beginning and end of all things meaningful, needs to be reminded again—and to think in terms of sharing it with the world—that God's purposes for his creation are not finished until he has brought our salvation to its consummation. Indeed, to deny the consummation is to deny what is essential to any meaningful Christian faith. Paul finds life meaningful precisely because he sees the future with great clarity, and the future has to do with beginnings—the (now redeemed) realization of God's creative purposes through Christ the Lord. There is no other prize; hence nothing else counts for much except *knowing Christ,* both now and with clear and certain hope for the future.

Application and Final Appeal (3:15—4:3) Although Paul's focus is altogether on the heavenly prize, his running shoes make regular contact with terra firma. So in the same way he did with Christ's story in 2:13-18, he applies his story to the situation in Philippi. Twice over he urges the Philippians to follow his example: first by having the same "mindset" as in his story (3:15-16), second by "joining together" in "walking" in his ways (v. 17). This is followed with a concluding set of stark contrasts: there are some who "walk" as *enemies of the cross,* whose *mind is on earthly things* and whose "future" is *destruction* (vv. 18-19), whereas as citizens of heaven we await from there our Lord and Savior, who at his coming will transform our earthly bodies into the likeness of his present heavenly glory (vv. 20-21).

Following this glorious wrap-up of his second excursion into the Philippians' "affairs," Paul concludes with two final appeals, which connect this one to the first one. He returns first (4:1) to the primary appeal from 1:27 to *stand firm in the Lord* and second (4:2-3) to its accompanying appeal from 2:2-5 to "have one mindset," this time specifically applying it to two leaders of the community. Thus Paul's final application of his story recalls the two major concerns addressed in the two sections of the letter given to their affairs: steadfastness (including their keeping a steady gaze on Christ and their sure future) and unity in the face of opposition.

The glue that holds together this application and final appeal is friendship and the three-way bond (between him, them and Christ) that gives the whole letter cohesion. Paul's story (3:4-14) was devoted altogether to his relationship with Christ; these appeals now link that with the other two sides of the triangle (see figure 1 in commentary on page 21). First, his secure relationship with the Philippians allows him to tell his story for purposes of imitation, as he now explicitly tells them (indeed, he begins [vv. 15-16] and ends [vv. 20-21] with first-person plural verbs [see commentary on 3:3], thus reinforcing that he and they are in this together). Second, the clear aim of all this has to do with the Philippians' relationship with Christ, which is specifically picked up in the final application (3:20-21) and two final appeals (4:1, 2-3). Also like the preceding narrative, all of this is placed in the context of friends having enemies in common (vv. 18-19): some who have rejected imitating Paul are in this case *enemies of the cross.*

First Application: Follow Paul's Mindset (3:15-16) Paul now concludes his story on the same note with which he began the story of Christ in 2:5, returning to the crucial verb *(phroneō)* that dominated the appeal in 2:1-5 (and will occur again in 3:19 and 4:2). Just as he urged them to a "mindset" *(phroneite)* in keeping with Christ's, so now he has told his story so that they will *take . . . a view [phronōmen] of things* in keeping with his own. It is thus hardly coincidental that Paul's story corresponds at several crucial points with Christ's. The present application is in three parts: a direct application (v. 15a), a qualification (v. 15b) and a rejoinder to the qualification (v. 16).

Paul begins with an inferential "therefore" (omitted in the NIV), which explains why Paul tells his story. "In consequence of what I have been narrating," he says, "let us now hear the application." Which begins: *All of us who are teleioi,* a play on "I have not yet arrived at the goal" in verse 12. This appears to be a bit tongue in cheek, since he includes himself in the present designation: he who is "not yet" *teleios* ("completed") in the sense of eschatological hope is "already" *teleios* ("mature"), along with them, in terms of how he lives in the present as he awaits the final glory. *Such a view of things* translates a simple "this," which probably refers to the whole narrative, including the rejection of his Jewish past. But it especially includes his "participation in Christ's sufferings by being conformed to his death" and his eager pursuit of the

3:15-16 These verses are sometimes read as though there were opposition to Paul in the eschatological prize, since that is the focus of verses 18-19 and 20-21: those who are *enemies of the cross* and who have set *their mind . . . on earthly things* are set in sharp contrast to *us,* whose *citizenship is in heaven,* from whence *we eagerly await* the *Savior.*

But then Paul makes a surprising qualification: *And if on some point you think [phroneite] differently, that too God will make clear to you.* Although some have seen here a hint of conflict between Paul and some in the community, that is most unlikely since Paul's tone carries not a whiff of the odor of controversy. Indeed, his words are almost nonchalant—a kind of "throwaway" sentence--which makes one think that no great issue can be in view. That not all of them would necessarily see things his way is implied, but that much has been implied throughout the letter.

Most likely this is another matter to be understood in the context of friendship. Paul is especially concerned that they follow his example, which happens also to be part and parcel of a patron-client friendship. But throughout the letter he studiously avoids any hint of this kind of superior-to-inferior expression of friendship; in fact he goes out of his way to make sure that their friendship is understood in terms of mutuality. That seems to be what is also going on here. He really is exhorting them to follow his example (as v. 17 will make even more clear); but exhortation in this case is not command, nor does it assume that all will see eye to eye with him on all matters. The emphasis in this sentence, after all, is on God's continuing to work among them through divine revelation. This would suggest that *on some point* does not so much reflect specifics that Paul has in mind, but generalities. Here is the offer of friendship; they may freely disagree with him at points—on many matters—and if any matter counts for something, Paul trusts God to bring them up to speed there as well.

Having allowed friends a difference of opinion, but stipulating that God will redirect their collective frame of mind in any case, Paul returns to his first point, expressed now in terms of behavior. "In any case," he rejoins, "on the matter at hand you need not wait for divine revelation." At the same time he returns also to the first-person plural, *only let us*

church (e.g., Hawthorne 1983:155-57), but that is to "mirror read" too much into too little.

live up to what we have already attained. Paul seems to be calling them to live in keeping with how they have already followed Christ, before they ever received this letter. Given his longtime—and loving—relationship with this church, and his frequent stops there, it is hard to imagine that in this letter he is telling them anything new. In fact in 3:1 he has said quite the opposite, that it is not burdensome for him to "write the same things" again as a "safeguard." Thus both the Christ narrative, which is foundational for his, and his own story are not new; rather they tell the "old, old story" all over again. This is what he and they have already attained, even if some are now slacking off in some way and for some reason.

The best explanation of the "why" of all this is the one suggested before, that in the face of opposition and some internal dissension, some of the Philippians have lost their vision for and focus on their crucified and risen Lord, including his coming again. Even in a Roman prison Paul has not lost his vision; here he urges them to follow his example and to see their participation in Christ's sufferings as Christ's way of "conforming them to his death," so that they, with Paul, may joyously gain the prize of his eternal presence.

Second Application—Follow Paul's Ways (3:17) For Paul correct thinking must lead to right living. Having thus concluded the first application by urging the Philippians to conform their behavior to what they have been doing in the past, he now presses that point again, but especially in light of some who do not. As in verse 13, he emphasizes the repetition with the vocative, *brothers [and sisters]*. At the same time he also returns to his more standard language of "walking" (NIV *live;* see commentary on 1:27) and "imitation" (NIV *following*). Thus, in keeping with his Jewish heritage, Paul urges his friends to *join* "together" (not *with others;* see note) in "imitating me," again emphasizing their

---

3:17 Although the compound *symmimētai* occurs only here, the concept of imitation occurs regularly in Paul's letters (1 Cor 4:16; 11:1; Eph 5:1; 1 Thess 1:6; 2:14; 2 Thess 3:7, 9). The language occurs in two kinds of contexts in Paul: suffering for the sake of Christ and the gospel, and behavior that conforms to the gospel. In every case imitation of Paul means "as I imitate Christ" (expressly so in 1 Cor 11:1; cf. 1 Thess 1:6). For the background of this idea in Judaism, see Fee 1995:363 n. 7.

There has been some debate on the sense of the compound, whether the *syn* implies "fellow imitators with him of Christ" or (as in the NIV) "fellow imitators of others who are

being united in doing so, by "walking" as Paul himself did.

What is in view from his heritage is the pupil who learned not simply by receiving instruction but by putting into practice the example of the teacher; the one who so imitates, internalizes and lives out the model presented by the teacher. Also in that heritage ethical life was thought of in terms of "walking in the ways of the Lord." Thus Paul urges the Philippians to *take note of those who* "walk just as you have us as a model." The grammar and language of this clause imply a group of people that extends beyond the Philippians themselves. Along with "watching out for" the itinerants who would "mutilate" them (3:2), they are to "take note of" or "be on the lookout for" people (probably other itinerants) who, like themselves, walk in keeping with the example they find in Paul.

Three matters are thus brought together in this second application: (1) that their behavior conform to the *pattern* Paul has just given them in his story (3:4-14); (2) that they corporately *join* together in imitating Paul in this way; and (3) that they *take note of* others who come along who "walk" this way, precisely because, as he will spell out in the next sentence, there are many who walk otherwise.

Indictment of Those Who Do Not (3:18-19) With an explanatory *for,* Paul proceeds to put his own model in contrast with that of some others, whose "walk" is quite the opposite of his. Who these people are has been grounds for considerable debate, no solution to which is totally satisfactory. More important for us is what Paul says of them and how they fit into the preceding application of his story and the succeeding appeals in 4:1-3. Whatever else, they exemplify a "mindset" (3:19) at odds with Paul's, and therefore with that being urged on the Philippians. Rather than living cruciform (3:10-11), they "walk" *as enemies of the cross of Christ* (v. 18); and rather than pressing on to gain the final prize (vv.

---

already imitating Paul." But neither of these work well grammatically (see Fee 1995:364 n. 10); and the one that fits both Paul's usage and the letter is the one accepted here.

3:18-19 This sentence has also generated a considerable bibliography in terms of "opponents" in Philippi. At issue is whether these are the same as those excoriated in verse 2; and if so, how to reconcile what is said here with verses 2-6, or if not, how many different kinds of opponents Paul is facing in this church. For a more complete defense of the view taken here, plus discussion of alternative views, see Fee 1995:366-75.

12-14) and thus eagerly awaiting *a Savior from* heaven (v. 20), *their mind is* set *on earthly things* and therefore *their destiny is destruction.* These three indictments, which so clearly fit the present context, frame two others whose meaning is more difficult to determine: *their god is their stomach* and *their glory is in their shame.*

In calling them *enemies of the cross of Christ* Paul is, as the first matter, intentionally setting them over against both Christ (2:8) and himself (2:10-11). According to 1 Corinthians 1:18-25, the cross stands as God's utter contradiction to human wisdom and power, and therefore inevitably creates enemies of those who refuse to go that route (which is why the triumphalists in Corinth opposed Paul's gospel and apostleship; see Fee 1987:165-82). Since any of two or three kinds of people would fit the description, the phrase helps very little with a specific identification. That *their destiny is destruction* makes it clear that Paul does not consider them to be followers of Christ at all; whether they once were so would at least make sense of his telling the Philippians about them once *again even with tears* (probably tears of sorrow for those who should know better; cf. Jer 9:1 in light of Phil 3:3 and 8). But in any case, as in 1:28, which it echoes, the language cannot be softened to mean anything other than eternal destruction. The contextual reason for its appearing second in this listing, as over against its logical place at the end, is probably rhetorical effect. Since the way of the cross is central to Paul's concern, the "end" for those who are *enemies of the cross* is brought forward to a place immediately following.

Their god is their stomach and its companion, *their glory is in their shame,* are especially difficult and therefore have led to all kinds of speculation. Only one thing seems certain: that these two phrases belong with the final one, giving concrete expression to what that one generalizes, namely that they live only for the present; they have set their minds on earthly, not on heavenly, things. The first phrase is very close to what Paul says of some divisive people in Romans 16:17-18 ("such people are not serving our Lord Christ, but their own appetites"); in both instances the imagery probably refers to some specific behavior. But to what? "Stomach" may be a metonymy for the craving after sumptuous fare, or perhaps for surfeiting. One cannot be sure. Perhaps it is intended to be more representative—of those who are so given over to present bodily desires of all kinds, represented by the appetites, that such has become a god to them.

From our distance, *their glory is in their shame* is even more cryptic. It is connected to *their god is their stomach* by a single relative pronoun, suggesting that this is the flip side of whatever that one means. *Glory* is what they delight in; *shame* is how they should perceive their behavior. The word *glory* is undoubtedly another wordplay, setting up the contrast to our being transformed into the likeness of Christ's present body "of glory" in Philippians 3:21. Hence it is an especially striking bit of irony, where not only are they not destined for glory at all, because of their present enmity to the cross, but what glory they have in the present lies precisely in what should be for them a matter of shame. But beyond that, in terms of specifics, we are largely in the dark.

With the final phrase, *their mind is on earthly things,* we come to where the whole indictment has been heading right along. Two things are significant for understanding. First, Paul once more uses the crucial verb from 2:2-5 and 3:15. They do not simply "think about" earthly things; their "minds are set on" *(phronountes)* such things, which stands in pointed antithesis to Paul's own mindset as portrayed in his personal story. His mind is set altogether on Christ, whose cross serves as pattern for his own life. Second, the *earthly things* their minds are set on sum up the former two; this is what it means finally to be given over to the *stomach* as one's deity and to *glory* in what should be shameful. By their fruit, Paul says, you will know them; by their focus you will also recognize that they are not walking according to the pattern of Christ and his apostle.

At the same time it sets up the contrast that follows. Here is the second crucial matter. These people over whom Paul weeps are first of all *enemies of the cross;* they are now characterized as those who have abandoned the pursuit of the heavenly prize, in favor of what belongs only to the present scheme of things.

Who these people are can only be speculated. Some things remind us of the "dogs" with which the section began; but their (apparently) libertine ways clearly do not. Most likely Paul is here picking up on the major concerns of his personal narrative in 3:4-14, by reminding the Philippians again of some about whom he has often told them in the past, who have left the way of the cross and are pursuing present, earthly concerns. He is probably describing some itinerants whose view of the faith allows them a great deal of undisciplined self-indulgence. In any case, they have not appeared heretofore in the letter and do not appear again. They have served their immediate purpose of standing in sharp relief to Paul's own "walk" and to his heavenly pursuit, so crucial to this letter, and toward which Paul now turns once more as he begins to draw this appeal to an end.

The Future of Those Who Do (3:20-21) Besides serving as Paul's immediate response to the "many" who "walk" contrary to the Pauline pattern, this sentence concludes the long exhortation that began in 3:1, returning to the theme of the eschatological prize (vv. 12-14) by underscoring its certainty. Whatever the current threat was, and whatever its source, Paul has apparently sensed an ebb in the Philippians' eschatological anticipation, a matter he has spoken to throughout the letter. At the same time, by picking up the play on their dual *citizenship* (cf. 1:27), plus the final affirmation that our *Savior* (a common title for the emperor) is the one who will also *bring everything under his control,* Paul puts their present situation—opposition in Philippi resulting in suffering—into divine perspective. All of this is said in a sentence that rises to extraordinary christological heights: not only is Christ the focus and center of everything, but his activities here are those ordinarily attributed to God the Father in Pauline salvation texts.

All kinds of contrasts mark the sentence: the inclusive *we* (cf. 3:3, 15-16) over against "them"; *heaven* over against *earthly things;* a *glorious* future over against *destruction;* and true glory over against the *shame* they *glory* in. Paul begins by emphasizing that *our* citizenship is *in heaven,* thus offering the ultimate reason for following his example and for looking out for others who do so as well (v. 17), while at the same time returning to the wordplay on *citizenship* from 1:27. In a classic expression of the "already/not yet" framework of his theology, Paul says in effect that "we are a colony of heaven" as we live the life of the future, our true homeland, while living presently in the Roman colony of Philippi.

Because heaven is our true homeland, we *eagerly await* our *Savior from there,* he goes on—in yet one more play on their Roman citizenship and clear attempt to encourage them in their present suffering. The primary title for the Roman emperor was "lord and savior"; Paul now puts those two words side by side: our *Savior* and *Lord,* Jesus Christ, who will not only *transform* our present humiliation into glory but do this in keeping with the *power that enables him to bring everything under his control* (including the Roman lord and savior, Nero Caesar!). All of this to reassure the Philippians that the heavenly prize is absolutely worth pursuing (vv. 12-14).

Now, however, instead of thinking about "attaining to the resurrection" (v. 11), Paul thinks in terms of Christ's return. The net result is the same. Our present earthly existence is expressed in terms of (literally) "the body of our [present] humble station" (NIV *lowly bodies,* same word as in 2:3 and 8), which for many of us is a constant reminder of our creatureliness. These Christ *will transform* so that they are (again literally) "conformed [*symmorphon;* cf. *symmorphizomenos* in 3:10] to the body of his glory." Therefore, just as knowing Christ now means being conformed into the likeness of his death (v. 10), so in our final glory we will be conformed into the likeness of his resurrection.

Christ's present existence is bodily in the sense of 1 Corinthians 15, that the body is the point of continuity between the present and the future. The form of that body is the point of discontinuity—a "mystery," Paul says—but adapted to the final life of the Spirit; hence it is a "supernatural body," or as here, "the body of his [present] glory." The good new is that the same future awaits those who are his, which is Paul's present concern. Our current lot, he has argued in 1:29-30 (cf. 2:17), is to suffer for Christ's sake. But we can "rejoice in the Lord" in the midst of such suffering (2:18; 3:1; 4:4) because our suffering itself is enabled by "the power of his resurrection" (3:10), which resurrection at the same time guarantees our certain future. Hence in our present "humiliation" we await the coming of the Savior, and with that coming the transformation of our humiliation into the likeness of his glory.

Moreover, the *power* by which Christ will bring about this transformation is "in keeping with [NIV *by*] the working" *that enables him* "also to subject all things to himself" (NIV *to bring everything under his control*). In some ways this is the most remarkable transformation of all, in that Paul here uses language about Christ that he elsewhere uses only of God the Father. The phrase "able to subject all things to himself" is Paul's eschatological interpretation of Psalm 8:7, where God will "subject all things" to his Messiah, who in turn, according to 1 Corinthians 15:28, will turn over all things to God the Father so that "God might be all and in all." Remarkably, in the present passage the subjecting of all things to himself is said to be by Christ's own power.

The little word "also" has unfortunately been omitted from many English translations, including the NIV. Here is the final word of assurance to the Philippians. By the same power by which he will transform their present bodies that are suffering at the hand of opposition in Philippi, Christ will likewise subject "all things" to himself, including the emperor and all those who in his name are causing the Philippians to suffer. As Paul has already said in 1:28, their own salvation from God will at the same time result in the destruction of the opposition.

It simply cannot be put any better than that. This passage reminds us that despite appearances often to the contrary, God is in control, that our salvation is not just for today but forever, that Christ is coming again, and that at his coming we inherit the final glory that belongs to Christ alone—and to those who are his. It means the final subjugation of all the "powers" to him as well, especially those responsible for the present affliction of God's people. With Paul we would do well not merely to await the end but eagerly to press on toward the goal, since the final prize is but the consummation of what God has already accomplished through the death and resurrection of our Savior, Jesus Christ the Lord.

Final Appeal I—Stand Firm (4:1) With two final appeals Paul brings 3:1-21 to conclusion. At the same time he reaches further back into the letter to bring closure to the twin issues raised in 1:27—2:18: that they remain steadfast in the gospel and do so as one person in the one Spirit. The appeals belong together; they are expressed with great skill, full of friendship indicators.

The first appeal is directed toward the whole community; simultaneously it applies the preceding word of future hope, recalls the primary exhortation of 1:27 with which the "their affairs" sections of the letter began, and leads into the specific appeal of 4:2-3.

Friendship here takes the form of a remarkable elaboration of Paul's ordinary vocative, *brothers [and sisters]:* it becomes *my* brothers and sisters, *whom I love and long for, my joy and crown*. This profusion of modifiers reminds them once again of his deep feelings for them and his deep concern for their present and future. The first set *(whom I love and long for)* recalls their primary relationship: his love for them accompanied by a deep longing for them. So much does this relational concern matter to him that he repeats—awkwardly from the perspective of grammar, but effectively from the perspective of relationship—the vocative "beloved" at the end of the sentence (NIV *dear friends,* evidence that English is not comfortable with such repetition). The second set is eschatological and is as prospective as the former is retrospective, looking toward the time when 3:20-21 will have come to fulfillment and the Philippians stand before Christ with Paul as *my joy and crown* (cf. 1 Thess 2:19), his "boast on the day of Christ" (2:16).

Nearly getting lost in this piling up of endearing vocatives is the appeal itself, *stand firm* (recalling 1:27), now modified with "thus" (NIV *this is how*) and *in the Lord*. During the Philippians' present distress they are to stand firm *in the Lord,* firmly planted in relationship with the same Lord whose coming they eagerly await and who will then subject all things to himself (3:20-21). And they are "thus" to *stand firm,* referring probably to the whole of 3:1-21, but especially to their imitation of Paul by their upright "walk" even as they bend every effort to attain the final prize.

Final Appeal II—Be of the Same Mind (4:2-3) Paul proceeds directly to his final appeal. Given its verbatim repetition of 2:2 and its specific naming of persons, very likely this is where much of the letter has been heading right along. In a media-saturated culture like ours, where naming the guilty or the grand is a way of life, it is hard for us to sense how extraordinary this moment is. Apart from greetings and the occasional mention of his coworkers or envoys, Paul rarely ever mentions anyone by name. But here he does, and not because Euodia and Syntyche are the "bad ones" who need to be singled out—precisely the opposite. That he names them at all is evidence of friendship, since one of the marks of enmity in polemical letters is that enemies are left unnamed, thus denigrated by anonymity.

These longtime friends and coworkers, *who have contended at my side in the cause of the gospel,* are no longer seeing eye to eye with each other. We know very little more about them. Syntyche was named after the goddess of fortune, indicating pagan origins; both were given names (roughly "Success" and "Lucky") indicative of parental desire for their making good in the world. That Paul had women as coworkers in Philippi should surprise us none, since the church there had its origins among some Gentile women who, as "God-fearers," met by the river on the Jewish sabbath for prayer (Acts 16:13-15). The evidence from Acts indicates that at her conversion Lydia became patron both of the small apostolic band and of the nascent Christian community. By the very nature of things, that meant she was also a leader in the church, since heads of households automatically assumed the same role in the church that was centered in that household. Moreover, Macedonian women in general had a much larger role in public life than one finds elsewhere in the Empire; in Philippi in particular they were also well-known for their religious devotion.

Paul now entreats these two leaders *to agree with each other* (*phronein* = "have the same mindset") *in the Lord.* Given (a) the brevity of this letter, (b) that the letter would have been read aloud in the gathered community in a single sitting, and (c) that appeals to "have the same mindset" are part of the stuff of letters of friendship, one can be sure that the present appeal is to be understood as the specific application of the earlier ones in Philippians 2:2 and 3:15. Given its position at the end, it is also probably related to the foregoing warning and appeal (3:1-21).

Paul refuses to take sides, thus maintaining friendship with all. He appeals to both women—indeed the identical repetition of their names followed by the verb has rhetorical effect—to bury their differences by adopting the "same mindset." As in the immediately preceding appeal, it is qualified *in the Lord,* evidence that we are not dealing with a personal matter but with "doing the gospel" in Philippi. Having "the same mindset" *in the Lord* has been specifically spelled out in the

4:3 Further adding to the plausibility that Luke is the "genuine" *yokefellow* addressed are the data from Colossians and Philemon. If my view of the date and place of this letter is correct (introduction, pp. 33-35), then Luke had been with Paul during the earlier period of this same imprisonment when Paul wrote these two letters (Col 4:14; Philem 23). The letter to Philippi, however, which appears to have been written toward the end of that imprisonment (see Phil 2:24) is especially notable for its lack of mention of the names of preceding paradigmatic narratives, where Christ (2:6-11) has humbled himself by taking the "form of a slave" and thus becoming obedient unto death on a cross, and Paul (3:4-14) has expressed his longing to know Christ in a cruciform way.

In another intriguing moment, Paul turns momentarily to address another coworker, asking him to *help* Euodia and Syntyche respond to the appeal: *Yes, and I ask you [singular] also, loyal yokefellow* (= "genuine companion"), *help these women*. What intrigues is that in a letter addressed to the whole church he should single out one person in this way (which he does nowhere else in his community-directed letters). Since the Philippians knew him well, rather than naming him Paul "authorizes" his assistance with the epithet "genuine companion." The appellation *yokefellow,* along with the adjective "genuine" (which he uses elsewhere to refer to intimate coworkers), indicates the closest kind of partnership between him and Paul. Although well-known and currently living there, he is almost certainly not a native of Philippi (since the others named and unnamed certainly are). Most likely he is one of Paul's itinerant coworkers who is presently on the scene there. Luke would fit the description perfectly. Not only was he such a "true companion," but in Acts 16 the "we" narrative takes Luke to Philippi, where it leaves off until Paul's return to Philippi some four to six years later in 20:1-5. The author of Acts surely intends his readers to understand that he had spent these intervening years in Philippi. If so, then as one of Paul's most trusted companions, he had given oversight to that work for some years in the past.

Paul's erstwhile companion is thus asked to help Euodia and Syntyche, obviously to "be of the same mind" *in the Lord*. It is perhaps significant for our day to note the mediatorial role that Paul's *yokefellow* was expected to play, rather than leaving the two women to work out the problem on their own. Even so, Paul's focus is still on Euodia and Syntyche, not on his yokefellow, and especially, as throughout the letter,

---

any of Paul's companions. All of this makes perfectly good sense if Luke had at some earlier point left for Philippi—and was perhaps the catalyst of their recent revival of material support (4:10). None of this can be proved, of course. Nonetheless, it fits all the available historical data, and the epithet *true yokefellow* would be especially fitting of Luke in light of the affectionate language in Colossians 4:14. At the same time the reason for addressing one person among them in the second-person singular is also resolved.

their (including the whole community) partnership with him *in the gospel.* His word order tells the story: inasmuch as in the gospel they have contended by my side. (On the athletic/military metaphor *contended at my side,* see commentary on 1:27; cf. 2:13-14.)

About *Clement and the rest of my fellow workers* we know nothing. The context demands that they are fellow Philippians. Why Paul should single out Clement is a singular mystery, made all the more so by the unusual way the phrase is attached to the former clause, *along with Clement and the rest.* This can only mean that these have also *contended at my side* along with Euodia and Syntyche *in the cause of the gospel* in Philippi. This is probably as close to an "aside" as one gets in Paul's letters. Having just mentioned Euodia and Syntyche in particular, he includes the others who were with him in that ministry from the beginning, for some good reason mentioning Clement in particular, perhaps not wanting to mention the rest by name lest he exclude any. In its own way, therefore, the clause probably functions as a gentle reminder to all who lead the believing community in Philippi to "have the same mindset in the Lord," even though that is not specifically said of or to them.

As so often in this letter, even here Paul concludes on an eschatological note. The ultimate reason for all of them (Euodia, Syntyche, Clement and the rest) to get it together in Philippi, as they await from heaven the coming of their Lord and Savior (3:20), is that their *names are in the book of life.* This unusual (for Paul) language is common stock from his Jewish heritage, where the faithful were understood to have their names recorded in the heavenly "book of the living," meaning the book that has recorded in it those who have received divine life (thus "the book of the living," Ps 68:29) and are thus destined for glory.

With these words Paul brings the specific hortatory sections of the letter to conclusion. In both verses 1 and 2-3 he has picked up the eschatological note from 3:20-21 that immediately precedes; and in both cases the note is affirmation and reassurance. If his concern in these exhortations is with the present—the believers' steadfastness and unity for the sake of the gospel in Philippi—his focus has regularly been on their certain future. He and they together have their names recorded *in the book of life,* and for that reason, as a colony of heaven in the Roman colony of Philippi, they need to live the life of the future now as they await its consummation.

When the dust clears and one gets beyond the specifics about names and "women in leadership," it is hard to imagine New Testament exhortations that are more contemporary—for every age and clime—than these. To *stand firm in the Lord* is not just a word for the individual believer, as such words are often taken, but for any local body of believers. The gospel is ever and always at stake in our world, and the call to God's people, whose *names are* written *in the book of life,* is to live that life now in whatever "Philippi" and in the face of whatever opposition it is found. But to do so effectively, its people, especially those in leadership, must learn to subordinate personal agendas to the larger agenda of the gospel, "to have the same mindset in the Lord." This means humbling, sacrificial giving of oneself for the sake of others; but then that is what the gospel is all about. So in effect these exhortations merely call us to genuine Christian life in the face of every form of pagan and religious opposition.

At the same time, here is one of those pieces of "mute" evidence for women in leadership in the New Testament, significant in this case for its offhanded, presuppositional way of speaking about them. To deny women's role in the church in Philippi is to fly full in the face of the text. Here is the evidence that the Holy Spirit is gender-blind, that he gifts as he wills. Our task is to recognize his gifting and to assist all such people, male and female, to "have the same mindset in the Lord," so that together they will be effective in doing the gospel.

☐ Concluding Matters (4:4-23)

Paul's basic concerns about the Philippians' "affairs" have now been addressed; but there is still one remaining item—an appropriate response to their gift. Thus far, in the framework of friendship, Paul has dealt with his affairs and with their affairs—twice. Now he moves toward a conclusion. Typically (in light of his extant letters), he begins his "concluding matters" with a series of brief exhortations (4:4-9). Also in typical fashion he concludes with a series of brief greetings (vv. 21-23). What is atypical, but turns out to be a rhetorical coup, is the insertion of his appreciation for their gift (vv. 10-20) between these two "typical" items (although it is not unlike the much shorter insertion about the letter-bearers in 1 Cor 16:15-18; so what is "typical"?).

The most likely reason for placement here is rhetorical, having to do with the orality of the culture. The letter was to be read aloud among the community gathered for worship. The last words left ringing in their ears before the (very brief) greetings would be the doxology of verse 20, a corporate response to their gift to Paul as a pleasing sacrifice to God, who in turn will "meet all your needs" according to his riches in glory "in Christ Jesus."

But even in these typical—and atypical—matters Paul's central focus remains the same: the Philippians' relationship with Christ as that is evidenced in their partnership with Paul in the gospel (vv. 14-17). Everything is still "in Christ Jesus/the Lord" (vv. 5, 7, 10, 13, 19, 21, 23); yet the brief exhortations themselves conclude by urging them once more to put into practice what they have learned, received, heard or seen in Paul (v. 9). Meanwhile "the peace of God" will guard them (v. 7) and "the God of peace" will be with them (v. 9).

Concluding Exhortations (4:4-9) These concluding exhortations, very like what one finds elsewhere (e.g., 1 Cor 16:13; 2 Cor 13:11; 1 Thess 5:12-24), are tailored to the situation in Philippi. Among other things they are to *rejoice in the Lord,* to let their "gentle forbearance" *be evident to all* (including those who oppose them) and to *not be anxious about anything* (given the present opposition and suffering), but let *prayer* and *thanksgiving* lead them to experience God's *peace*. The exhortations fall into two clear parts: verses 4-7, in which Paul appropriates his Jewish heritage, and verses 8-9, which reflect both his Hellenistic Jewish background (Jewish wisdom) and the best of Greco-Roman philosophical virtues.

The heart of the first set reflects the threefold expression of Jewish piety—rejoicing in the Lord, prayer and thanksgiving—which are basic to the Psalter: "the righteous rejoice in the LORD" (Ps 64:10; 97:12) as they "come before him with thanksgiving" (Ps 95:2; 100:4) to pray in his sanctuary (Ps 61:1-4; 84:1-8). For Paul these are the work of the Holy Spirit in the life of the believer and especially of the believing congregation. They are expressed as imperatives because, in keeping with the

Old Testament, devotion and ethics are inseparable responses to grace. The truly godly person both longs for God's presence, where one pours out one's heart to God in joy, prayer and thanksgiving, and lives in God's presence by "doing" the righteousness of God. Otherwise piety is merely religion, not devotion.

Also in keeping with the Psalter, these (second-person plural) imperatives exemplify the conjunction between individual and corporate piety (see commentary on 2:4 and 13). For Paul joy, prayer and thanksgiving, evidenced outwardly by *gentleness* (v. 5) and inwardly by God's *peace* in their midst (v. 9), have first to do with the (gathered) people of God; but the fact that God's peace will serve as a garrison for *your hearts and minds* reminds us that what is to be reflected in the gathered community must first of all be the experience of each believer.

Rejoice, Give Thanks and Pray (4:4-7) As elsewhere (2 Cor 13:11; 1 Thess 5:16), Paul begins with *rejoice,* here repeating 3:1 exactly, *rejoice in the Lord*—with the adverbial addition *always* (from 1 Thess 5:16). Thus it serves both to frame the preceding section on "their affairs," giving a context for the warnings and appeals in that section, and to introduce the final series of encouragements and exhortations. The two adverbs *always* and *again* tell us much, especially that this is not just "typical" and therefore to be passed over as a nice Christian platitude, but crucial to the whole of this letter.

Joy, unmitigated, untrammeled joy, is—or at least should be—the distinctive mark of the believer in Christ Jesus. The wearing of black and the long face, which so often came to typify some later expressions of Christian piety, are totally foreign to Paul's version; Paul the theologian of grace is equally the theologian of joy. Christian joy does not come and go with one's circumstances; rather it is predicated altogether on one's relationship with the Lord and is thus an abiding, deeply spiritual quality of life. It finds expression in "rejoicing," which is an imperative, not an option. With its concentration *in the Lord,* rejoicing is *always* to mark individual and corporate life in Philippi. They who "serve by the Spirit of God" (3:3) do so in part by *rejoicing in the Lord,* whatever else may be their lot. In this letter "whatever else" includes opposition and suffering at the hands of the local citizens of the Empire, where Caesar was honored as "lord." In the face of such, the Philippians are to rejoice in *the* Lord *always*." (See further comment on 1:18; 2:2, 17-18; 3:1.)

The second imperative, *let your gentleness be evident to all,* follows from the first. The Lord to whom they belong has graciously set them free for joy—always. At the same time others should know them for their "gentle forbearance" (NIV *gentleness*) toward one another and toward all, including those who are currently making life miserable for them. *Gentleness* is used by Hellenistic writers and in the LXX primarily to refer to God (or the gods) or to the "noble," who are characterized by their "gentle forbearance" toward others. That is most likely its sense here, only now as the disposition of all of God's people.

This is the Pauline version of 1 Peter 2:23, spoken of Christ but urged on Christian slaves: "when they hurled their insults at him, he did not retaliate; when he suffered, he made no threats. Instead, he entrusted himself to him who judges justly." It is this gentle forbearance and meekness of Christ, to which Paul appealed in 2 Corinthians 10:1, which he here calls the believers to exhibit in Philippi.

The sudden appearance of an indicative *(the Lord is near)* is as surprising as its intent is obscure. Does Paul intend "Rejoice in the Lord always; *and* let your gentleness be evident to all, *for* the [coming of] the Lord is near"? Or "*Because* the Lord is [always] near, do not be anxious about anything"? Or does he intend a bit of both, perhaps something as close to intentional double-entendre as one finds in the apostle?

On the one hand, this looks very much like another instance of intertextuality, purposely echoing Psalm 145:18, "The LORD is near to all who call on him." In this case it introduces verses 6-7 as an expression of realized eschatology: "Because the Lord is ever present, do not be anxious but pray." On the other hand (or perhaps at the same time), it also echoes the apocalyptic language of Zephaniah 1:7 and 14 ("the day of the LORD is near"), picked up by Paul in Romans 13:12, and found in James 5:8, regarding the coming of the Lord.

On the whole it seems likely that this is primarily intended as the last in the series of eschatological words to this suffering congregation, again

4:6 The verb translated *present (gnōrizesthō)* means to "let God know." There is perhaps a wordplay with *gnōsthetō* (be evident) in verse 5. Although this is something of a colloquialism—God hardly needs to be informed about our requests—our doing so

reminding them of their sure future despite present difficulties. It thus functions as encouragement and affirmation. Since the Philippians' present suffering is at the hands of those who proclaim Caesar as Lord, they are reminded that the true *Lord is near*. Their eschatological vindication is close at hand. At the same time, by using the language of the Psalter, Paul is encouraging them to pray in the midst of their present distress, because *the Lord is near* in a very real way to those who call on him now.

Borrowing from the Jesus tradition, that the children of the kingdom are to live without care—but not "uncaring" or "careless"—Paul turns to one consequence of the Lord's being *near*. They are to live without anxiety, instead entrusting their lives to God with *prayer* and *thanksgiving*. Apprehension and fear mark the life of the unbelieving, the untrusting, for whom the present is all there is, and for whom the present is so uncertain—or for many filled with distress and suffering, like the Philippians. On the contrary, Paul urges, *in everything, by prayer and petition, with thanksgiving, present your requests to God. In everything* stands in contrast to *not . . . about anything* and means "in all the details and circumstances of life." The three words for prayer are not significantly distinguishable; *requests (aitēmata)* are "made known" before God by *prayer (proseuchē)* and *petition (deēsis)*. In so doing one acknowledges utter dependence on God while at the same time expressing complete trust in him.

Petition accompanied by *thanksgiving* puts both prayer and our lives into proper theological perspective. *Thanksgiving* is a recognition that everything comes as gift, the verbalization before God of his goodness and generosity. Gratitude thus acknowledged begets generosity. Indeed, lack of gratitude is the first step to idolatry (Rom 1:21). Paul's own life was accentuated by thanksgiving; and he could not imagine Christian life that was not a constant outpouring of gratitude to God. Thus *thanksgiving* does not mean to say "thank you" in advance for gifts to be received; rather, it is the absolutely basic posture of the believer and the proper context for petitioning God. It is also the key to the affirmation

---

nonetheless carries theological importance. For the believer it is an expression of humility and dependence.

that follows.

Paul deliberately conjoins *the peace of God* with the exhortation to pray in trusting submission *with thanksgiving*. This is God's alternative to anxiety, in the form of affirmation and promise. As we submit our situation to God in *prayer, with thanksgiving, . . . the peace of God* in turn *will guard* our *hearts and minds*—because we are *in Christ Jesus*. That Paul expresses *peace* in such terms is probably an indication that one can make too much of the differences within this believing community, implied in 2:1-4 and made explicit in 4:2. He is indeed concerned that all of them "have the same mindset" as they "do" the gospel in Philippi; but in contrast to other letters, he does not express peace as an imperative (cf. Col 3:15) but as an indicative, closely related to their trusting God in prayer.

Like joy, peace is a fruit of the Spirit (Gal 5:22). It is especially associated with God and his relationship to his people. Here it is *the peace of God* because God is *the God of peace* (Phil 4:9), the God who dwells in total *shalom* (wholeness, well-being) and who gives such shalom to his people. Such peace *transcends all understanding*. This could mean "beyond all human comprehension," which in one sense is certainly true. More likely Paul intends that God's peace totally transcends the merely human, unbelieving mind, which is full of anxiety because it cannot think higher than itself. Our prayer to the God who is totally trustworthy is accompanied by his *peace*, not because he answers according to our wishes but because his peace totally transcends our merely human way of perceiving the world. Fortunately, God's people do not need to have it all figured out in order to trust him!

Such peace will therefore *guard* our *hearts* and thoughts (NIV *minds*). In the Hebrew view the heart is the center of one's being, out of which flows all of life (e.g., Mk 7:21). God's *peace* will do what instruction in "wisdom" urged the young to do: "Above all else, guard your heart, for it is the wellspring of life" (Prov 4:23). In the present context God's peace will be his "garrison" (a striking military metaphor) around our *hearts* when anxiety threatens. It will also guard our

---

4:8-9 These two sentences bear remarkable structural similarity (lost in most English translations) that probably indicates some kind of close relationship between them: "Whatever things are [repeated six times] . . . , if there be any true virtue, these things put

"thoughts"—those very thoughts that lead to fear and distress and that keep one from trusting prayer. As so often in this letter, such protection is *in* (or "by") *Christ Jesus*. It is the Philippians' relationship to God through Christ, in whom they trust and in whom they rejoice, that is the key to all of these imperatives and this affirming indicative.

Even though the experience of God's peace happens first of all at the individual level, it is doubtful whether in this context it refers only to "the well-arranged heart." For Paul peace is primarily a community matter. As noted below (Phil 4:9), the ascription *God of peace* occurs in contexts where community unrest is lurking. Indeed, apart from the standard salutation the mention of peace in Paul's letters occurs most often in community or relational settings (e.g., Rom 14:19; Eph 2:14-17; 4:3; Col 3:15). Thus the Philippians need not have anxiety in the face of opposition, because they together will experience the protection of God's *peace* in the midst of that conflict; and they who have been urged over and again to "have the same mindset" are here assured that the peace of God which surpasses merely human understanding will also protect their thoughts as they live out the gospel together in Philippi.

Joy, prayer, thanksgiving, peace—these identify Pauline spirituality. Such lives are further marked by gentle forbearance and no anxiety. The key lies with the indicative, *the Lord is near*—now and to come. In a post-Christian, postmodern world, which has generally lost its bearings because it has generally abandoned its God, such spirituality is very often the key to effective evangelism. In a world where fear is a much greater reality than joy, our privilege is to live out the gospel of true shalom, wholeness in every sense of that word, and to point others to its source. We can do that because the Lord is near in this first sense, by the Spirit who turns our present circumstances into joy and peace and who prompts our prayer and thanksgiving. And we should be at that task with greater concern than many of us are, because *the Lord is near* in the eschatological sense as well.

On Good Thoughts and Following Paul (4:8-9) With a *finally, brothers [and sisters]*, Paul brings the hortatory part of the letter to

---

your minds to," compared to "what things you have both . . . and [repeated four times] . . . in me, these things also put into practice."

conclusion. There remains but the acknowledgment of their gift. These final two sentences need to be held tightly together, not only because their structural similarity suggests as much, but especially because the truth of the one is to be assessed in light of the other.

For many who were raised in evangelical traditions, verse 8 ought to be a breath of fresh air. Contrary to what is often taught, implicitly if not explicitly, there is a place in Christian life for taking into serious account the best of the world in which we live, even though it may not be (perish the thought!) overtly Christian. Or to put it another way, it is decidedly not Paul's view that only what is explicitly Christian (be it literature, art, music, movies or whatever) is worth seeing or hearing. Truth and beauty are where you find them. But at all times the gospel is the ultimate paradigm for what is *true, noble* or *admirable*. Or perhaps you have not noticed that many truly great movies (e.g., *Spitfire Grill*) find their greatness because they tell our story (redemption through self-sacrifice), probably without even knowing it.

There is nothing else like verse 8 in Paul's extant letters. It reflects a world with which the Philippians were familiar before they had ever become followers of Christ and friends of Paul; for although some of these words are common stock in Jewish wisdom, they are especially the language of Hellenistic moralism (and would be quite at home in Epictetus's *Discourses*). In effect Paul tells the Philippian believers to take into account the best of their Greco-Roman heritage, as long as it has moral excellence and is *praiseworthy*. Verse 9 puts that into perspective: they comply with the first set of exhortations by putting into practice what they have learned from Paul as teacher and have seen modeled in his life. The whole concludes with the promise of God's abiding presence as *the God of peace*.

The verb *logizomai* ordinarily means "to reckon" in the sense of "take into account," rather than simply to think about. Since the first four words already point to what is virtuous (NIV *excellent*) and *praiseworthy*, Paul most likely adds the proviso because he intends them to select out what is morally *excellent* and *praiseworthy* from *whatever* belongs to the world around them, and to do so on the basis of Christ.

They should thus give consideration first to whatever is *true*, a word that is narrowly circumscribed in Paul's letters, finding its measure in

God (Rom 1:18, 25) and the gospel (Gal 2:5; 5:7). *Noble* is a word that most often has a "sacred" sense ("revered" or "majestic") but here probably denotes "honorable," "noble" or "worthy of respect." Like truth, *right* for Paul is always defined by God and his character. Thus even though this is one of the cardinal virtues of Greek antiquity, in Paul it carries the further sense of "righteousness," so that it is not defined by merely human understanding of what is "right" or "just" but by God and his relationship with his people. *Pure* is a word that originated in the religious cultus, where what had been sanctified for the temple could not have blemishes. Here it has to do with whatever is not besmirched or tainted in some way by evil. Like *truth* (1:18), it occurs earlier in this letter (1:17), referring to the "impure" motives of those wishing to afflict Paul.

With the fifth and sixth words *(lovely* and *admirable)* we step off New Testament turf altogether—linguistically, at least—onto the unfamiliar ground of Hellenism. Nonetheless, these words remind us that common grace is a New Testament reality. *Lovely* refers to what people consider "lovable" in the sense of having a friendly disposition toward. Here is the word that throws the net broadly, so as to include conduct that has little to do with morality in itself but is recognized as admirable by the world at large. It could refer to a Beethoven symphony as well as to the work of Mother Teresa among the poor of Calcutta; the former is lovely and enjoyable, the latter admirable as well as moral. *Admirable,* although not quite a synonym of *lovely,* belongs to the same general category of "virtues." Rather than referring to a virtue in the moral sense, it represents the kind of conduct that is worth considering because it is well spoken of by people in general.

It is probably the lack of inherent morality in the last two words that called forth the interrupting double proviso: *if anything is excellent,* if anything is *praiseworthy. Aretē (excellent)* is the primary Greek word for "virtue" or "moral excellence" and is generally avoided by the LXX translators. Although it is not found elsewhere in Paul, the present usage, along with "contentment" in verse 11, is clear evidence that he felt no need to shy away from the language of the Greek moralists. What he intends, of course, is that "virtue" be filled with Christian content, exemplified by his own life and teaching (v. 9). Likewise with *praise-*

worthy. Although this word probably refers to the approval of others, the basis has been changed from general ethical judgment to conduct that is in keeping with God's own righteousness. While not inherent in verse 8 itself, such an understanding of these words comes from the immediately following exhortation to imitate Paul, which in turn must be understood in light of what has been said to this point.

It is not surprising that the concluding exhortations in this letter should end on the note of imitation. In effect verse 9 summarizes, as well as concludes, the letter. Paul's concern throughout has been the gospel, especially its lived-out expression in the world. To get there he has informed the Philippians of his response to his own present suffering (1:12-26), reminded them of the "way of Christ" (2:6-11) and told his own story (3:4-14), all of which were intended to appeal, warn and encourage them to steadfastness and unity in the face of opposition. Now he puts it to them plainly, as the final proviso to the preceding list of virtues that they should take into account. Read that list, he now tells them, in light of what *you have learned* and *received* and *heard* and *seen in me,* and above all else *put* these things (what *you have learned,* etc.) *into practice.*

Learned and *received* reflect Paul's Jewish tradition, where what is *learned* is thus *received* by students; *heard* and *seen in me* appeared in this way in 1:30 in the context of their common struggle of suffering for Christ's sake. Given the overall context of this letter, one may rightly assume that Paul is once again calling the Philippians to the kind of cruciform existence (see note on 1:11) he has been commending and urging throughout. Only as they are "conformed to Christ's death" as Paul himself seeks continually to be, even as they eagerly await the final consummation at Christ's coming, will they truly live what is *excellent* and *praiseworthy* from Paul's distinctively "in Christ" perspective.

The exhortations are thus finished; so Paul rightly concludes with a "wish of peace," which here takes the form of ultimate benediction, that *the God of peace will be with you.* The ascription *God of peace* is derived from the Old Testament; every occurrence in Paul's letters is in contexts where strife or unrest is close at hand (cf. Rom 16:20; 1 Cor 14:33; 2 Thess 3:16). Although "strife" is hardly the word to describe the Philippian scene, he nonetheless signs off with this affirmation, perhaps significantly so in light of the repeated exhortation to "have the same mindset."

Will be with you reflects the motif of God's presence, the desire for which determines so much in Jewish piety and theology, both in the Old Testament and in the intertestamental period. For Paul, and the rest of the New Testament, the way God is now present is by his Spirit, who is the fulfillment of the promises that God will put his Spirit into his people's hearts so that they will obey him (Ezek 36:27). In Paul's understanding this is how *the God of peace will be*—and already is—*with you*. And the fruit of the Spirit is *peace* (Phil 4:7).

These concluding exhortations call us to embrace what is good wherever we find it, including the culture with which we are most intimately familiar, but to do so in a discriminating way, the key to which is the gospel Paul preached and lived—about a crucified Messiah, whose death on a cross served both to redeem us and to reveal the character of God into which we are continually being transformed.

This is an especially relevant word in our postmodern, media-saturated world, where truth is relative and morality is up for grabs. The most common response to such a culture, unfortunately, is not discrimination but rejection or absorption. This text suggests a better way, that we approach the marketplace, the arts, the media, the university looking for what is *true* and *noble* and *admirable,* but that we do so with a discriminating eye and heart, for which the Crucified One serves as the template. Indeed, if one does not consider carefully and then discriminate on the basis of the gospel, what is rejected very often are the mere trappings, the more visible expressions, of the "world," while its antigospel values (relativism, materialism, hedonism, nationalism, individualism, to name but a few) are absorbed into the believer through cultural osmosis. This text reminds us that the head counts for something, after all; but it must be a sanctified head, ready to *practice* the gospel it knows through what has been *learned* and *received.*

Acknowledging Their Gift: Friendship and the Gospel (4:10-20)

So how would you feel? Your financially strapped college group has scraped together a considerable amount of cash in order to help a former member do humanitarian missionary work in Central Africa. After some time you receive word back—a long letter in fact—which goes on and on about how the group might better serve the Lord on its own campus, but nary a word about the gift. And then at the end, with a kind of "by the way," the gift is mentioned; but even so more time is spent on how little the gift was really needed than on thanksgiving itself. You would have a right to be a bit miffed. Both our secular and spiritual cultures expect something better of friends, and no one likes an ingrate. Which is exactly how many feel about Paul at this point in the letter.

Carrying our own feelings about our "missionary friend" back into Paul's letter to the Philippians, however, is its own form of cultural gaffe, a clear reflection that we cannot really imagine a culture in which such things might be done differently. But different they were indeed; and we know this because many of the philosophers wrote treatises on friendship and on the benefits of friendship that were a part of their cultural presuppositions. It turns out in fact that the placement of Paul's gratitude for their gift at the end, his avoidance of the word meaning "thank you" and the way he wrestles with reciprocity (the "giving and receiving" [v. 15] of benefits) are all perfectly explainable on the grounds of Greco-Roman friendship, which is presupposed at every point in this letter, and now especially in this passage.

With his major concerns about the Philippians' affairs now addressed, and the concluding exhortations given, Paul turns at last then to the first reason for the letter—to acknowledge their recent gift and thus to rejoice over this evidence of friendship renewed. To this point he has not thanked them directly, although his gratitude is clearly implied in 1:3-7 and 2:25, 30 (perhaps 2:17). But now he does so, and at the end (4:18-20) does so in a profuse way.

Three matters thus intertwine. First is his genuine gratitude for their recent gift, expressed three times in three variations (vv. 10, 14, 18). This is set, second, in the primary context of friendship: mutuality and reciprocity, evidenced by "giving and receiving" (v. 15)—a theme that gets strained in this case because of (1) his being on the receiving end of that for which he has nothing to give in return and (2) his and their

---

4:10-20 For a thorough discussion of the reciprocity of "giving and receiving" in Greco-Roman friendship, plus an overview of the many views that have been offered on this passage, see Peterman 1997. He has also demonstrated convincingly that this mutuality also carries some of the baggage of a patron-client relationship, due to his role as apostle of Jesus Christ. Third, and most significant (and typical!), this sociological reality is subsumed under the greater reality of the gospel; thus the whole climaxes in doxology. All of this is fashioned with consummate artistry, so that their "giving," his "receiving," and the long-term partnership in the gospel which their gift reaffirms climax in verses 18-20 with gratitude (from Paul), accolade and promise (from God to them), and doxology (from both to God).

A passage like this should also be read in light of Paul's unsolicited, lavish praise of this church in 2 Corinthians 8:1-5, with its (thoroughly Christian) equation "affliction + poverty = abounding in generosity." It is unlikely that the Philippians have changed radically in the intervening few years. Indeed, it is precisely this quality of their Christian life, expressed toward him within the cultural context of friendship, that leads Paul to give thanks in this way—as "rejoicing in the Lord" (see v. 10) and as an outburst of praise to God's glory (v. 20). Here is a community where the gospel had done its certain work.

Their Gift and Paul's "Need" (4:10-13) Two matters are taken up in these opening sentences. First (v. 10a), Paul rejoices over their renewing the first feature of friendship, giving and receiving. But having expressed that in terms of *at last,* he is quick to caution that they must not hear him wrongly (v. 10b). He knows that the long hiatus in this tangible evidence of their partnership in the gospel was due to the lack of *opportunity*. Second (vv. 11-13), Paul wants to make sure that they do not understand his joy as based on *need*. This demurral is his way of reminding the Philippians that theirs was true friendship, without utilitarian origins based on mutual usefulness.

1. *Their Gift—Friendship Renewed (4:10).* There is nothing quite so buoyant to the weary soul as an unexpected visit from an old friend. No wonder as Paul turns to express gratitude for their gift, he starts by telling them that he did then what he has been urging them to do throughout: "I rejoiced" (NIV *rejoice*) *greatly in the Lord.* The reason for his great joy is expressed with a botanical metaphor, meaning to

---

thanksgiving is not "thankless," as many have argued.

4:10 The NIV understands *echarēn* ("I rejoiced") to refer to the time of writing (thus reading the verb as an "epistolary aorist," written about the present but put in the past because that

"blossom again"—like perennials or the spring shoots of deciduous trees and bushes. After a period of some dormancy in the matter of giving and receiving, the Philippians *have* thus *renewed* this dimension of their friendship with Paul. The adverb *at last* likewise implies a hiatus in their giving, not meaning—as he suddenly realizes they may take it—"finally, at last," as though he had been expecting something in the meantime, but points to the conclusion of the hiatus. Thus "now, finally, you were able to do what for a long time you could not."

This in turn is expressed in language special to this letter: to show *concern for me*. Here begins a series of word repetitions and wordplays that appear regularly in this final section of the letter. The verb *phroneō* appeared first in the thanksgiving (1:7) to refer to Paul's "feeling this way" about them. Elsewhere in the letter it means "have a (certain) mindset." Here it carries the sense of a mind set toward the care of another; hence the NIV's *you have been concerned.* This is made certain by the qualifier *indeed, you have been concerned, but you had no opportunity to show it.* Two points of grammar indicate he is trying to deflect possible misunderstanding of the first clause. He begins, first, with a contraction that picks up *your concern* and intensifies it; second, both verbs in this clause are Greek imperfects, implying a continual *concern* for Paul with a likewise ongoing lack of *opportunity* to do anything about it. Together they mean something like "with reference to which [concern] you were indeed continually concerned." Thus he recognizes—and acknowledges—that the hiatus had nothing to do with their lack of *concern* but with a lack of *opportunity*.

2. *Paul's "Need" and Christ's Sufficiency (4:11-13).* Typically, Paul adds qualifier to qualifier, now putting the entire event into christological perspective. It would be wrong for the Philippians to infer that he rejoiced over their gift *because I am in need,* that his joy was over their gift as such, as though it had to do with finally being able to eat again. Rather, his joy is over friendship's having had opportunity to blossom again; and their friendship, he points out further, is not utilitarian in the sense of what he can secure from it.

---

will be the perspective of the reader). More likely, however, this is a true aorist; Paul is recalling his rejoicing when Epaphroditus arrived.

Here is the second in the series of word repetitions and wordplays. He had told them in 2:30 that he did have "lack"—of their presence!—which was made up in part by Epaphroditus's coming. Now he says that his joy is *not* over their filling his "lack" in the material sense (although he gladly acknowledges in 4:18 that he was "filled to the full" by their gift). But that also calls for further explanation; so rather than take up the matter of what his joy is all about (which comes next in vv. 14-17), he instead goes on to elaborate why their ministering to his *need* was not the reason for his joy.

And with that he launches into one of his finer moments. With the language of Stoicism still ringing in his own mind (from v. 8), he moves into the Stoic stronghold of *autarkeia* (contentment based on self-sufficiency) and transforms it by means of the gospel into "Christ-sufficiency." To be sure, the outward expression and inner result between him and the Stoics appear much the same; but in fact Paul and Seneca are a thousand leagues apart. The Stoic's (and Cynic's) sufficiency or contentment comes from within; Paul's comes from without, from his being a man in Christ, on whom he is totally dependent and thus not independent at all in the Stoic sense. Because Paul and the Philippians are both "in Christ," neither is dependent on the other for life in the world; but also because they are both "in Christ," Paul received their gift with joy.

He begins with the premise: *I have learned to be content [autarkēs] whatever the circumstances.* The rest is explanation. His *circumstances* run the gamut from being "humbled" (NIV *in need*) to "abounding" (NIV *have plenty*). These are then elaborated—and partly repeated—in light of his present imprisonment as *well fed or hungry* and, now in reverse order, "abounding" (NIV *in plenty*) or "lacking" (NIV *in want*). Although we do not know how much hunger he experienced before Epaphroditus arrived, he does pick up the verb "abound" again in verse 18 specifically to refer to how the Philippians' gift has altered his circumstances: *I have received full payment* and abound (NIV *and even more*); *I am amply supplied, now that I have received from Epaphroditus the gifts you sent.*

4:11 For a brief collection of Stoic-Cynic texts that idealize *autarkēs,* see Fee 1995:431 n. 37.

By starting with *I know* (by experience) *what it is to be* humbled, Paul says such an "un-Stoic" thing that one suspects he is making sure his premise is not understood in a Stoic way. Not only is "humbled" not the ordinary verb for being *in need,* it is in fact something to be avoided. Some Stoics may have reveled in "want"; none of them could tolerate the "humiliation of humility." Thus even though the broad term is used to embrace his being *in need,* with this word Paul is also embracing a way of life similar to that of his Lord (2:8; cf. Mt 11:28), a way of life that finds expression elsewhere in his various "hardship lists" (e.g., 1 Cor 4:11-13; 2 Cor 6:4-10).

The broader vocabulary of *need* and *plenty* implies "in every which way"; so in light of his present circumstances he specifies, *whether well fed or hungry.* The Philippians themselves have often been party to his being *well fed:* when he and his coworkers lived in Philippi under the generous patronage of Lydia (Acts 16:15) and when the Philippians repeatedly supplied his material needs in Thessalonica (Phil 4:15 below) and Corinth (2 Cor 11:9), and perhaps elsewhere. But in a prison system where prisoners must secure their own food supply, he also has had plenty of opportunity to go *hungry.* Indeed, he has *learned the secret* of both, a verb used primarily for initiation into the mystery cults. Thus "I have gotten in on the secret of both having a full stomach and going hungry."

But Paul is neither reveling in the one nor complaining of the other. His various hardship lists make it clear he had experienced "plenty" of "want." But in contrast to some of the Cynics, he did not choose "want" as a way of life, so as to demonstrate himself *autarkēs;* rather he had learned to accept whatever came his way, knowing that his life was not conditioned by either. His relationship to Christ made them both essentially irrelevant. Thus he concludes: *I can do everything through him who gives me strength.* With that he transforms his very Stoic-sounding sentences into a sufficiency quite beyond himself, in Christ, the basis and source of everything for Paul. Thus "self-sufficiency" becomes contentment because of his "Christ-sufficiency."

Here is a much-used sentence from Paul that is often taken out of context and thus abused. While *everything* seems to be all-embracing and is often applied to one's activities (especially those that are personally demanding—athletics, learning to drive and the like), in context it refers primarily to living in *want* or *plenty*. Paul finds Christ sufficient in times of bounty as well as in times of need! Thus, rather than being a christianized version of the Stoic ideal, this passage points up the absolute Christ-centeredness of Paul's whole life. He is a man in Christ. As such he takes what Christ brings. If it means "plenty," he is a man in Christ, and that alone; if it means "want," he is still a man in Christ, and he accepts deprivation as part of his understanding of discipleship.

Given the context, this brief autobiographical moment probably also serves as a paradigm. He has just urged them to practice what he both taught and modeled (4:9). In the midst of their own present difficulties, here is what they too should learn of life in Christ, that being "in him who enables" means to be "content" whatever their circumstances.

Their Gift as Partnership in the Gospel (4:14-17) Returning to the language of the thanksgiving in 1:3-8, Paul resumes what he began in 4:10, moving it a step forward. In verse 10 he joyfully received the Philippians' gift as tangible evidence that their *concern for* him had "blossomed afresh." Since their gift met his material needs during imprisonment, it serves as evidence of their being "partners with him" *(synkoinōneō)* in his "affliction" *(thlipsis;* NIV *share in my troubles);* in verses 15-16 it is likewise evidence of their partnership with him in the work of the gospel. As in 1:5-7, their love for Paul and serving the cause of the gospel blend. After all, to love Paul is to love the gospel. But also as in the preceding paragraph, he qualifies what he says about the gift itself; again, it is not that he is not grateful (4:18-20 makes that abundantly clear) but that the gift is secondary to their relationship, in this case expressed in terms of how their gift to him is seen from above—a point that gets full elaboration in verses 18-19.

To speak of their gift in terms of "being partners with him in his affliction" echoes both his and their "participation in Christ's sufferings" (3:10) and the mutuality of their suffering together from 1:29-30 and 2:17—although in this case the emphasis is on their succoring him in his time of need. The language *it was good of you* (4:14) also appears on a regular basis in letters of friendship in reference to a benefit that one has received from the other.

The use of *koinōnia* language in verse 14 in turn brings Paul back to the first use of this word in 1:5 (their "participation/partnership with him in the gospel"), but now with specifics. Indeed, the next sentence (4:15-16) holds the key that unlocks many of the mysteries of our letter. Four important reminders are noted. First, *you Philippians . . . shared* (aorist of *koinōneō*) *with me in the matter of giving and receiving* uses the technical language for the mutual giving and receiving of benefits in Greco-Roman friendship. Second, this "partnership" is related to *the gospel* and goes back to their *early days;* third, they are the only church that has entered into this kind of "partnership" with him *(not one church . . . except you only).* And fourth, the earliest evidence for it occurred at his very next stop in Macedonia, *in Thessalonica,* where *you sent me aid* more than once *when I was in need.* Unpacking these four items will tell a lot of the story between Paul and this church—and other churches as well.

First, the crucial matter is Paul's metaphorical use of commercial language that begins here and goes through verse 18: *the matter of giving and receiving* (v. 15); *what may be credited to your account* (v. 17); *I have received full payment* (v. 18). This sudden proliferation of commercial language has long been recognized; only recently has it also been recognized that well before Paul came by it, the language of verse 15 had been co-opted by the philosophers to express the reciprocity of benefits—*the matter of giving and receiving*—in true friendship. In the Greco-Roman world one could not understand genuine friendship without friends' benefit to one another; hence goodwill included mutual "benefits." But since benefits could easily deteriorate into something more utilitarian, Seneca, for example, actually wrote treatises on benefits, both to expound on their nature and necessity and to safeguard them from such deterioration. "Benefits" simply meant that friends could be counted on to help each other out, often at some degree of personal sacrifice—by caring for family, for example (see the sample letter on p. 14, or coming to one's aid in time of need or crisis, or embarking on activities that were of mutual benefit.

The language that had become common parlance for this social phenomenon was borrowed from the world of commerce, which is what Paul is now picking up. His use of this technical language in conjunction with *koinōnia* in this matter implies a friendship agreement that both sides have intentionally entered into. The rest of his plays on the commercial dimension of the metaphor are his own.

Second, as already noted in the thanksgiving (1:5, *your partnership in the gospel from the first day until now),* this relationship goes back to the beginning, and thus to *the early days of your acquaintance with the gospel* (literally "in the beginning of the gospel when I set out from Macedonia"). Although there is some stickiness here in terms of details, together with 1:5 this passage makes clear that the friendship existed while Paul was first among them; it later became a bond between them, as this passage (cf. 1 Thess 2:2) and 2 Corinthians 11:8-9 make certain. This is what leads him in Philippians 4:10 to mention the hiatus, and now renewal, of this partnership.

Third, that *not one church . . . except you only* entered into this relationship with Paul can be taken in at least two ways: as a pejorative swipe at other churches or as a way of reminding the Philippians of the unique relationship he had with them. In light of the evidence especially from 1 and 2 Corinthians, where that church also wanted such a relationship but it was not granted (1 Cor 9:1-18; 2 Cor 11:7-11), the latter of these is surely the more likely. Why Paul chose such a relationship with this one church only is a matter of speculation, most likely related both to his choice to maintain himself hereafter by "working with his own hands" (1 Cor 4:12; 2 Thess 3:6-12) and to the special relationship he had developed with this first Christian congregation on European soil.

Fourth, this relationship, in which their part of the reciprocity was to minister to Paul's physical needs while his was to let this be their way of partnering with him in the advance of the gospel, began *even when I was in Thessalonica.* According to 1 Thessalonians 2:2, his early memory of his time in Philippi had also to do with his suffering and ill treatment there by the authorities; according to Acts 17:1-7, similar ill treatment happened again in Thessalonica—under the charge of treason. So the Philippians' material help during those rough days is now fondly recalled, this time in terms of his *need.* That they gave such help "more than once" (the NIV's *again and again* stretches the idiom a bit) indicates the level of their commitment to him in this matter.

But just as in Philippians 4:10-13, this mention of his *need* immediately calls forth another *not that* qualifier against possible misunderstanding. His short recital of their exemplary history of friendship with him in the matter of *giving and receiving* is not to be taken as an indirect request for more help. Exactly the opposite, and now picking up on the commercial metaphor itself, what he "seeks" (NIV *looking for*), he tells them, is (literally) "the fruit that increases into your account," by which he means metaphorically "an accrual of 'interest' against your divine 'account.' "

When unpacked, the metaphor expresses Paul's real concern for them, found as early as 1:25 in terms of "your progress in the faith." Their giving to him is an expression of love, of the gospel at work in their midst. For Paul every time they do so, it is also evidence of "fruitfulness," of the kind for which he prayed in 1:11. Such fruitfulness has the effect of being entered on the divine ledger as "interest," as the certain indication of the increase of their fruitfulness, which will find its full expression at the coming of Christ. They themselves will be Paul's eschatological "reward" (2:16; 4:1); their gift to him has the effect of accumulating "interest" toward *their* eschatological reward. Their gift, which serves his physical health, serves more significantly as evidence of their spiritual health. What else would one seek, one wonders, in a relationship such as theirs, which is predicated altogether on their mutual belonging to Christ?

Many years ago I heard a wise preacher counsel some younger ministers that Satan has three hounds with which he pursues those in ministry: pride, money and sex. Money is surely not the least of these. It is therefore of some interest for us to note how sensitive Paul is on this matter. He can scarcely speak about it, and especially his relationship to receiving it, without offering a demurral such as one finds in verse 17. This may well account for his (apparent) change of policy when he got to Thessalonica. There were enough itinerant religious and philosophical hucksters about, who according to Dio Chrysostom "used flattery as a cloak for greed" (cf. 1 Thess 2:4), for Paul to set out on a different course of maintenance upon leaving Philippi. Thus he can remind those in both Thessalonica and Corinth that his motives were totally free of pecuniary interests (1 Thess 2:1-10; 2 Cor 12:14-15). Paul did not "seek what is yours, but you" (2 Cor 12:14)—a paradigm for all who are in Christian ministry of any kind.

Gratitude and Divine Reciprocity (4:18-19) These final sentences in Paul's letter to his friends are certain evidence that those who have accused Paul of offering "thankless thanks" in this section (vv. 10-20) have read him poorly—through their own cultural biases. For now he mentions their gift directly. In doing so he soars, piling up verbs at the beginning by which he indicates how richly his own needs have been met by their lavish generosity, and concluding with a change of metaphors expressing God's pleasure over their gift.

The first clause, *I have received full payment,* reflects his final use of the commercial/friendship metaphor, indicating that his "receipt" of what they have "given" puts the "obligation" of friendship back on his side. To this he adds the verb from verse 12; "I abound" (NIV *and even more*), he says, meaning that with the coming of Epaphroditus *with the gifts you sent,* "I have more than enough."

As further indication that the passage is not "thankless," Paul starts all over again. *I am amply supplied,* "filled to the full," he says, and then mentions Epaphroditus and their *gifts* ("the things from you") directly. But in doing so he describes their gift by means of a rich metaphor from the Old Testament sacrifices *(a fragrant offering, an acceptable sacrifice, pleasing to God),* so as also to indicate divine approval for what they have done. The imagery is of the burnt offering, which was understood as a *fragrant offering* to God. The picture is of the "aroma" of the sacrificial fire wafting heavenward—into God's "nostrils," as it were. Properly offered, it becomes *an acceptable sacrifice, pleasing to* him. This, Paul says, is what their gift has amounted to from the divine perspective.

In its own way this sentence thus responds directly to verse 17. Although Paul does not seek the *gift* as such, in fact he has received their gifts, which have resulted in his now "having plenty" (see v. 12). What he does seek, he told them, is "an accrual of interest against your divine account." That, he now tells them with this splendid shift of metaphors, is exactly what has happened. Their gift, which has met Paul's material needs, has by that very fact pleased God, who becomes the focus of the rest of the passage.

The mention of God at the end of verse 18 leads directly to Paul's great master stroke—verse 19. The reciprocity of friendship is now back in Paul's court. But he is in prison and cannot reciprocate directly. So he does an even better thing: Since their gift had the effect of being a sweet-smelling sacrifice, *pleasing to God,* Paul assures them that God, whom he deliberately designates as *my* God, will assume responsibility for reciprocity. Thus, picking up the language "my need" from verse 16 and "fill to the full" from verse 18, he promises them that "my God will fill up every need of yours" (NIV *meet all your needs*).

From his point of view, they obviously have the better of it! First, he promises that God's reciprocation will cover "every need of yours," especially their material needs, as the context demands—but also every other kind of need, as the language demands. One cannot imagine a more fitting way for this letter to conclude, in terms of Paul's final word to them personally. In the midst of their "poverty" (2 Cor 8:2), God will richly supply their material needs. In their present suffering in the face of opposition (1:27-30), God will richly supply what is needed (steadfastness, joy, encouragement). In their need to advance in the faith with one mindset (1:25; 2:1-4; 4:2-3), God will richly supply the grace and humility necessary for it. In the place of both "grumbling" (2:14) and "anxiety" (4:6) God will be present with them as the "God of peace" (4:7, 9). *My God,* Paul says, will act for me on your behalf by "filling to the full" *all your needs.*

And God will do so, Paul says, *according to* his riches in glory (NIV *glorious riches*) *in Christ Jesus.* The Philippians' generosity toward Paul, expressed lavishly at the beginning of verse 18, is exceeded beyond all imagination by the lavish "wealth" of the eternal God, who dwells "in glory" full of *riches* made available to his own *in Christ Jesus.* God's riches are those inherent to his being God, Creator and Lord of all; nothing lies outside his rightful ownership and domain. They are his "in glory" in the sense that they exist in the sphere of God's glory, where God dwells in infinite splendor and majesty, the *glory* that is his as God alone (v. 20). It is *according to* all of this—not "out of" his riches but

4:19 Because "glory" seems to be such a slippery word in English, there is a tendency on the part of recent interpreters and translations to take a phrase like the "in glory" in this sentence and make an adjective *(glorious)* out of it. But that seems to miss too much.

"in accordance with this norm," the infinite riches of grace that belong to God's own glory—that God's full supply will come their way to meet their every need. The language is deliberately expansive; after all, Paul is trying to say something concrete about the eternal God and God's relationship to his people.

Which is why the final word is not the heavenly one, "in glory," but the combined earthly and heavenly one, *in Christ Jesus*. Because Paul has beheld the "glory of God in the face of Christ Jesus" (2 Cor 4:6), expressed in this letter in the majestic Christ narrative in 2:6-11, Paul sees clearly that Christ Jesus is the way God has made his love known and available to his human creatures. This is what the letter has ultimately been all about. It began *in Christ Jesus;* it now concludes *in Christ Jesus*. For Paul "to live is Christ and to die is gain." Thus the final word in the body of the letter proper is this one, "every need of yours *according to* the wealth that is God's in glory made available to you *in Christ Jesus*."

Doxology (4:20) Verses 18-19 say it all; nothing more can be added. So Paul simply bursts into doxology. The indicative yields to the imperative of worship. When one thinks on God's *riches* lavished on us in Christ Jesus, what else is there to do but praise and worship?

Christ is indeed the focus of everything that God has done and is doing in this world and the next, but God the Father is always the first and last word in Paul's theology. *My God* is now *our God and Father;* and the living God, the everlasting One who belongs to the "ages of ages" and who dwells "in glory," is now ascribed the *glory* that is due his name.

All of this because the Philippians have sent Paul material assistance to help him through his imprisonment! True theology is expressed in doxology, and doxology is always the proper response to God, even—especially?—in response to God's prompting friends to minister to friends.

This passage thus belongs to several such doxologies in the Pauline corpus, which come at varied moments and reflect Paul's true theological

"Glory" is a thoroughly biblical word, both to describe what characterizes the God who cannot be seen and to designate thus the sphere of his existence. God dwells "in glory"; and it is in keeping with that norm that he lavishes his grace upon his people.

orientation. The *amen* with which they conclude, taken over by Christians from the Jewish synagogue, is the last word, our "so be it," not only to the doxology itself but especially to the ultimate eschatological words, *for ever and ever.* This is our way of acknowledging that "glory to God for ever and ever" is the way it is and ever will be world without end, no matter what we do. So let us, God's people in all times and climes, join the chorus.

Closing Greetings (4:21-23) As in most of his letters, and in keeping with the conventions of letter-writing in the Greco-Roman world, Paul concludes with the standard greetings (vv. 21-22)—plus a grace-benediction (v. 23). Despite their diversity, the Pauline greetings have three basic components, all of which occur here in their tersest expression:

1. The imperative to *greet all the saints* (which is the way he greets each of them).
2. *Greetings* from his immediate companions.
3. *Greetings* from other *saints* in his present location.

Here the only elaboration, and only surprise, is the inclusion of *those who belong to Caesar's household* in the final greeting. Such greetings are one of the ways Paul kept the various churches aware of and in touch with one another. In their own small way, therefore, they function as part of his concern for the unity of the body of Christ.

Greetings to Each One in Philippi (4:21a) The imperative to *greet* (= "give my greetings to") each one of (NIV *all*) *the saints in Christ Jesus* is notable for both its uniqueness and its brevity. For a community with whom Paul is on such friendly terms, one might have expected more. The brevity is explicable in light of the preceding theological-doxological conclusion. Further greetings would be intrusive, detracting from the words he most wants to leave with them—God's glory out of which he lavishes riches on them in Christ Jesus, to whom all glory is now due.

On the meaning of "saint(s)" see commentary on 1:1. In saying "every saint," Paul is thus not greeting the community lumped together as a

4:22 On *the saints . . . who belong to Caesar's household,* see the introduction, p. 34. Both this phrase and the mention of the Praetorian Guard in 1:13 play havoc with what is currently the most popular view of Paul's place of imprisonment—Ephesus. The problem with this view is that Ephesus was one of the capitals of the province of Asia, which was a senatorial

whole but each member of the community individually. He does not single anyone out, but he does greet each of them in this fashion. It is not clear whether *in Christ Jesus* modifies "every saint" or "give my greetings." The word order would seem to favor the former; but that creates an unusual—and unnecessary—redundancy. To be a saint is to be *in* fellowship with *Christ Jesus.* Moreover, this phrase, which is especially frequent in this letter, usually modifies the verb in its sentence (although 4:19 is a notable exception). Most likely, therefore, Paul intends the greeting to be *in* the name of *Christ Jesus.* They are thus to pass on Paul's greetings to one another, and the greeting is to be *in Christ Jesus,* who is both the source and the focus of their common life together.

Greetings from Believers in Rome (4:21b-22) Next Paul sends greetings from two sets of believers in Rome: *the brothers who are with me* and *all the saints.* His failure to mention the names of his associates in this case is in keeping with the terseness of these greetings. Just as he does not mention anyone in Philippi by name, neither does he mention any of his companions, even though this greeting makes it clear that some of them are still with him (see further commentary on 2:20-21).

The next greeting reaches out to the broader circle of believers in Rome. Here he does indeed say *all the saints,* and he surely intends that, even if many of them do not even know they are being included—and in light of 1:15 and 17 some of those might not wish to be included! But they are all included simply because they all belong to one another, those in Rome to each other and those in Rome to those in Philippi as well.

But in this case Paul adds the intriguing *especially those who belong to Caesar's household. Household* would include household slaves as well as family members, but in either case it refers in particular to those who actually lived in Nero's palace in Rome (now uncovered by archaeologists and accessible to tourists). Two matters are noteworthy.

First, this little phrase joins with mention of the Praetorian Guard in

---

province. The historic tensions between the Senate and the emperor make it altogether unlikely that there were members of the emperor's household in Ephesus in such numbers that Paul would single them out as sending greetings.

1:13 as the strongest kind of evidence for the Roman origins of this letter. Every objection to this takes the form of trying to gainsay a simple historical reality, namely, that both of these groups are especially "at home" in Rome. All other views must seek to discredit the obvious and thereby discount the significance of this notation.

Second, the import of this greeting could hardly be lost on the Philippian believers, whose opposition in part at least stems from the fact that Philippi is a Roman colony, where devotion to Caesar had a long history. Paul and the Philippians have a common source of opposition: they suffer at the hands of Roman citizens loyal to Caesar, Paul as an actual prisoner of Caesar. But by incarcerating him at the heart of the Empire, they have thus brought in a member of the "opposition" who is in the process of creating a "fifth column" within the very walls of the emperor's domicile. Paul either has found or has made disciples of the Lord Jesus among members of the imperial household, who are thus on the Philippians' side in the struggle against those who proclaim Caesar as lord!

Paul is an indomitable apostle of Christ Jesus. Let him loose and he will be among those "who turn the world upside-down" (Acts 17:6; a charge of sedition!) for his Christ; imprison him too close to home and he will turn Caesar's household upside-down as well. Here is a word of encouragement. The "word of life" to which the Philippians hold firm (Phil 2:15-16) has already penetrated the heart of the Empire. They have brothers and sisters in Caesar's own household, who are on their side and now send them greetings; and therefore the Savior whom they await (3:20) will gather some from Caesar's household as well as from Caesar's Philippi when he comes.

The Grace-Benediction (4:23) In all of the extant letters that bear Paul's name, he signs off with this, or a similar, grace-benediction. Like his salutations, Paul's closing greetings are Christianized. Instead of the standard goodbye in Greek letters (*errōso* [literally "be strong"]; cf. the letter of James in Acts 15:29), it is *grace* that he wishes for the Philippians. Although *grace* is primarily from God in Paul's letters, in the grace-benedictions it is invariably *the grace of our Lord Jesus Christ* that he prays will be with them. Thus the final grace serves to "bookend" his letters, which begin with "grace and peace" as part of the greeting (see on 1:2).

On this note the letter comes to an end. One hesitates to draw out too much theology from these rather conventional closing formulas. But as noted at the beginning and elsewhere (e.g., 4:8, 11-13, 15-16) in Paul's hand conventions are never merely conventional. Eventually everything, including these conventions, is brought under the influence of Christ and the gospel. Thus the final greetings of Philippians, which by their threefold elaboration presuppose the church as the body of Christ, are to be given and received as *in Christ Jesus*. And the final *grace* is also from *the Lord Jesus Christ,* so that the whole letter, from beginning to end and everywhere in between, focuses on Christ, who as Paul's life (1:21) is magnified both in his language and in the two narratives that point specifically to him (Christ's in 2:5-11 and Paul's in 3:4-14). To miss this central focus on Christ would be to miss the letter altogether, and to miss the heart of Pauline theology. May we who read this letter as the Word of God follow in Paul's train.

Bibliography

Alexander, Loveday
1989 "Hellenistic Letter-Forms and the Structure of Philippians." *Journal for the Study of the New Testament* 37:87-101.

Barth, Karl
1962 *The Epistle to the Philippians*. Translated by J. W. Leitch. London: SCM Press.

Bauer, Walter
1979 *Greek-English Lexicon of the New Testament and Other Early Christian Literature*. Translation and adaptation of W. Bauer's 4th ed. by W. F. Arndt and F. W. Gingrich; 2nd ed. revised by F. W. Gingrich and F. W. Danker. Chicago: University of Chicago Press.

Beare, Frank W.
1959 *The Epistle to the Philippians*. Black's New Testament Commentaries. New York: Harper.

Bloomquist, L. Gregory
1993 *The Function of Suffering in Philippians*. Journal for the Study of the New Testament Supplements 78. Sheffield, U.K.: JSOT Press.

Bockmuehl, Markus
1997 *The Epistle to the Philippians*. Black's New Testament Commentaries. 4th ed. Peabody, Mass.: Hendrickson (replaces Beare).

Borman, Lukas
1995 *Philippi: Stadt und Christengemeinde ur Zeit des Paulus*. Novum Testamentum Supplements 78. Leiden: Brill.

Collange, Jean-François
1979 *The Epistle of Saint Paul to the Philippians*. Translated by A. W. Heathcote. London: Epworth.

Deissmann, Adolf
1927 *Light from the Ancient East*. 4th English ed. New York: George Doran.

Dunn, J. D. G.
1980 *Christology in the Making*. London: SCM Press.

1991 "Once More, ΠΙΣΤΙΣ ΧΡΙΣΤΟΥ." In *Society of Biblical Literature 1991 Seminar Papers,* pp. 730-44. Edited by E. H. Lovering Jr. Atlanta: Scholars.

Fee, Gordon D.

1967 *The First Epistle to the Corinthians.* Grand Rapids, Mich.: Eerdmans.

1995 *Paul's Letter to the Philippians.* Grand Rapids, Mich.: Eerdmans.

1996 *Paul, the Spirit and the People of God.* Peabody, Mass.: Hendrickson.

Feinberg, Paul D.

1980 "The Kenosis and Christology: An Exegetical-Theological Analysis of Phil 2:6-11." *Trinity Journal* 1:21-46.

Garland, David E.

1985 "The Composition and Unity of Philippians: Some Neglected Literary Factors." *Novum Testamentum* 27:141-73.

Gnilka, Joachim

1976 *Der Philipperbrief.* Freiburg, Germany: Herder.

Green, Joel B.

1993 "Crucifixion." In *Dictionary of Paul and His Letters,* pp. 177-79. Edited by Gerald F. Hawthorne, Ralph P. Martin and Daniel G. Reid. Downers Grove, Ill.: InterVarsity Press.

Gundry, Robert H.

1976 *"SŌMA" in Biblical Theology with Emphasis on Pauline Anthropology.* Cambridge: Cambridge University Press.

Hainz, J.

1990 "κοινωνία." In *Exegetical Dictionary of the New Testament,* 2:303-5. Edited by Horst Balz and Gerhard Schneider. 3 vols. Grand Rapids, Mich.: Eerdmans.

Hawthorne, Gerald F.

1983 *Philippians.* Waco, Tex.: Word.

Hays, Richard B.

1989 *Echoes of Scripture in the Letters of Paul.* New Haven, Conn.: Yale University Press.

1991 "ΠΙΣΤΙΣ and Pauline Christology: What Is at Stake?" In *Society of Biblical Literature 1991 Seminar Papers,* pp. 714-29. Edited by E. H. Lovering Jr. Atlanta: Scholars.

Hendriksen, William

1962 *Philippians.* Grand Rapids, Mich.: Baker.

Hengel, Martin

1977 *Crucifixion.* Philadelphia: Fortress.

Hooker, Morna D.
1978 "Philippians 2:6-11." In *Jesus und Paulus: Festschrift für Werner Georg Kümmel zum 70—Geburstag,* pp. 151-64. Edited by E. E. Ellis and E. Grässer. 2nd ed. Göttingen, Germany: Vandenhoeck und Ruprecht.

Hoover, Roy W.
1971 "The *Harpagmos* Enigma: A Philosophical Solution." *Harvard Theological Review* 64:95-119.

Hurtado, Larry W.
1984 "Jesus as Lordly Example in Philippians 2:5-11." In *From Jesus to Paul: Studies in Honour of Francis Wright Beare,* pp. 113-26. Edited by P. Richardson and J. C. Hurd. Waterloo, Ont.: Wilfrid Laurier University Press.

Käsemann, Ernst
1968 "A Critical Analysis of Philippians 2:5-11." *Journal for Theology and the Church* 5:45-88.

Kertelge, Karl
1990 "δικαιοσυνή." In *Exegetical Dictionary of the New Testament,* 1:325-30. Edited by Horst Balz and Gerhard Schneider. 3 vols. Grand Rapids, Mich.: Eerdmans.

Koester, Helmut
1962 "The Purpose of the Polemic of a Pauline Fragment (Philippians III)." *New Testament Studies* 8:317-32.

Koperski, Veronica
1996 *The Knowledge of Christ Jesus My Lord: The High Christology of Philippians 3:7-11.* Contributions to Biblical Exegesis and Theology 16. Kampen, Netherlands: Kok Pharos.

Lightfoot, J. B.
1881 *Saint Paul's Epistle to the Philippians.* 4th ed. London: Macmillan. Reprint Grand Rapids, Mich.: Zondervan, 1956.

Malherbe, Abraham J.
1988 *Ancient Epistolary Theorists.* Society of Biblical Literature Sources for Biblical Study 19. Atlanta: Scholars.

Martin, Ralph P.
1980 *Philippians.* Grand Rapids, Mich.: Eerdmans.
1997 *A Hymn of Christ: Philippians 2:5-11 in Recent Interpretation and in the Setting of Early Christian Worship.* Downers Grove, Ill.: InterVarsity Press (originally published as *Carmen Christi,* Society of New Testament Studies Monograph Series 4, Cambridge: Cambridge University Press, 1967; 2nd ed. with new preface. Grand Rapids, Mich.: Eerdmans, 1983).

Mayer, Bernhard
1987 "Paulus als Vermittler zwischen Epaphroditus und der Gemeinde von Philippi: Bemerkungen zu Phil 2,25-30." *Biblische Zeitschrift* 31:176-88.

Michael, J. Hugh
1928 *The Epistle to the Philippians*. London: Hodder & Stoughton.

Moule, C. F. D.
1970 "Further Reflexions on Philippians 2:5-11." In *Apostolic History and the Gospel: Biblical and Historical Essays Presented to F. F. Bruce on His 60th Birthday*, pp. 264-76. Edited by W. W. Gasque and Ralph P. Martin. Grand Rapids, Mich.: Eerdmans.

Murphy-O'Connor, Jerome
1976 "Christological Anthropology in Phil. II, 6-11." *Revue Biblique* 83:25-50.
1995 *Paul the Letter-Writer: His World, His Options, His Skills*. Collegeville, Minn.: Liturgical.

O'Brien, Peter T.
1991 *Commentary on Philippians*. Grand Rapids, Mich.: Eerdmans.

Otto, Randall E.
1995 " 'If Possible I May Attain the Resurrection from the Dead' (Philippians 3:11)." *Catholic Biblical Quarterly* 57:324-40.

Peterlin, Davorin
1995 *Paul's Letter to the Philippians in the Light of Disunity in the Church*. Novum Testamentum Supplements 79. Leiden: Brill.

Peterman, G. W.
1997 *Paul's Gift from Philippi: Conventions of Gift Exchange and Christian Giving*. Society for New Testament Studies Monograph Series 92. Cambridge: University Press.

Pfitzner, V. C.
1967 *Paul and the Agon Motif*. Novum Testamentum Supplements 15. Leiden: Brill.

Pilhofer, Peter
1995 *Philippi*. Vol. 1: *Die erste christliche Gemeinde Europas*. Wissenschaftliche Untersuchungen zum Neuen Testament 87. Tübingen: J. C. B. Mohr (Siebeck).

Porter, Stanley E.
1993 "Word Order and Clause Structure in New Testament Greek: An Unexplored Area of Greek Linguistics Using Philippians as a Test Case." *Filología Neotestamentaria* 6:177-206.

Rapske, Brian
1994 *The Book of Acts and Paul in Roman Custody*. Grand Rapids, Mich.: Eerdmans.

Reed, Jeffrey T.
1991 "The Infinitive with Two Substantival Accusatives: An Ambiguous Construction?" *Novum Testamentum* 33:1-27.

Silva, Moisés
1992 *Philippians*. Grand Rapids, Mich.: Baker.

Stowers, Stanley K.
1985 *Letter Writing in Greco-Roman Antiquity*. Library of Early Christianity 5. Philadelphia: Westminster Press.
1991 "Friends and Enemies in the Politics of Heaven: Reading Theology in Philippians." In *Pauline Theology*, 1:105-21. Edited by J. M. Bassler. Minneapolis: Fortress.

Strimple, Robert B.
1979 "Philippians 2:5-11 in Recent Studies: Some Exegetical Conclusions." *Westminster Theological Journal* 41:247-68.

Tellbe, Mikael
1994 "The Sociological Factors Behind Phil 3:1-11 and the Conflict at Philippi." *Journal for the Study of the New Testament* 55:97-121.

Vincent, M. R.
1897 *Critical and Exegetical Commentary on the Epistles to the Philippians and to Philemon*. International Critical Commentary. Edinburgh: T & T Clark.

Watson, D. F.
1988 "A Rhetorical Analysis of Philippians and Its Implications for the Unity Question." *Novum Testamentum* 30:57-88.

Weima, Jeffrey A. D.
1997 "What Does Aristotle Have to Do with Paul? An Evaluation of Rhetorical Criticism." *Calvin Theological Journal* 32:458-68.

White, John L.
1972 *The Form and Function of the Body of the Greek Letter*. Society of Biblical Literature Dissertation Series 2. Missoula, Mont.: Scholars.

White, L. Michael
1990 "Morality Between Two Worlds: A Paradigm of Friendship in Philippians." In *Greeks, Romans and Christians: Essays in Honor of Abraham J. Malherbe*, pp. 201-15. Edited by D. L. Balch, E. Ferguson and W. A. Meeks. Minneapolis: Fortress.

Witherington, Ben, III
1994 *Friendship and Finances in Philippi: The Letter of Paul to the Philippians*. Valley Forge, Penn.: Trinity Press International.

Wright, N. T.
1986 "ἁρπαγμός and the Meaning of Philippians 2:5-11." *Journal of Theological Studies* 37:321-52.

Ziesler, John A.
1972 *The Meaning of Righteousness in Paul: A Linguistic and Theological Enquiry*. Society for New Testament Studies Monograph Series 20. Cambridge: Cambridge University Press.

Zmijewski, J.
1991 "κοινωνία." In *Exegetical Dictionary of the New Testament,* 2:276-79. Edited by Horst Balz and Gerhard Schneider. 3 vols. Grand Rapids, Mich.: Eerdmans.